Religion and Politics in America's Borderlands

Religion and Politics in America's Borderlands

Edited by Sarah Azaransky

LEXINGTON BOOKS
Lanham • Boulder • New York • Toronto • Plymouth, UK

Published by Lexington Books
A wholly owned subsidiary of The Rowman & Littlefield Publishing Group, Inc.
4501 Forbes Boulevard, Suite 200, Lanham, Maryland 20706
www.rowman.com

10 Thornbury Road, Plymouth PL6 7PP, United Kingdom

Copyright © 2013 by Lexington Books

All rights reserved. No part of this book may be reproduced in any form or by any electronic or mechanical means, including information storage and retrieval systems, without written permission from the publisher, except by a reviewer who may quote passages in a review.

British Library Cataloguing in Publication Information Available

Library of Congress Cataloging-in-Publication Data Available

ISBN 978-0-7391-7862-1 (cloth : alk. paper)

∞™ The paper used in this publication meets the minimum requirements of American National Standard for Information Sciences Permanence of Paper for Printed Library Materials, ANSI/NISO Z39.48-1992.

Printed in the United States of America

Contents

Acknowledgments	vii
Introduction: The Border and the Borderlands *Sarah Azaransky*	1

I: The Borderlands as a Religious Resource

1	Immigration and Some of Its Implications for Christian Identity and Doctrine *Orlando O. Espín*	19
2	Alternately Documented Theologies: Mapping Border, Exile and Diaspora *Carmen M. Nanko-Fernández*	33
3	How to Shape Christian Perspectives on Immigration?: Strategies for Communicating Biblical Teaching *M. Daniel Carroll R.*	57

II: The Borderlands as a Political and Religious Reality

4	Borderlife and the Religious Imagination *Daisy L. Machado*	81
5	A Tour of the Border in San Diego: Militarization of the Line and Criminalization of Immigrants *Pedro Rios*	99
6	Spiritualities of Social Engagement: Women Resisting Violence in Mexico and Honduras *Monica A. Maher*	121

III: The Borderlands as a Call to Action

7	The Subversive Act of Breaking Bread: How the Eucharist Transforms the Immigration Conversation *Craig Wong*	145
8	A Divided Friendship: Friendship Park: The Past, Present, and Future of the U.S.-Mexico Border *John Fanestil*	163

9 Vicissitudes of the Margins: An HIV/AIDS Theological
 Journey 177
 Ángel F. Méndez Montoya

Index 185
Index of Bible Passages 191
About the Contributors 193

Acknowledgments

My deepest gratitude goes to Charles Marsh and the Project on Lived Theology, which sponsored the "Spring Institute for Lived Theology: Theology, Immigration, and the Borderlands," which planted the seeds for this volume. Charles' encouragement and the generous grant from the Project on Lived Theology made it possible to bring together leading academic specialists and grassroots activists to do what is at the heart of the Project on Lived Theology: to understand the way theological commitments shape the social patterns and practices of everyday life and to encourage theologians and scholars of religion to embrace theological life as a form of public responsibility.

I thank all the contributors to this volume. Their personal, theological, and academic commitments to justice on the border and in the borderlands enlivened the Institute and shine through in their chapters. It was a privilege and a joy to work with them on this project.

The chapters of this book did indeed begin in conversations, which also entailed planning, catering, and travel arrangements. Thank you to Kristina Garcia Wade and Kelly Figueroa Ray of the Project on Lived Theology and to David Alejandro Cervantes of the University of San Diego for their help with the innumerable details that they got perfectly right. A special, heartfelt thank you to Lynn Keenan and Ann Hill who looked after baby Lucy in the weeks after she was born and while I was preparing for the Institute. Lynn and Ann made these conversations—and so this book—possible.

I am grateful to the participants of the "Spring Institute for Lived Theology: Theology, Immigration, and the Borderlands," including Michael Akong, Maria Pilar Aquino, Art Cribbs, Carl Crider, Elaine Elliott, Jamie Gates, Jess Jollett, Rebecca Moore, Barbara Quinn, Bill Radatz, Madison Shockley, Christauria Welland, and Theresa Yugar, for bringing their expertise, creativity, and incisive theological reflections about the border to intense and diverse collaboration.

Thank you to David Rosado at the New York Public Library, Kimberly David at the Library of Congress, and Marilyn Scott at the Billy Ireland Cartoon and Library Muscum at Ohio State University for their help in securing electronic copies of historical photos and cartoons. Thank you also to Charles Henderson for permission to reprint Angel F. Mendez Montoya's "Vissisitudes of the Margins: An HIV/AIDS Theological Journey," *Cross Currents* 61, no. 4 (December 2011): 549–56.

I thank Julie Falk and Karen Teel for their encouragement and support on this and other projects. Thanks to Shea Tuttle of the Project on Lived Theology for her help with permissions and to Michelle Poveda of USD's Theology and Religious Studies Department for help with printing and all kinds of administrative support. Thank you also to Melissa Wilks, formerly of Rowman & Littlefield, and my current editor, Eric Wrona, who shepherded the book to publication.

I am always grateful to my family—my son Finn Keenan, my daughter Lucy Azaransky, and my husband Kevin Keenan—for their loving patience and support, ever more so when deadlines loom and they inspire me to finish up and come home.

Introduction

The Border and the Borderlands

Sarah Azaransky

Immigration from Mexico and Central America shapes life in border communities and, increasingly, throughout the United States. In California, Texas, and Arizona, border policy has prompted environmental lawsuits, land disputes, and an almost-twenty-year humanitarian crisis of border crossing deaths; in Alabama, Georgia, and Utah, among other states, legislatures have passed laws that target people without proper papers. Immigration has become a national political issue, concerned with who is entitled to live and work in the United States and the efficacy of current strategies to "control" the border.[1]

Immigration also poses religious questions for Christians about how to "welcome the stranger" and challenges congregations to develop programs to meet the needs of immigrants and refugees in their midst. Calls to protect the stranger and even to treat her as a citizen span the Testaments. Official positions of the U.S. Conferences of Catholic Bishops, mainline Protestant churches, and the evangelical Christians for Immigration Reform echo this rich scriptural tradition when they call their followers to provide justice for immigrants and for humane political reforms.

More than simply an issue that demands congregational response, immigration is transforming American churches. While the millions of documented and undocumented immigrants in the United States hail from all over the globe, the political discussion about immigration focuses on people from Mexico and Central America. Indeed, this focus makes demographic sense. A third of all immigrants presently living in the United States are from Mexico, while it is estimated that of immigrants without proper papers who live in the United States, 60 percent are from Mexico.[2] Herein lies a profound religious challenge: the growth of the Latino population in the United States is "transforming the nation's religious landscape."[3] Through a joint series of public opinion surveys, the Pew Hispanic Center and the Pew Forum on Religion and Public Life found that "about a third of all Catholics in the U.S. are now Latinos" and noted the "growth of evangelical and pentecostal Christianity among Latinos."[4] In short, immigration shapes political and religious realities in twenty-first century America.

Religion and Politics in America's Borderlands engages these political and religious realities through critical analysis about how religious commitments are displayed, professed, and embodied in experiences of immigration and in life at the border and in the borderlands. It investigates how these commitments shape patterns of everyday living, including economic, political, and racial perceptions. This book shows how religious practices are shaped by life in the borderlands, how the realities of migration shape an American theological perspective, and how religious reasons provide a different starting point for conversations about immigration. It also offers concrete and practical lessons for how professors can talk about immigration in their classrooms and how church leaders— whether the pastor of a congregation or lay leader—can strengthen their congregations in their contributions to civic wholeness and human flourishing.

The contributors to this volume are leading academic specialists about immigration and the borderlands and nationally-recognized grassroots activists, who reflect on their varied experiences of living, working, and teaching on the U.S.-Mexico border and in the borderlands. These authors demonstrate how the border and the borderlands reshape religious thinking. They call on theologians, ethicists, and other scholars in religious studies to recognize how immigration is a social reality that affects the life of many American Christians and their churches. In conversation with sociologists, historians, and policymakers, the volume's authors demonstrate how Christian faith animates historical and political understanding of life in the borderlands. In order to engage with authors' accounts of the border and borderlands, it is necessary to provide some context. Here, a discussion of the U.S.-Mexico border serves as a starting point, rather than a limiting frame, for considerations of immigration, the border, and the borderlands. First, we turn to contemporary consequences of border policy and the history of the borderline.

DETERRENCE PROVOKES A HUMANITARIAN CRISIS

The border is the almost-2,000-mile international boundary between the United States and Mexico. On the U.S. side, in urban areas like San Diego, Nogales, and El Paso, walls and military technology bulwark the international boundary. For instance, in San Diego the international border is fortified by a ten-foot steel wall that cuts a jagged path for fourteen miles from the Pacific Ocean into the foothills of the Laguna Mountains. This wall has transformed the immigration experience for hundreds of thousands of North and Central Americans and spurred a humanitarian crisis.[5]

The wall is the result of a change in border policy. In 1994, U.S. border policy shifted its emphasis from apprehension of people who had crossed the border without papers to deterrence. To deter unauthorized border crossers, border policy focuses on technology, a majority of agents, and increased surveillance on urban corridors. A corollary of deterrence is that technology and manpower employed in urban areas will result in border crossers being "forced over the more hostile terrain" of desert and mountains.[6] The strategy assumes that natural barriers will deter crossers and those undeterred will be easier to apprehend. Neither assumption has proved correct.

People have been deterred from crossing the border in the fourteen-mile urban corridor between San Diego and Tijuana, an area that before 1994 accounted for more than half of all apprehensions of unauthorized border crossers along the entire 2,000-mile length of the U.S. border with Mexico. But deterrence has not dissuaded people from crossing; instead it has changed migration routes. Increased patrols of urban corridors have pushed people into the desert. Immediately following the implementation of deterrence, there was an increase in the number of attempted crossings by people without papers in the desert and mountains east of San Diego.[7] As a result, border deaths increased dramatically. The majority of deaths have occurred in California and Arizona. Apart from the urban area surrounding the city of San Diego, the borderlands between Baja and Alta California are a labyrinth of canyons, many of which remain uncharted, making travel on foot difficult and vehicular rescue sometimes impossible. The border's desert lowlands that rise into the mountains provide little to no natural shelter or water and are home to scorpions, rattlesnakes, and mountain lions. In order to cross the border east of the city of San Diego, a person needs to travel fifteen to thirty miles through the desert on foot before she reaches any road. In winter months, nighttime temperatures fall below freezing; in summer months, daytime temperatures consistently reach above 110 degrees.

Before 1994, traffic fatalities were the leading cause of death of people attempting unauthorized border crossings. Since 1994, the leading cause of border deaths is exposure. In summer months, border crossers inevitably run out of water and can be forced to drink their own urine to stay alive in the extreme heat.[8] In winter months, border crossers can be caught up in fast-moving snowstorms. For people crossing the border in the Imperial Desert, drowning is the second-greatest cause of death. People who cross the border here have to contend with the All America Canal, an eighty-two-mile aqueduct that runs parallel to the border. The Canal's depth fluctuates between seven and twenty feet and can be as wide as several football fields. The Canal's often vicious undertow can quickly sweep swimmers underwater.[9]

No one knows the number of people who have died in the process of crossing the border, because the federal government does not prescribe standard methods for charting the rise in border crossing deaths.[10] The Government Accounting Office nevertheless estimates that the number of border crossing deaths doubled between 1995 and 2005, the decade following the implementation of deterrence.[11] According to noted immigration scholar Wayne Cornelius, there have been 5,000 documented deaths of people who were in the process of crossing the border between 1995 and early 2009.[12] The lack of an agreed-upon metric for counting border deaths gives us "an incomplete picture of the human toll of unauthorized crossing" and results in a "strongly suspected undercount."[13] Many of the people who have died while crossing without papers "remain unknown at death or are identified as 'Mexican.' Collectively, they have become the *desparecidos* (the disappeared) of the border."[14] Even as an economic downturn in the United States has meant fewer people crossing the border, the rate of border crossing deaths has risen.[15]

The increase in border crossing deaths should not be treated as an unforeseen consequence, for the risks of crossing the border in the desert and mountains are an integral part of prevention through deterrence.[16] The strategy recognizes the risks of desert and mountain crossings and employs them as a threatened cost. The federal government's refusal to develop a standard method for determining the number of border crossing deaths means that the Department of Homeland Security cannot consider what number of border crossing deaths are an acceptable consequence of a particular border policy.

Deterrence also contributes to the construction of the social location of "illegal aliens." While border policies necessarily address social boundaries of insider and outsider, deterrence does so in such a way that it targets a population that is poor and Latino. Joseph Nevins reminds us that we cannot "divorce growing emphasis on 'illegal aliens' from the long history in the United States of largely race-based anti-immigrant sentiment rooted in fear and/or rejection of those deemed as outsiders, a history that is inextricably tied to a context of exploitation and political and economic marginalization of certain immigrant populations."[17] The social construction that designates a person as illegal may mitigate against engaging with failures in the policy. Following the "subhuman construction" of illegal alien, argues Steven Bender, "migrant deaths do not warrant a change in national border policy, no matter the death toll."[18]

What occasioned the sea change in border policy in the mid-1990s? News accounts of border and immigration policies are rife with crisis rhetoric: there is a crisis of people without papers—so-called "illegal" human beings—who stream across the border, and a crisis of failed security on the borderline itself. Deterrence was the result of a constellation of factors that made border enforcement a political focus in California in the early 1990s. Anti-immigrant sentiment has been attributed to an economic downturn and to shifting demographics, which by the early 1990s made it clear that California was soon to become a "minority-majority" state.[19] The clearest expression of a growing nativism came in the 1994 ballot initiative Proposition 187, which called on school administrators, health care workers, and local police to deny public services to any person with "apparent illegal status."[20] Political rhetoric leading up the 1994 vote helped to shape public imagination about people with and without papers who have crossed the border. Linguist Otto Santa Ana sifted through all the articles in the *Los Angeles Times* between 1992 and 1994 devoted to Proposition 187 and uncovered patterns in how reporters described people who cross the border and people of Latin American origin who live in the United States. A set of dominant metaphors in the *LA Times* described Latin American immigrants as "a sea of brown faces," a "human surge," and a "brown tide."[21] A secondary set of metaphors described immigration as an "alien invasion" that put California under a "state of siege."[22] A context of deterrence, therefore, was dominant political rhetoric that portrayed non-white persons as threatening to overwhelm the state.

Douglas Massey insists that the crisis rhetoric that developed in the 1990s—and continues to be used today—is not in response to any sociological fact, for "despite all the rhetoric about floods and invasion, the rate of undocumented in-migration from Mexico has not changed in three decades."[23] So why call it a crisis? Massey attributes at least an aspect of contemporary anxieties about immigration to the passage of the North American Free Trade Agreement (NAFTA) in 1994. He argues, "the current immigration 'crisis' stems from a fundamental contradiction lying at the heart of American policy toward Mexico—our schizophrenic attempt to create an integrated North American market within which borders are rendered" permeable for goods, capital, and information "but impermeable with respect to the movement of workers."[24] This fundamental contradiction is evidenced in San Ysidro, the land crossing between San Diego and Tijuana, which is the busiest land crossing in the world and the most fortified.

HOW THE LINE WAS DRAWN

Anxiety about the border—and the people who cross it—is nothing new, as the history of the border itself and of immigration policies in the early twentieth century show. The current international boundary emerged after a war that began as a border dispute in 1846 between the United States and Mexico in what is now Texas. According to the United States, the border between the countries was the Rio Grande. According to Mexico, it was the Nueces River, to the north. After Americans troops ventured south of the Nueces, Mexican troops attacked them. In response, the United States declared war on Mexico. A year and a half later, the United States "prevailed and demanded an enormous swath of northern

Mexico, including the future states of Nevada, California, and Utah, and parts of Arizona, New Mexico, Colorado and Wyoming."[25] The 1848 Treaty of Hidalgo drew the line that is the current international boundary and also guaranteed U.S. citizenship to anyone living in the vast region ceded to the United States.

In the earliest years after the current border was drawn, life continued much as it had before. Families who had lived for generations along the Rio Grande or farmed in Tijuana River Valley continued to travel back and forth across the international boundary with no fanfare. Policing the southern border with Mexico only became a concern for American politicians in the second decade of the new century. After the outbreak of the Mexican revolution in 1910, Mexican generals sought control of Mexican cities on the southern side of the border as way to collect customs duties and import arms and ammunition.[26] The first significant American presence along the border were U.S. Army troops sent by President Taft to "enforce neutrality laws, prevent arms smuggling, suppress banditry, calm apprehensive civilians, and protect American border towns."[27] By the end of 1915, President Wilson had stationed 20,600 soldiers along the border. In response to Pancho Villa's raid in 1916, Wilson sent an additional 100,000 National Guard troops.[28] At the end of the Mexican Revolution in 1920, National Guard and Army troops were recalled, but political anxieties attached to the border persisted. In response to Prohibition, the United States began to patrol its borders formally. In 1924, the Border Patrol was created with "the purpose of controlling the border between inspection stations."[29]

There were mixed reactions to people who crossed the border. During the turmoil of the Revolution, many Mexicans fled north to find safety and work. At the same time appeared the first increased immigration requirements to affect Mexicans.[30] The 1917 Immigration Act required a literacy test for all people entering the United States and restricted entry of people with "a loathsome or contagious disease," people who are "paupers" and would likely need government assistance, or who are found to be "mentally or physically defective."[31] Immigration officials were charged, therefore, with inspecting people who wanted to cross the line to see if they met new immigration standards. Drawing from "stereotypes of Mexicans as carriers of disease who threatened both the health of the nation and its charity system (and also as a fertile population ready to take over the nation)," immigration officials subjected immigrants to "humiliating medical inspections at border crossing stations."[32]

Economic pressures, however, encouraged immigration. By the time the United States entered World War I, Mexican immigrants were welcomed as a much-needed labor force. Business lobbies, especially for agribusiness and the railroad industry, pushed for cheap labor. While Mexicans were welcome to the United States to work, American immigration law did not permit them to become citizens. While there were not limits on immigration from Mexico (or Central or South American countries), American immigration law placed immigrants from Central and South Americas in a racial quandary. According to the Naturalization Act of 1790 and its revision in 1870, only those people who were deemed white or black could become citizens.[33] In a binary racial taxonomy, it was not readily apparent where Mexican citizens, who displayed a range of hues, would fit.

The very treaty that drew the border complicated racialized standards for citizenship. The Treaty of Hidalgo granted U.S. citizenship to all those people who lived in the regions that had formerly been part of Mexico. The circumstances of the Treaty guaranteed citizenship to a multiracial group of people of Spanish and indigenous descent and thus indicated a precedent for non-white and non-black American citizens. The Treaty itself is a historical marker that frames the borderlands and foreshadows systems of exclusion or belonging.

WHERE ARE THE BORDERLANDS?

While the border is physical line with a particular history, the term *borderlands* can describe a place, a process, or a condition. As a place, the borderlands has traditionally described the wide region that straddles the international border between Mexico and the United States. In the century and more after the Treaty of Hidalgo, people continued to travel freely between the countries and shared family, cultural, and religious ties. By 2020, the population of the borderlands, what is sometimes described as "*el tercer païs*" or "the third country," is expected to reach 36 million.[34] In the borderlands zone has emerged a bi-national community, where U.S. citizen borderlands dwellers can have more in common with their Mexican neighbors than they do with fellow citizens from Seattle, Atlanta, or Cleveland. (A similar point can be made about Mexican borderlands dwellers and fellow citizens in Mexico City, Tuxtla Guitierrez, or La Paz.) Of course, what happens in this border zone affects the identities and histories of the United State and Mexico, even as it has not traditionally been an object of historical interest.

The term "borderlands" was first used in 1921 by historian Eugene Bolton to challenge the traditional American historiography that traced American beginnings to the arrival of Anglo-Saxon immigrants in the northeast and followed their westward migration. Shifting the axis from east-west to south-north, Bolton emphasized vast Spanish colonial holdings that reached from South America to northern California. Indeed, for Americans who live near what is now the U.S.-Mexico border, "Spain is stamped on our land surveys. From Sacramento to St. Augustine nearly everybody holds his acres by a title going back to Mexico or Madrid.

Most of the farms, in a wide swath along the border, are divisions of famous grants which are still known by their original Spanish names."[35]

To make sense of the importance of Spanish colonial interests to American history and their continued cultural sway, Bolton advocated that U.S. history focus on the borderlands. Bolton recognized that "borderland zones are vital not only in the determination of international relations, but also in the development of culture. . . . By borderland areas not solely geographical regions are meant; borderlands studies of many kinds are similarly fruitful."[36] Exhorting fellow historians to rethink the Turner thesis that predicated American history and identity on Westward expansion, Bolton insisted that historians in the United States not let international borders circumscribe their field of study.[37] To understand so-called American history, Bolton argued that American historians needed to consider the full breadth of American experience, including Mexican and Spanish history in the New World. Bolton's entreaty that we transform our historical imagination is also relevant to American religious history, in which south-north axis "is repeatedly overlooked in historical reconstructions of American religion."[38]

Since Bolton's work in the early twentieth century, the term "borderlands" has been appropriated by legal scholars, anthropologists, and literary critics as an object of study. While each discipline brings a different set of methods and tools to studying the borderlands, shared conclusions emerge about the borderlands as a place of conflict and contradiction that produces particular social and political identities. For example, in an account of how the construction of the American border shapes a legal borderlands, Mary L. Duziak and Leti Volpp argue that "national borders are not only material and territorial they are also rhetorical. Conventional renderings of our national narrative cast the immigrant as the desiring subject, longing to come and to belong to America."[39] Borders must be regulated, because if borders were left open the United States would suffer an influx of desirous immigrants. The assumption that would-be immigrants are longing to come to the United States discounts the actual habits of many seasonal workers, for example, who wish to return to their homes and families at the end of a harvest, building project, or for the holidays.[40]

Meanwhile, anthropologist Robert Alvarez designates the borderlands as a place and a process, as "a region and set of practices defined and determined by this border that are characterized by conflict and contradiction, material and ideational."[41] The borderlands produced at this particular international boundary are unique, according to Alvarez, because "no other border in the world exhibits the [same] inequality of power, economics, and the human condition."[42]

Chicana feminist Gloria Anzaldúa has written perhaps the most influential account of the borderlands, which she describes as "physically present wherever two or more cultures edge each other, where people of different races occupy the same territory."[43] For Anzaldúa, the border "*es una herida abierta* [is an open wound] where the Third World grates against the first and bleeds. And before a scab forms it hemorrhages again, the lifeblood of two worlds merging to form a third country—a border culture."[44] For Anzaldúa the borderlands is a place—connected to the international boundary—and a process—the interaction of races and cultures.

As a process and a condition, the borderlands also describes a broader region that has been affected by the economic, political, and religious realities of pan-American migrations. The borderlands describes communities in California and Texas, but also refers to patterns of migration that challenge congregations in Colorado and community service organizations in Boston. Borderlands may describe, then, locations that are more than 1,000 miles from the international boundary. These particular places are transformed into borderlands when realities of migration challenge existing understandings of political and religious life.

ENGAGING POLITICAL AND RELIGIOUS REALITIES

The chapters in this book address these challenges from various standpoints and by employing different methods. This volume is unique because it includes an ecumenical conversation among Roman Catholic, mainline Protestant, and evangelical voices. The contributors use historical, theological, and hermeneutical approaches, as well as human rights documentation of current realities on the ground. In spite of their diversity of standpoints and disciplines, the contributors share a focus on the lived dimensions of religious and political commitments. Whether an evangelical scholar whose research focus is the Old Testament, a Roman Catholic feminist theologian, or a grassroots advocate for immigrants' rights, the volume's contributors model a kind of engaged scholarship. The scholarship is engaged in two primary ways: each author is self-conscious about the standpoint from which she writes and the communities to which her work is responsible, and each author is aware of participating in a larger conversation that seeks to advance the public good around understandings of immigration and the borderlands.

Earlier versions of this volume's chapters were presented at the "Spring Institute for Lived Theology: Theology, Migration, and the Borderlands" that took place in April 2010 in San Diego. Sponsored by the Project on Lived Theology, a research institute that embraces theological life as a form of public responsibility, the Spring Institute gathered academic specialists and grassroots activists to explore together the U.S.-Mexico border as a rich theological text and seek to understand how religious commitments and convictions shape social patterns and practices of everyday life in the borderlands and beyond. The volume's contributors agree that "the details of one's lived experience, the details of one's social, cultural, historical, political, and religious realities shape one's understanding of self, world, and God."[45] Their chapters reflect necessary and ongoing dialogue between academics and activists (even as the volume demonstrates this to be an imperfect distinction) to forward transformative and emancipatory models of life on the border and in the borderlands.

In the opening section, "The Borderlands as a Religious Resource," Orlando Espín, Carmen Nanko-Fernández, and Daniel Carroll demonstrate how religious reflection and activism are transformed when they self-consciously reflect on their social location in the borderlands. Realities of immigration challenge Christian doctrine, according to Espín, who argues that if American Christian theology is to focus on who Christians are, then it must turn its attention to immigrants. Espín insists that it is not the theologian's task to discern what the Christian doctrine may say about immigration; rather, American theologians are called to discern what immigration means for the Christian doctrine. Read together, the chapters of Espín, Nanko-Fernández, and Carroll model how the location of the borderlands transforms religious reflection.

In a remarkable summary of who she calls "academia's undocumented scholars," Nanko-Fernández explores a diversity of Latin@ theological scholarship and biblical interpretation about migration. Focusing particularly on the themes of border, exile, and diaspora, Nanko-Fernández maps differences between Chicano, Cuban-American, and Puerto Rican scholars to demonstrate how particular social locations inform the directions they follow and shape understandings of Jesus, God, and church. Nanko-Fernández has documented a "rich body of scholarship that is consummately aware of its grounded yet translocal character."

Carroll's chapter explores how immigrant realities transform our reading of Scripture. Drawing from his experiences of leading discussions with evangelical audiences all over the country about Scripture and immigration, Carroll has identified three primary audiences who have concerns about immigration: people who are suspicious or scared of immigrants, people in the majority culture who want to use Scripture to help them make sense of current realities, and immigrants themselves. Carroll's chapter identifies the best starting place to begin a Scripture-based conversation about immigration and offers specific readings of Biblical narrative and law that help contemporary audiences reflects on current realities.

Chapters by Daisy Machado, Pedro Rios, and Monica Maher analyze the concept of the borderlands and investigate how contemporary U.S. border and foreign policy shape political and religious identities. Machado investigates historical and contemporary religious practices that have emerged in the borderlands. The career of turn-of-the-century *curandera*

Teresa Urrea convinces Machado that the U.S.-Mexico borderlands were—and continue to be—a place where boundaries of religious belief and practice are fluid, while contemporary *comités guadalupanos* that organize a relay between Mexico City and New York City are evidence that the borderlands are not limited to the Southwest. Establishing an argument that is central to the volume, Machado attests that the Latino borderlands are "where culture, race, identity, politics, and religion intersect in complicated and even violent ways."

Like other contributors, Pedro Rios grounds his argument in personal experience. Born and raised just miles from the international boundary between Mexico and the United States, Rios argues that violence on the border results from government policies and actions, not from people who cross without proper papers. As the executive director of the U.S.-Mexico Border program of the American Friends Service Committee, Rios regularly leads tours of the international boundary. In his chapter, Rios leads readers through specific locations along the San Diego-Tijuana border to chart its growing militarization, analyze border and immigrations policies effects on border communities, and to document Border Patrol's involvement in immigrants' deaths. Rios shares with Machado a concern to broaden our moral imagination about citizenship. Both authors question the narrow framework of juridical citizenship and propose instead a concept of citizenship grounded in practices of belonging.

Read together, the chapters of Rios and Monica Maher show how U.S. policies shape the practices of citizenship in the U.S. borderlands and far beyond. Drawing from extensive fieldwork in Mexico and Honduras, Maher argues that borderlands extend as far south as Honduras, where she connects a rise in gender violence in with U.S. economic and military policies. Maher documents how Mexican and Honduran women transform traditional religious practices, such as pilgrimage, prayer, and lament, to protest the murders of hundreds of women in each country. Maher celebrates the women's theological creativity and transgressive spiritual practices as methods for women to make democratic demands for murderers to be brought to justice and for women's safety to be assured.

In the book's final section, "The Borderlands as a Call to Action," Craig Wong, John Fanestil, and Ángel Méndez-Montoya offer concrete examples on how life in the borderlands shapes congregations and individuals. Just as Pedro Rios reflects on his upbringing on the border, Craig Wong frames his chapter with his Chinese grandmother's experience of immigrating to California. Calling the Chinese the "original 'illegal aliens' under federal law," Wong connects his family's story to the experiences of contemporary undocumented people. The executive director of Grace Urban Ministries, an evangelical and congregation-based nonprofit that serves immigrants in San Francisco, Wong proposes sharing the Eucharistic table as a religious practice that promotes solidarity with immigrants and visions of more just U.S. policies. Since sharing the table is in opposition to public culture, Wong indicates how it gives us new ways of thinking about immigration.

In conversation with Wong's discussion of the table and Rios' account of the border in San Diego, John Fanestil's chapter focuses on the history of Friendship Park, the most southwesterly point in the continental United States and a place where Americans and Mexicans can meet face to face, with only a mesh fence separating them. Fanestil calls the park the "birthplace of 'the borderlands'" because of the ongoing negotiation of the borderline that occurs at this location and continues to the date of this writing. As a way to bridge the *de jure* border, Fanestil, who is a Methodist minister, offered Communion through the fence every weekend for more than six months. In his chapter, Fanestil characterizes his serving communion through the border fence as a way to "juxtapose in sharp relief the inherently universal demands of the Christian sacraments and the inherently restrictive demands of the nation-state."

Ángel Méndez Montoya witnesses the effects of immigration policies on an individual. A Mexican citizen, Méndez reflects on his own experiences being labeled an "inadmissible other," when he is prevented from reentering the United States because of his HIV status. Méndez uses his experience of borderlife and his frustrations with immigration policy as a *locus theologicus*, a location from which theological proofs may be deduced. Similar to how Wong sees transformational possibility in sharing the table and Carroll in reading Scripture, Méndez suggests that the border prompts a new way of understanding the relationship between human and divine. Méndez's "queer decolonial alternative" points to "our perpetual condition of being on the border . . . between divine and human agency."

NOTES

1. The movement of peoples across the border between Mexico and the United States is perhaps better referred to as im/migration, denoting a complex phenomenon: some people want to move permanently to the United States, many others want simply to work in the United States as seasonal workers, and are unwilling immigrants, who remain in the United States out of economic necessity or because border and immigration policies make trips across the border too difficult.

2. Douglas S. Massey, "Understanding America's Immigration 'Crisis'" *Proceedings of the American Philosophical Society* 151, no. 3 (September 2007): 309.

3. Pew Hispanic Center and Pew Forum on Religion and Public Life, "Changing Faiths: Latinos and the Transformation of American Religion," April 25, 2007, available at http://pewhispanic.org/reports/report.php?ReportID=75(accessed July 12, 2011).

4. Ibid.

5. Maria Jimenez, "Humanitarian Crisis: Migrant Deaths at U.S.-Mexico Border" October 1, 2009, joint report sponsored by ACLU of San Diego and Imperial Counties and Mexico's National Commission of Human Rights, available at http://www.

aclusandiego.org/article_downloads/000888/Humanitarian%20Crisis%20Report%209-30-09.pdf(accessed July 22, 2011).

6. U.S. Border Patrol, "Border Patrol Strategic Plan 1994 and Beyond: National Strategy," 1994: 7. (Available through the I.N.S. Historical Reference Library. Copy in author's possession.)

7. The most common metric for charting the number of unauthorized crossing is to consider the number of apprehensions as indicative of the number of crossings generally. In 1993, the year before deterrence, there were 531,589 apprehensions of unauthorized border crossers in San Diego; in 1998, there were 248,092. In 1993, there were 30,045 apprehensions in El Centro (the largest border town in Imperial County, the neighboring county to the east of San Diego); in 1998, there were 226,695 apprehensions in El Centro. While San Diego apprehensions fell by 66 percent, apprehensions in El Centro rose by 761 percent. Yuma and Tucson, border cities in neighboring Arizona, saw increases at similar rates to El Centro, in Bill Ong Hing, "The Darker Side of Operation Gatekeeper," *UC Davis Journal of International Law and Policy* 7, no. 2 (Spring 2001): 131.

8. John Annerino, *Dead in their Tracks: Crossing America's Desert Borderlands* (New York: Four Walls Eight Windows, 1999), 130.

9. See Wayne Cornelius, "Death at the Border: Efficacy and Unintended Consequences of US Immigration Control Policy," *Population and Development Review* 27, no. 4 (December 2001): 671 and Madeleine Hinkes, "Migrant Deaths Along the California-Mexico Border: An Anthropological Perspective," *Journal of Forensic Sciences* 53, no. 1 (January 2008): 18.

10. A 2008 Congressional Research Service Report argues that accurate collection of migrant death is a challenge due to the large number of federal, state, and local jurisdictions involved. The reports admits that "the Border Patrol did not begin formally collecting information until 1998," four years after the implementation of Operation Gatekeeper, in CRS Report for Congress, 2008.

11. U.S. Government Accountability Office, *Illegal Immigration: Border-Crossing Deaths Have Doubled Since 1995; Border Patrol's Efforts to Prevent Deaths Have Not Been Fully Evaluated* (August 2006), 42, available at: www.gao.gov/new.items/d06770.pdf (accessed July 12, 2011).

12. Wayne Cornelius, "Looking Forward to a Smarter and More Just U.S. Immigration Policy: What Mexican Migrants Can Tell Us," Paper presented at Religion, Migration, and National Identity Conference (April 16–17, 2009), University of San Diego.http://www.sandiego.edu/peacestudies/documents/tbi/Corneliusreducedoptimized.pdf(accessed July 13, 2011).

13. Karl Eschbach, "Death at the Border," *International Migration Review* 33, no. 2 (1999): 438.

14. Ibid., 437.

15. Tim Stellar, "Border Deaths at Historic Highs Even As Crossing Plunge," *Arizona Daily Star* August 19, 2012,http://azstarnet.com/news/local/border/border-deaths-at-historic-highs-even-as-crossings-plunge/article_90dd06a4-63cd-5ca2-b40a-f499909bf7ae.html(accessed December 20, 2012); Ted Robbins, "Illegal Border Crossings Fewer But Just As Deadly" *National Public Radio: Weekend Edition Sunday* August 7, 2011,http://www.npr.org/2011/08/07/138959162/illegal-border-crossings-fewer-but-just-as-deadly(accessed December 20, 2012).

16. Eschbach argues that border deaths "should not be treated as 'unintended' consequences, since they were an integral part of the INS's 'prevention through deterrence' strategy from its inception" in Eschbach, "Death at the Border," 437.

17. Joseph Nevins, *Operation Gatekeeper: The Rise of the "Illegal Alien" and the Making of the U.S.-Mexico Boundary* (New York: Routledge, 2002), 96.

18. Steven Bender, *Greasers and Gringos: Latinos, Law, and the American Imagination* (New York: New York University Press, 2003), 124.

19. For anti-immigrant sentiment as response to economy, see Michael Alvarez and Tara L. Butterfield, "The Resurgence of Nativism in California? The Case of Proposi-

tion 187 and Illegal Immigration," Social Science Working Paper 1020 of the California Institute of Technology (October 1997): 2–11. As response to demographics, see Jennifer Cheng, et al., *A Portrait of Race and Ethnicity in California* (San Francisco: Public Policy Institute of California, 2001), vii.

20. See "Proposition 187: Text of the Proposed Law,"www.usc.edu/libraries/archives/ethnicstudies/historicdocs/prop187.txt(accessed December 30, 2008).

21. Santa Ana notes that the *Los Angeles Times* took an editorial state against Prop. 187, calling it morally and politically wrong. In spite of the paper's editorial position, articles used racist metaphors to describe immigration. See Otto Santa Ana, *Brown Tide Rising: Metaphors of Latinos in Contemporary American Public Discourse* (Austin, TX: University of Texas Press, 2002), 72–4.

22. Ibid., 70.

23. Massey, "Understanding America's Immigration 'Crisis,'" 310.

24. Ibid.

25. Joel Levanetz, "A Compromised Country: Redefining the US-Mexico Border," *The Journal of San Diego History* 54, no. 1 (Winter 2008): 40.

26. David Work, "Enforcing Neutrality: The Tenth US Cavalry on the Mexican Border, 1913-1919." *Western Historical Quarterly* 40, no. 2 (Summer 2009): 181.

27. Ibid., 179–80.

28. Ibid., 181.

29. "The Origins of the Border Patrol," available at http://www.cbp.gov/xp/cgov/border_security/border_patrol/border_patrol_ohs/history.xml(accessed July 13, 2011).

30. Natalia Molina, "In A Race All Their Own: The Quest to Make Mexicans Ineligible for US Citizenship," *Pacific Historical Review* 79, no. 2 (May 2010): 187.

31. The text of the 1917 Immigration act is available at http://library.uwb.edu/guides/USimmigration/39%20stat%20874.pdf(accessed July 13, 2011).

32. Molina, "In A Race All Their Own," 187.

33. Ibid., 168.

34. Daisy Machado, "Promoting Solidarity with Migrants," in *Justice in a Global Economy: Strategies for Home, Community, and World*, edited by Pamela K. Brubaker, Rebecca Todd Peters, Laura A. Stivers (Louisville: Westminster John Knox Press: 2006), 118. For an account of the shifting demographics in the borderlands since 1950, see James B. Pick, Nanda Viswanatha, James Hettrick, "The US-Mexican Borderlands Region: A Binational Spatial Analysis," *The Social Science Journal* 38 (2001): 567–95.

35. Herbert E. Bolton, *Wider Horizons of American History* (New York: Appleton Century Company, 1936), 100.

36. Ibid., 52.

37. For more on Bolton's influence, see Albert L. Hurtado, "Parkmanizing the Spanish Borderlands: Bolton, Turner, and the Historians' World," *The Western Historical Quarterly* 26, no. 2 (Summer 1995): 149–67; and David J. Weber, "Turner, the Boltonians, and the Borderlands," *The American Historical Review* 91, no. 1 (Feb. 1986): 66–81.

38. Luis D. Léon, "Metaphor and Place: the US-Mexico Border as Center and Periphery in the Interpretation of Religion," *Journal of the American Academy of Religion* 67, no. 3 (Sept. 1999): 543.

39. Mary L. Duziak and Leti Volpp, "Introduction—Legal Borderlands: Law and the Construction of American Borders," *American Quarterly* 57, no. 3 (Sept. 2005): 599.

40. Massey, "Understanding America's Immigration 'Crisis,'" 324.

41. Robert R. Alvarez, Jr. "The Mexican-US Border: The Making of an Anthropology of Borderlands," *Annual Review of Anthropology* 24 (1994): 448.

42. Ibid., 451.

43. Gloria Anzaldúa, *Borderlands/La Frontera: The New Mestiza*, Third edition (San Francisco: Aunt Lute Books, 2007), 20.

44. Ibid., 25.

45. Lori Hale, "Lived Theology 101: Exploring the Claim 'What We Believe Really Matters' with Undergraduates," paper presented at the 2011 "Spring Institute for Lived Theology: Lived Theology in Method, Style and Pedagogy" in Charlottesville, Virginia (May 27, 2011).

SELECTED BIBLIOGRAPHY

Annerino, John. *Dead in their Tracks: Crossing America's Desert Borderlands*. New York: Four Walls Eight Windows, 1999.

Anzaldúa, Gloria. *Borderlands/La Frontera: The New Mestiza*, Third edition. San Francisco: Aunt Lute Books, 2007.

Bender, Steven. *Greasers and Gringos: Latinos, Law, and the American Imagination*. New York: New York University Press, 2003.

Bolton, Herbert E. *Wider Horizons of American History*. New York: Appleton Century Company, 1936.

Jimenez, Maria. "Humanitarian Crisis: Migrant Deaths at US-Mexico Border." October 1, 2009, joint report sponsored by ACLU of San Diego and Imperial Counties and Mexico's National Commission of Human Rights, available at http://www.aclusandiego.org/article_downloads/000888/Humanitarian%20Crisis%20Report%209-30-09.pdf.

Nevins, Joseph. *Operation Gatekeeper: The Rise of the "Illegal Alien" and the Making of the U.S.-Mexico Boundary*. New York: Routledge, 2002.

Santa Ana, Otto. *Brown Tide Rising: Metaphors of Latinos in Contemporary American Public Discourse*. Austin: University of Texas Press, 2002.

I

The Borderlands as a Religious Resource

ONE

Immigration and Some of Its Implications for Christian Identity and Doctrine

Orlando O. Espín

How does one "set the theological stage" for what follows in the present volume? By pointing to reality and by letting that reality raise serious questions for Christian doctrines and theologies, and identity. Living next to the most-crossed border in the world, it is impossible to ignore the realities of bi-nationality, of the artificiality of borders, and of migration in both directions. I know many visitors to southern California visit the northern side of that imaginary line we call "the border." Unfortunately, most will not see that same imaginary line from the southern side where they have planted crosses for each person killed by the U.S. Border Patrol in incidents that are all too frequently blamed on the victims. The number of crosses increases every year. For a well-written and very disturbing story of immigration, I suggest *Enrique's Journey* by Sonia Nazario. For theological studies on immigration, see the works of U.S. Latino/a theologians, biblical scholars and historians who have been seriously reflecting on immigration for at least two decades.[1]

My intent here is not to address what Christian doctrine might or might not say *about* immigration. Rather, I hope to raise some questions on what immigration might say *about* the meaning and consequences of Christian doctrine. In my view, the border and immigration are important dogmatic issues, in the strictest theological sense. The questions, I hope, might prove important for those of us who engage in the scholarly study of Christianity and its doctrines and practices, as well as for those engaged in ministry or other social services. *Who* and *what* is "Christian" might turn out to be important for debates on immigration. I suspect that some of the questions might be uncomfortable, but in the world of theology (and higher education, in general) we cannot afford to pretend that uncomfortable issues do not exist.

I also hope that these reflections and questions will help set the stage for the present volume on the mutually implicating relationship of theology, immigration, and border reality.

I am a theologian, not a social scientist. More specifically, I do systematic, constructive theology, and not social ethics. My interest on immigration is focused on the inescapable challenge posed by immigration to the usual doctrinal, theological, pastoral, and institutional meaning of "Church." I should also add that, for me, to reflect on immigration is not a theoretical exercise or a reflection on someone else's experience. I am an immigrant, who arrived in the United States as a young teenager, and who has never forgotten the experiences of uprootedness and discrimination that most immigrants and their children can still identify as their own. My life is implicated in my remarks.

Relevant to the debates regarding immigration is the fact that at least 65 percent of the U.S. population self-identifies as Christian. So, why should U.S. Christians and churches, as well as U.S. scholars of Christianity, reflect on immigration? Why should they take the experience of immigration very seriously?

REASONS FOR TAKING IMMIGRATION SERIOUSLY WITHIN CHRISTIAN THEOLOGIES AND MINISTRIES

There are a number of very important reasons. Let me very briefly discuss three. The first reason to take immigration seriously is that half of all Roman Catholics in the United States are Latinos/as. About twelve percent of all American Episcopalians are Latinos/as. Approximately a third of the membership of U.S. Pentecostal denominations is Latino/a. Latinos/as are, already, the largest ethnic group in the country, after European descendants; and in some states Latinos/as are fast becoming the majority population (already surpassing European Americans among those under age thirty-five). Latinos/as are younger and have larger families than any other ethnic or racial group in the country. Although the vast majority of Latinos/as (about seventy-eight percent) are *not* immigrants, millions of us are immigrants or the children of immigrants. Immigration is never far from our families and communities.[2] Immigration, however, is not solely a Latino/a issue. Consider too the millions of Canadian, Filipino, Vietnamese, African, Near Eastern, *and* European immigrants and their children in the United States today. Immigration is not the experience of one group or of one generation, certainly not if you are the child of immigrants. U.S. Christianity remains, as strongly as it was in the nineteenth century, a religion of immigrants.

Please ask yourselves: How can we honestly and ethically do *American* Christian ministry or *American* Christian theology, and disregard the most traumatic experience in the life of millions of members of *American* Christian churches? How can we do American Christian anything and ignore the reality of millions of immigrant Christians in this country, and across the world? For those who are Roman Catholic this means, for example, half of the members of their Church in the United States.

A second reason to take immigration seriously stems from a central Christian metaphor. The Christian theological tradition has often spoken of the Church as a "pilgrim people," a people on the move.[3] These images are not merely poetic phrases. Rather, they indicate a reality that lies at the very foundations of Christianity. They remind us of some crucial consequences of Jesus's preaching on the Reign of God. They point to Christianity's approach to and understanding of reality, and to its experience of God. Or put differently, it is impossible to be a Christian and be "stuck" in the past or in the present. The "pilgrim people of God" are living witness to the precarious and always penultimate quality of all human societies, of all human explanations, of all human institutions, of all human decisions, and of all human expectations. Only God is final and absolute. Not our churches and not their doctrines. And not our nation.

Indeed, it is part of the genius of Christianity to value that which is truly human while at the same time critiquing its claims to finality. Only God is final and absolute, and nothing and no one else can make such claims. This double genius of Christianity has pushed it forward in spite of its own follies and sins. The image of a "pilgrim people," therefore, is not just a poetic phrase but a doctrinal insight that touches the dogmatic core of who we are as a Christian people. "Pilgrimage" into the future Reign of God is, therefore, of the very essence of Christian identity and practice.

But can we be on a "pilgrimage" without ever "moving"? Can a people "move" into the future without somehow becoming "immigrants" into that very future? Can we do theology or ministry without somehow reflecting on the meaning of "migrating" (even if only from the known to the unknown)? Can we be Christian without *ourselves* becoming "immigrants" into the promised future of humankind? Can we speak seriously and responsibly about the future fulfillment of the Reign of God without realizing that it requires *our* "migrating" into the future, and thus *our* becoming "immigrants" in and to the Reign? No one can hope to participate in the Reign of God without first admitting that he/she is an "immigrant" in that Reign, and that no one has a "birth right" to the Reign of God. Before God and God's Reign we are all *and only* immigrants.

These are not poetic or homiletic phrases, but explicitly *dogmatic* statements (in the strictest theological sense of "dogmatic") that have to do with the definition of what is "Christian." Theological reflection on immigration is not just about those who have crossed geographic borders and their children; it is not just for those who are pastorally engaged with immigrants and their families, or who study them as "objects" for the furthering of (probably dominant) knowledge. Theological reflection on immigration must be part and parcel of what *all* Christian theologies and institutions do. Because being "pilgrim," that is being "immigrant" toward the Reign of God, is a necessary, indispensable, non-negotiable and foundational reality of the Church of Christ.

Can we understand ourselves as Church without incorporating "immigration" into that understanding? Of course not. Can institutions that claim to be Christian be, in fact, "Christian" if they do fail to incorporate "immigration" and immigrants into their daily mission and reality? You know the answer: Churches must be formed by the realities of immigration—and not because of political correctness or momentary convenience, but—because this is of the very essence of Christianity.

A third reason to take immigration seriously is Christianity's aversion to idol worship. As I indicated above, all Christians claim that only God is God, that only God is absolute. But if we debate the issue of immigration (as immigration is usually understood today), it is because another decision preceded it, the decision to establish and recognize a border. Any border (our local southern California border, the one with Canada, and every other border between nations anywhere else) is an imaginary, human creation. Creation did not come packaged with borders. Earth did not evolve with borders. Human decisions made a few rivers and a few mountains into "borders," and in other cases (as in our local San Diego case) human decisions made an imaginary line into a "border."

"That is yours, and this is ours": that is a border, established by human decisions. More precisely, borders are established by decisions made by a handful of humans who have the power to make those decisions and to claim the authority to defend them. *Established borders are the result of power decisions by the powerful.* And this reference to dominant (and asymmetric) power must be part of any discussion on borders and immigration.

But Christians, I argue, are compelled to ask the following questions: What do we do with human power decisions that are the cause of thousands of human deaths? How many deaths are too many for American Christians? Are the human decisions that created and still maintain the borders absolute decisions? Are these decisions so extraordinarily necessary or absolute that human lives can or should be sacrificed to maintain the borders created by a handful of powerful humans? To defend borders born of conquest must we continue to sacrifice humans? Human beings are being killed, hunted, persecuted, separated from their children, imprisoned, raped, traded as merchandise, and at times treated as slaves or animals, because of earlier human decisions that established an imaginary line called a "border" and now that human decision has to be defended and protected at any cost . . . or has to be crossed in the hope of finding a future worthy of humans. Who, may I ask, can claim that human politicians can make decisions that not even God would make, decisions that are blatantly against the most basic of God's commandments: To love every neighbor as we love ourselves?[4]

Human persons are the living "images of God," endowed by their Creator with a dignity that no human law can give or take away, are persecuted because they have dared cross an imaginary line established by politicians through the use of force and solely for the furtherance of human (political and economic) interests. Have we endowed a human decision by human politicians with an absolute character that can only be claimed by and for God? Can one be Christian and not see the transparently clear idolatry in much of today's debate regarding immigration? Or do we think that some idols are okay as long as they are ours and benefit us?

What I argue here is not primarily about politics. Instead, it is basic Christianity. This has to do with the Christian response to the Gospel of Jesus Christ. This is basic Christianity: idolatry is not acceptable. And idolatry is to claim the quality of absoluteness for what is no more than a human creation. To put a human law or a human decision above real respect for shared humanity (a shared humanity that *is* God's creation and God's image) is not acceptable. It is even less acceptable when adherence to a human political decision requires the infliction of death or suffering on other human persons. We cannot in good conscience think this is doctrinally or ethically irrelevant.

That we not commit idolatry, that we be "immigrants" towards the Reign of God, and thereby that we affirm "immigration" as an indispensable component of the Church's identity and reality, all of these are non-negotiable. But how do we let these fundamental doctrines shape the mission and daily reality of Christian institutions? I suggest that only by including the immigrant, because without the immigrant there is no real inclusion of "immigration." How we include the immigrant (and the immigrant's experience of, and perspective on, immigration), however, cannot be achieved by exclusively or mainly listening to those who benefit from the existence of borders. We must listen to those whose lives are sacrificed daily before we listen to those who benefit from this sacrifice, or who justify the deaths of thousands. Why? Because, among Christians, there is no question that salvation came and comes from a once unknown Crucified and not from those who legally condemned him to death.

If being "pilgrim" (being an "immigrant") is of the essence of Christianity, then the inclusion of immigrants and their experience cannot be taken as secondary, as cosmetic, or as an excuse for one more committee or statement for institutional marketing purposes, or to make us feel good as we continue to cover-up our ethical mediocrity and our idolatries. We can pretend that we haven't seen and heard. We can pretend that what we have seen and heard doesn't apply to us, to our theologies and to our institutions, for whatever reason. We can pretend that it is possible to be Christian while ignoring crucially essential dimensions of Christian self-identity and Gospel. We might even think that we are already doing everything that needs to be done, thereby absolving ourselves of any further change. Or we can honestly wrestle with the issues, with the call of the Gospel, and with the real lives of immigrant women and men, with their children, and with the real future of the churches. There are no easy answers. Only questions that we can no longer avoid, and facts that demand attention.

IMMIGRATION AND CHRISTIAN THEOLOGY

Anyone who has read the Hebrew and Christian Scriptures knows that theological reflection on immigration is as old as the Bible. However, the present context and reasons for immigration are not what they were in the biblical or ecclesial past, and so with biblical and ecclesial insights we must also take into consideration today the new issues and realities that our forebears did not and could not have considered.

While I have highlighted three important reasons for American theologians to reflect on immigration, I now want to point briefly to a question of method. Theology is not a monologue. From the very beginning of our discipline, theologians have assumed as necessary their dialogue with other fields of learning, and indeed with human experience as the latter is understood and explained by the social and human sciences: that is why philosophy has always been so important for theology, and why increasingly today the social sciences have become important dialogue partners for theologians. I mention this because I will need to refer very briefly here to the economy and to human culture in light of the contemporary realities of globalization, before addressing specifically theological issues.

GLOBALIZATION AND SOME OF ITS CONSEQUENCES

Globalization is a theoretical paradigm that attempts to describe humanity's current stage, with special emphasis on the development of worldwide capitalism as the new cultural context.[5] There is no commonly agreed definition of "globalization," but most scholars agree that globalization at least refers to "the increasingly interconnected character of the political, economic, and social life of the peoples on this planet." More concretely, globalization is the extension of the effects of modernity to the entire world, accompanied by the compression of time and space brought about by communication technologies.[6]

Globalization has brought a decrease in the functions and power of nations and of national governments. The globalized economy has become "de-territorialized." Contemporary capitalism has become global, thereby surpassing the strictly national, international or multinational. Territorial states no longer have the determining power to control transnational corporations. The transnational corporations are no longer tied to a territory, a culture, or a nation. The consequences of this new reality are enormous on the national states, on the labor market, on the very concept of nation, on human cultures, and on immigration.

In the process of the "de-territorialization" of capital, what becomes globalized are not only economic strategies and institutions, but also ideas, thought processes, and socio-cultural patterns of behavior are also globalized and "de-territorialized." Breaking cultural, social, political, and ideological barriers (which had been built over the centuries), the mass media and other means of massive and instant communication have shaped (and continue to shape) a truly global mass culture. A whole universe of symbols and signs is now broadcast and distributed globally by the modern means of communications, thereby defining anew the manner in which millions of persons throughout the world think, feel, desire, imagine, believe, and act. Signs and symbols are increasingly disconnected from historical, religious, ethnic, national or linguistic particularities, becoming "de-territorialized" and "global."

There is little doubt that globalization has appropriated those elements of modernity and post-modernity that serve its "de-territorializing," global project, although globalization should not be confused with the historical stages usually referred to as "modernity" and "post-modernity." Thus, for example, globalization emphasizes the very "post-modern" attitude that relativizes all claims to truth or to universal validity in order to bring down the cultural, political or religious barriers that may stand in the way of the methods and activities of the transnational corporations. But at the same time, globalization emphasizes the very "modern" and universalizing scientific and technological claims made by Western societies, since the 18th century, in their quest to control knowledge and the creation of knowledge in the world, thereby denying scientific and technological legitimacy or equality to any scientific or technological alternative from outside the Western world.

The evident success of the transnational, globalization model in *some* corners of the world, however, has made the rest of the world (that is, the vast majority of humans, which are deemed to be "not successful" by the standards of globalization) wish to have the success they see elsewhere for themselves. It would be utterly naive to think that the "de-territorialization" of the economy, of cultural imagination, and even of human identities, somehow follows or obeys the dynamics of equality or democracy. In fact, globalization seems to imply and assume the construction of new hierarchies of power across the world. What globalization brings is a new, asymmetric distribution of privileges and exclusions, of possibilities and of hopelessness, of freedoms and slaveries. During the last three millennia, asymmetric power relations in the world were organized so that the rich needed the poor (whether it was for the rich to "save their souls" through works of charity on behalf of the poor, or to exploit the poor through labor in order to further increase the rich's wealth). Now, in these globalized times, the poor seem to be no longer necessary. Wealth and capital increase without the work of the poor (among other reasons because the labor force needed in the globalized economy is a trained labor force which, almost by definition, prevents the participation of the poor). Globalization is a new way of producing wealth, but it is also (and concomitantly) a new way of producing poverty.

Let me argue that while the "physicality" of territory has been important to humans, its importance has not been mainly due to the "physicality" of the land, but, rather, its importance resided mostly on a people's ability to sustain their lives and their identity as a people "there." Put differently: "territory" is the condition that sustained human life and helped identify a people as such in a given "place." While on the other hand, globalization is intimately connected with "de-territorialization." In other words, globalization causes and is caused (among other reasons) by the possibility of *not needing* a "place" which would identify and sustain a people as "this" people.

Identity and sustenance, in the new economy, come from the possibilities opened by being members of the so-called global village. Identity and sustenance, thus conceived, dramatically alter (and clearly subvert) what has been traditionally understood by "identity" and "sustenance"—and, consequently, also impact such categories as "loyalty," "honor," "citizenship," "nationality" and "immigration." The very notion of "immigration," after all, assumes a set of cultural and political definitions (such as "border") that, thanks to the globalized economy, are gradually losing their hold on human experience. Boundaries between states become increasingly insignificant in the flow of information and capital. The movement of peoples, especially rural peoples in search of the benefits of globalization, makes the meaning of home as ancestral place less significant. If boundaries have played an important role in identity by helping us define who we are by who we are not, they are now so crisscrossed by globalization processes that they seem to have lost their identity-conferring power.

I find it highly ironic that the individuals and groups who enthusiastically and uncritically endorse the economic and cultural conditions which foster globalization (likely because they are benefiting from them) are often the same individuals and groups who wish to hold back the consequences of the transformation of the traditional cultural definitions and political structures which globalization is quickly dismantling. In other words, it is impossible to support an unbridled global market economy (or the conditions for and benefits thereof) without compromising family and communal values, beliefs and expectations, and without actively promoting the migration of millions.

Given what I've been arguing about globalization and "de-territorialization," immigration cannot be simply or naively viewed today as the movement of individuals who individually decided to move from one geographic location to another, even when crossing national boundaries. Globalization inevitably forces millions to migrate, and is the cause of most present-day immigration. The global economy is a reality. The global labor market is a reality. The global distribution of symbolic and material products is a reality. Global mass culture is an increasing reality. The power of nations is no longer what it used to be prior to the emergence of the transnational corporations. And, and as consequence, identity and sustenance are no longer necessarily tied to a geographic location for millions of people

People migrate because they need to find employment in order to feed their families, educate their children, and be able to afford healthcare—these are human, moral rights, and Christian ethics has consistently affirmed this. Consequently, we may ask, do people have the moral right to migrate across borders when their very existence and livelihood is at risk? Can national laws ultimately prevent immigration when pervasive globalization, supported by the very governments and power groups that want to stop the migratory flow, is forcing millions of humans to migrate in order to simply live?

The growing reality of exchange and engagement through immigration (of building and rebuilding, and of defining and redefining, the human community), as well as the "pilgrim" foundations of Christianity, make me wonder if we are not also urgently in need of a new ecclesiology, which is the branch of theology that considers the nature and functions of the church. While reflecting on the usual topics of any substantive ecclesiology, a contemporary ecclesiology that responds to immigrant realities would take seriously the experience of and doctrinal issues raised by immigration, viewing the entire ecclesiological construct from the perspective of immigration.

FURTHER THEOLOGICAL REFLECTIONS ON IMMIGRATION

While we consider that new ecclesiology, I will recommend here a few questions to guide and foster the reflection, as well as a renewed understanding of catholicity. Since the councils of Christian antiquity, Christian doctrine has consistently taught that the Church must recognize itself as both "catholic" and "one." There is no choice possible between these two marks of the Church—catholicity and unity are non-negotiable and are equally necessary. History reminds us, however, that there is no easy way of fostering both catholicity and unity.

Catholicity, which means universality, is not a question of geography. In other words, the catholicity of the Church does not depend on the latter's presence in every corner of the planet. If this were so, how could we claim that early Christianity was indeed "catholic"? Catholicity is a quality of the Church that describes a constitutive and indispensable dimension of the Church's mission and foundational grace. Catholicity has to do with universality as quality, as attitude, as vocation. The Church is "catholic" because its doors are open to every human being, and to every human group, without distinction and without barriers. The Church is "catholic" because it refuses to assume that one human culture is superior to others, or that one human culture or nation is "better suited" as witness and bearer of the Christian gospel, or that one theology is the standard for all others. Indeed, it is part of the very definition of catholicity that national, cultural, racial, political, gender, economic and theological barriers and imperial/colonizing attitudes must come down as a direct consequence of God's revelation in Christ.

Catholicity does not stamp out diversity. On the contrary, it assumes the legitimacy of diversity. Universality does no necessitate uniformity—but it does require the end of prejudice and of all claims of superiority over others. In some ways, it is possible to argue that catholicity offers the Church the ground on which to understand and engage contemporary globalization while at the same time allowing the Church to prophetically critique globalization's inhuman consequences. Where globalization attempts to erase diversity, catholicity can strongly support diversity. Where globalization would implement unfair power and class relations, catholicity can demand equality and respect for the rights of all humans. Indeed, the Church's catholicity can play this prophetic role precisely because the Church too is a global community, whose identity does not depend on nationalities, territories, racial categories, or borders that serve as barriers.

It is indeed part of the genius of Christianity to engage and dialogue with every culture, every race, every people, every idea. The Church will not necessarily come to agree with all, but agreement or disagreement cannot occur without prior discernment, and discernment cannot happen without prior knowledge. Knowledge, in turn, cannot come about without serious engagement and exchange. The catholicity of the Church can and does transcend and critique the barriers established by human societies throughout the centuries precisely because it assumes and engages human diversity.

Welcoming the stranger or foreigner (the "immigrant," we could say today) is the most often repeated commandment in the Hebrew Scriptures, with the exception of the imperative to worship only the one God.

And the love of neighbor (especially of the more vulnerable neighbor) is doubtlessly the New Testament's constant demand. Furthermore, the best Christian social ethics has consistently defended not only the human rights of immigrants but their right to migrate across borders in order to find security and livelihood. Whatever the cause of immigration today, there can be no doubt as to where the Church must stand when it comes to defending the immigrant.

In mainstream Christian teaching, immigrants are *not* and *cannot* be considered "aliens" or "foreigners" among Christians. Immigrants, on the contrary, are always valued as "neighbors," and we all know the New Testament's repeated and emphatic command to love our neighbor, regardless of the neighbor's virtues or lack thereof. From the apostolic Church through the great bishops of Christian antiquity to our own generation, we find a constant, broad, and powerful stream of voices insisting that the neighbor in need must be loved and protected, and treated as equal. The moral demands on Christians seem clear. The doctrinal explanation and grounding of these moral demands are solid. The particularities of each situation will dictate *how* immigrants' rights will be defended and protected, but there is no question on *whether* they should be defended and protected.

Finally, I want to turn to questions to guide and promote a new ecclesiological construct. In addition to my reflections on the necessary Christian attitude toward immigrants, and arguably much more important in the long run, are the following theological, dogmatic questions that might appropriately ground and guide the construction of a theology of immigration within a fundamental ecclesiology:

1. Given the global economy and the "de-territorialization" it has brought about, could we argue that immigration is *the* indispensable "sacrament" of the Church's catholicity today? Can we have catholicity today without immigration?
2. Can we be "catholic" without recognizing in ourselves and in our immigrant neighbors the "pilgrim" condition so emphatically taught by the Scriptures and required of all who hope to participate in the Reign of God, thereby making immigration the contemporary definition of "pilgrim Church" with all the latter implies (or should imply) in ecclesiology?
3. Can we discover in the immigrant (and in the experience of immigration) the very dimension of catholicity that defines Christianity, thereby making the fair treatment of the immigrant, and our understanding of the experience of immigration, *necessary* to Christianity (not just pastorally but dogmatically)?

Immigration will not stop; given contemporary globalization, it cannot stop. And yet a thorough, systematic theological reflection on immigration is still in the future. Theologians have been dealing with immigration from the perspective of ethics (social or personal), but the questions posed to dogmatic or systematic theologians by globalization, "de-territorialization," and immigration have frequently gone unheard and consequently unanswered. I cannot and do not pretend to have done here more than a quick "scratch of the surface." In fact, I know that I have done nothing but suggest that immigration, and its contemporary global context, merit careful study on the part of theologians—not just as an ethical or pastoral issue, but as a profoundly dogmatic one. And I hope to have adequately made the point.

I hope to have helped all of us begin to confront (or continue to confront) some of the consequences that millions of our fellow Christians bring to our door. I know it's not easy to deal with immigration as Christians, but as Christians we have no choice. The present volume will continue raising questions and challenging our answers.

NOTES

1. An easily accessible online bibliography is found at http://www.latinobibliography.org. I would more emphatically recommend these titles by U.S. Latino/a scholars: J.-P. Ruiz, *Readings from the Edges: The Bible and People on the Move* (Maryknoll, NY: Orbis Books, 2011); G.L. Cuéllar, *Voices of Marginality: Exile and Return in Second Isaiah 40-55, and the Mexican Immigrant Experience* (New York: Peter Lang Publishing, 2008); C. Nanko-Fernández, *Theologizing en Espanglish: Context, Community and Ministry* (Maryknoll, NY: Orbis Books, 2010); O. Espín, "Migrations and Unexpected Inter-Religious Dialogue," in *eJournal of Hispanic/Latino Theology*, I: 5/25/07 (ISSN: 1930-9147); idem., "La experiencia de lo sagrado en el contexto contemporáneo de globalización," in R. Fornet-Betancourt, ed., *Resistencia y solidaridad* (Madrid: Editorial Trotta, 2003), 171–90; idem., "Immigration, Territory, and Globalization: Theological Reflections." In: *Journal of Hispanic/Latino Theology*, 7:3 (2000), 46–59. All of these publications include bibliographies on many of the issues raised in the present paper.

2. All demographic figures are from studies sponsored (although not necessarily published) by the Center for the Study of Latino/a Catholicism (University of San Diego, 2009), projected to 2011.

3. From the vast possible bibliography, see: Second Vatican Council (1963–1965). *Lumen Gentium*, 1, 48; idem., *Gaudium et Spes*, 45, 57, 58; S. Nash, *The Church as a Pilgrim People: Hebrews-Revelation* (Macon, GA: Smyth & Welwys, 2001).

4. I want to remind the reader, it is an explicit and repeated command in the Bible that God's People must also love the foreigner and treat the foreigner as they would treat a fellow-citizen.

5. This definition of globalization (with greater problematization thereof) I owe to Robert Schreiter. See his *The New Catholicity* (Maryknoll, NY: Orbis Books, 1997).

6. For further developments of some key ideas briefly presented in this section on globalization and its consequences, and for ample bibliographical references, see O. Espín, "Immigration, Territory, and Globalization: Theological Reflections," cit.; and several chapters in: idem, *Grace and Humanness: Theological Reflections Because of Culture* (Maryknoll, NY: Orbis Books, 2007).

SELECTED BIBLIOGRAPHY

Cuéllar, Gregory Lee. *Voices of Marginality: Exile and Return in Second Isaiah 40-55, and the Mexican Immigrant Experience*. New York: Peter Lang Publishing, 2008.
Espín, Orlando. *Grace and Humanness: Theological Reflections Because of Culture*. Maryknoll, NY: Orbis Books, 2007.
Nanko-Fernández, Carmen. *Theologizing en Espanglish: Context, Community and Ministry*. Maryknoll, NY: Orbis Books, 2010.
Ruiz, Jean-Pierre. *Readings from the Edges: The Bible and People on the Move*. Maryknoll, NY: Orbis Books, 2011.

TWO
Alternately Documented Theologies
Mapping Border, Exile and Diaspora

Carmen M. Nanko-Fernández

In a September 2009 article in *Theological Studies*, Catholic theologian Daniel Groody writes, "Some research has been done on migration and religion from a sociological perspective, but there is virtually nothing on the topic from a theological perspective. Theology seems to enter the academic territory from the outside, as if it were a 'disciplinary refugee' with no official recognition in the overall discourse about migration."[1] He continues, "Even among theologians the topic of migration is largely undocumented. The Vatican and various episcopal conferences have notable writings about the pastoral care of immigrants, but to date little has been written about migration as a theological reality."[2]

With all due respect, I am left to wonder what exactly constitutes theological reflection on *migration* and who counts as a *documented* theologian? Scholarship in the United States of America and Canada by a number of Latin@,[3] Asian American, African American, and diasporic theologians and biblical scholars is embedded in the matrices of peoples on the move, so much so that migrations, in all their complexities, shape hermeneutical lenses that engage not only texts but contexts. These theologians and biblical interpreters remain academia's undocumented scholars. The failure to acknowledge even the existence of these theologies of migrations authored by those whose own diasporic experiences often shape their theological perspectives and hermeneutical optics replicates the very marginalization often experienced by the communities these theologians represent. Postcolonial biblical interpreter and theologian

R.S. Sugirtharajah speculates that the dismissal of the writings of scholars from racially and ethnically underrepresented constituencies relates to the sources of their theologizing, in other words, "their life-experiences of being vilified and demeaned."[4] These loci theologici result in articulations that "reveal a great deal of emotion, passion, and expressions of anger, and they may at times seem confrontational" thus generating discomfort and irritation with these scholars who "unashamedly and openly declare their presuppositions and preferential options..." in works considered "lamentations" by mainstream academia rather than "rational" discourse.[5]

In light of this "racism of omission,"[6] the words of theologian Fumitaka Matsuoka contain a haunting claim: "When theology moves into the public arena of discourse out of the womb of the faith community, it challenges both the public itself and theology's own credibility."[7] I would further emphasize that the unnerving challenge comes when our particular theologies nurtured in the wombs of our particular ethnic/racial/cultural and diasporic communities insist that for us theology is and always has been part of the public weave.

Theologizing out of particularity, the so-called contextual, local, or vernacular theologies are well over a quarter of a century old. Diasporic interpreters, as Sugirtharajah observes, "represent a new breed of professionally trained scholars addressing and challenging the academy. Their works show how they constantly translate in both directions—from the home they left behind and the new home they are trying to make sense of."[8] Chicago-based Argentinian theologian Nancy Bedford offers another perspective by shifting attention from place to movement. "The experience of migration questions fixed ontological categories and tidy linguistic solutions. As migrants who are theologians and theologians who are migrants, our experience is by definition more that of a way or a path than of a place. We might think therefore in terms of a *via theologica* as a possible variation on a *locus theologicus.*"[9]

One need only pick up the anthology *Realizing the America in Our Hearts: Theological Voices of Asian Americans* (2003) to appreciate the diversity of perspectives that arise from the multiple and varying experiences of migrations often homogenized under the umbrella term Asian North American. What emerges in this anthology is a "quilt of many colors and many patterns."[10] From Chinese-Canadian Greer Anne Wenh-In Ng's proposition of a bamboo theology[11] to Peter Phan's exploration of Vietnamese-Americans caught between Eagle and Dragon,[12] the reflections in this volume challenge the temptation to create a *theology of migration* by insisting on the distinctiveness of each migration and its respective context. These essays demonstrate that one size does not fit all; there is no *universal* experience of migration.

African American theological reflections further problematize simplistic constructions of migrations. For example, theological and biblical interpretations of Exodus, especially as shaped by historical experiences such as the Middle Passage, flights from slavery, the great northern migrations, and internal movements precipitated by events like Hurricane Katrina introduce a range of lenses from liberation to forced displacement all shrouded in the sin of racism.

The diversity encompassed beneath the umbrellas of "Latino/a" or "Hispanic" is far more complicated than the homogeneity implied by the terms. La comunidad latina includes immigrants, those of us recognized by the U.S. government as well as those of us who are alternately documented; refugees and exiles, guest workers and migrant laborers; those of us made citizens by choice or fast-tracked through military service; those of us born citizens by virtue of our birth in the United States or Puerto Rico or to U.S. citizen parents.

How migrations are experienced varies, and so should the theologies that emerge from the particularities of their contexts. There is no ubiquitous experience of displacement, and the movement of peoples affects not only those on the move, but those encountered along the way as well as the sending and receiving communities. Recognizing the experiential differences in/of migrations should result in more than just nuanced discourse on an assumed universal theme and such cognizance is especially vital in the development of pastoral ministries and in the dialogue that shapes public policies.

LATIN@ THEOLOGIES AND PEOPLE ON THE MOVE

This chapter documents theological and biblical reflections on migration(s) from the perspectives of Latin@ scholars. A survey of Latin@ theological and biblical scholarship reveals an array of experiences behind such familiar categories as border/frontera, exile and diaspora. These terms affirm a distinctiveness of experience that challenges any overarching construction of a "theology of migration" even if done latinamente.[13] Miguel Díaz, a Cuban American theologian and, as of 2009, the U.S. Ambassador to the Holy See, queries, "How might we construct a theology of migration meaningful to the displaced who among themselves did not experience perilous journeys (e.g., longstanding Cuban exiles or Haitian refugees in South Florida or the Hmong in Minnesota)? Other particular geographical, political, and religious factors similarly should impact our theology of migration."[14]

Along with other aspects of our theologizing latinamente, our own social locations as hermeneuts inform the directions we tend to follow. The *border* surfaces as primary focus for many of our Mexican-American and Tejan@ theologians. The theologies of Virgilio Elizondo, Arturo Bañuelas, Nancy Pineda-Madrid and others reflect the fluidity of life along contested fronteras. It should come as no surprise that reflections on *exile* are especially predominant among many of our Cuban-American interlocutors, see for example the work of biblical and culture studies scholar Fernando Segovia, theologian Justo González as well as mujerisata theologian Ada María Isasi-Díaz. For our Boricuas, Nuyoricans and other dispersed Puerto Ricans like theologians Samuel Solivan, Edwin Aponte, Luis Rivera Rodríguez and biblical scholar Jean-Pierre Ruiz postcolonial interpretations open up experiences of *diaspora* and internal migrations—a complex relationship of being simultaneously colonized and imperial citizen, yet suspect enough to be detained in Arizona without probable cause.

For Latin@'s, our own theologies bring perspectives that offer alternate insights precisely because our theologizing claims an intimacy with the daily lived experiences of our complex networks of accountability. Latin@ theologies are grounded in la vida cotidiana; complex daily lived realities are our theological loci. From this stance, theologians are insiders, implicated and embedded. On matters of migrations, three coordinates deserve attention as we more intentionally map our place in the theological plaza: frontera/border, exile, diaspora. The treatment of these coordinates in this context is by no means exhaustive but it is intended to document the existence of a substantial body of theological reflection and biblical interpretation on migrations and a constellation of experiences that result from the voluntary and forced movements and settlements of peoples.

MAPPING COORDINATES: BORDER/LA FRONTERA

For many Latin@ theologians the motif of border has been especially provocative. First-generation theological reflections characterize Latin@ theology as "border theology."[15] In part this is due to the social locations of these theologians by virtue of their own ethnicities as Mexican, Mexican American, Tejan@ or Chican@; their geographic location, particularly in the southwestern region of the United States and/or in border towns like San Diego/Tijuana or El Paso/Juárez; their pastoral accompaniment of im/migrant communities. These experiences shape the hermeneutical lenses used in the construction of Latin@ theologies en conjunto and these borderlands and border-crossing experiences function as ground from which such theologizing arises.

Historical Context

On the U.S.-Mexican border the people are not only "on the move" but have historically been *moved in on*. These lands, carved out on both sides of the current border, are the product of multiple conquests and varying movements of peoples for centuries. This reality complicates any reflection latinamente and can create conflicted responses to the ongoing migrations that have shaped and continue to reshape the west and southwestern regions of the United States. The region absorbed and reflects the impact of Spanish explorations, Catholic evangelization and too often violence against indigenous people. Nineteenth-century migrations from the eastern and midwestern United States brought countless English-speakers, U.S. imperial aspirations, and various Christian faith traditions, including Mormonism. Migrations of the twentieth and twenty-first centuries continue to bring not only Mexicans, but relocated Vietnamese refugees as well as Central Americans crossing the southern border of Mexico fleeing oppressions across the economic and political spectrum and an assortment of natural disasters.

In a twist on the U.S. national equating of "Mexican" with "illegal alien," historically "it was white U.S. citizens who were the 'illegal aliens' whose undocumented incursions into Mexican national territory" set the stage for the invasion and seizure of Mexican lands and the subsequent disenfranchisement of former Mexican citizens who now found themselves in the United States without ever moving.[16] Ironically the "foreigners" were not the "strangers" who settled from the east and Midwest but the Mexicans who had long occupied the annexed territories, and, even though they are granted U.S. citizenship, they and their descendants remain aliens in their own land. This establishment of a contested border allowed for the "coupling of 'Mexican'-ness and migrant 'illegality,'" that to this day "has rendered Mexicans in the United States as permanent 'outsiders,'" and "has insured that the politics of citizenship is always a thoroughly racialized matter."[17]

Latin@ Theological Directions

In Latin@ theological and biblical studies, the border functions as both lens and locus. As lens this body of scholarship engages the works of Chican@, postcolonial and culture studies. La frontera is perceived as liminal space, with all the ambiguities, possibilities and violence contested places of intersections, encounters and clashes hold. The influences of Chican@ theorists such as Gloria Anzaldúa are especially noticeable in the writings of theologians like Virgilio Elizondo.[18] For Anzaldúa the convergence of histories and peoples at the U.S.-Mexican border "*es una berida* [sic] *abierta* where the Third World grates against the First and bleeds. And before a scab forms it hemorrhages again, the lifeblood of two worlds merging to form a third country—a border culture."[19] Borderlands are characterized by spatial, human, and material hybridity. From the historical reality of the Spanish conquest of indigenous populations, "*nació una nueva raza, el mexicano* (people of mixed Indian and Spanish blood), a race that had never existed before."[20] From a theological perspective, this creates a new historical moment, "the unique *mestizo* border reality is a *kairos*, a moment of grace and opportunity experienced in the decisive action to act as bridge people between the Americas."[21]

Movement of peoples, in all its good and sinfulness, in this case has soteriological and eschatological implications. From the standpoint of mestizaje, Mexican American theologian and Catholic pastor Arturo Bañuelas contends that the role of bridge "has as its task the elimination of all cultural, political, sexual, and economic boundaries to pave the way for the fashioning of a new historical project that subsists in the unfolding of God's reign."[22] Using his own experience of being a mestizo who is from the borderlands as hermeneutical optic for reading the gospels, Virgilio Elizondo finds theological significance in his construction of Galilee as a borderland, peripheral to Jerusalem as center of Jewish life.[23] He posits a hybridity to the Galilean region and its people that corresponds to U.S.-Mexican borderlands and the mestizaje that characterizes his people. For Elizondo, on these borders with these peoples despised because of their embodied mixture God acts in a self-revelatory manner that invites inclusivity. Cuban American theologian Roberto Goizueta, whose own scholarship is influenced by Elizondo, captures the christological connection: "In the person of Jesus Christ, who comes from and, resurrected, returns to Galilee, the *mestizo* victim is revealed as the sacrament of God's reign, the witness to a truly global *ekklesia*."[24]

The borderlands and the peoples created by migrations and encounters, provide images for comprehending Jesus Christ and the church as well. The concept of mestizo/a as bridge is theologically significant in redefining the humanity of a people despised and discriminated against because of their embodied hybridity. This in turn informs Christological trajectories which image Jesus as border crosser and/or interprets his Galilean pedigree as ancient mestizaje. While these trajectories have been necessarily challenged and critiqued, for example by Guatemalan theologian and Canadian immigrant Néstor Medina[25] and Nuyorican bibical scholar Jean-Pierre Ruiz,[26] they, and the critiques they engender, are nonetheless illustrative of a body of theological scholarship on matters related to migrations by scholars from racial, ethnic, cultural and diasporic communities traditionally under-represented in academia.

Moving Beyond the Border

There are limitations to border metaphors, and cautions that require attention if theologies seek to contribute to public discourse and to the formulation of public policy. It is important to avoid fetishizing or romanticizing the southern border of the United States. Spiritualizing interpretations of others' real life dangers has a voyeuristic quality and camouflages the ugliness of socio-economic injustices and violence that characterizes life on the edge. In some ways, this is similar to appropriations of the preferential option for the poor that missed the point and instead romanticized poverty.

The theological scholarship of Nancy Pineda-Madrid, a self-described "mujer fronterizada,"[27] offers an example of yet another direction in theologizing with the borderlands as context. In her book *Suffering and Salvation in Cuidad Juárez* Pineda-Madrid confronts the complexity of contemporary border violence by focusing on what she terms *feminicide*, "the killing of girls and women by men in exceptionally brutal manner, on a massive scale and with impunity for the perpetrators."[28] Employing a hermeneutic of social-suffering she carefully analyzes this ongoing atrocity as well as the ritualized practices of resistance by the victims' families and supporters. From these responses to suffering she proposes that "community is the condition that makes salvation possible."[29] Pineda-Madrid is one of the few theologians to take seriously violence in the borderlands, a reality intertwined with migrations and the drug trade that has a long reaching impact because as transborder performance artist Guillermo Gómez-Peña observes an "empire of violence does not stop at the border."[30]

Too narrow a focus on the U.S.-Mexican border alone distracts attention from other sites of struggle that constitute complex networks of international relations requiring political address, for example the southern border of Mexico, the Straits of Mona, the northern border of the United States, even the practices at sea ports and airports. Borders are contested spaces however they are rarely the final destination. The tragic consequences of failed or misguided public policies are felt in the heartland and en los barrios as the daily rhythms of life are disrupted with workplace raids and neighborhood sweeps. Lives lived in the shadows can unravel in even the most comfortable of circumstances. Theological contributions to the public conversation will remain limited if we stay fixated on the crossing but neglect to attend to the living, to the mundane perils and anxieties associated with going to school, earning a just wage in a safe workplace, renting an apartment, opening a bank account, getting married, driving a car.

Borders, like hyphens, focus attention on binary relationships. While these have value, our metaphors need to expand lest we perpetually insure that only certain people will stereotypically become the other. Furthermore borders and hyphens too often are used more as minus signs rather than as an indication of equals, and in such equations, one side inevitably is found lacking. Why else the move?

MAPPING COORDINATES: EXILE/EXILIO

The metaphor of exile resonates acutely with Cuban Americans, especially those whose own stories include journeys to the United States, sometimes via Spain. These experiences create a theological weave threaded with a powerful autobiographical strand that underscores distinctiveness among migrations yet shares collective elements among those who identify as exiles. In the scholarship of these primarily first generation Cuban immigrants, the Babylonian exile provides a biblical referent, a text read and reread through hermeneutical bifocals that interpret what Fernando Segovia has described as being from two places but with no place to stand.[31]

Historical Context

Memories of exile are engrained in the Cuban national and diasporic imagination. The relationships with both the United States and Spain are conflicted because each nation historically is/has been both colonizer and refuge to Cubans.[32] In the twentieth century, the rise to power of Fidel Castro unleashes several streams of emigration that create exilic communities of Cubans particularly in the New York metropolitan area and in Florida. But this is not a new phenomenon. In the nineteenth century, émigrés from the Spanish colony to New York are also motivated by political forces. Driven into exile by their advocacy for independence, often times these Cuban intellectuals continue their revolutionary activities in New York.[33] Among the most prominent of these Cuban national heroes are Félix Varela y Morales[34] and José Martí.[35]

Arriving in New York in 1823, Varela, a Catholic priest, ministered among the Irish immigrants of New York City and his advocacy for human rights and social reform in both his home and exilic lands caused fellow countryman José Martí to refer to him as "the Cuban saint." Varela died in in 1853 in exile, yet he remained faithful to his native land, as evident in the closing words of the first volume of his *Letters to Elpidio*: "Guided by the torch of faith, I go to the tomb, on the edge of which I hope, with God's grace, to make with my last breath a profession of my firm belief and a fervent prayer for the good of my country."[36]

These exilic experiences are often marked by a longing for the homeland. "Deeply embedded in the Cuban psyche exists the realization that they have lost the land of their birth and that when their bodies are finally laid to rest, they will be interred as foreigners in an alien soil."[37] This sense of displacement, complicated by memories of what no longer is or in many cases even never was, is not necessarily the experience of generations born in the United States. However the loss that accompanies dislocation crosses generations and creates an impoverishment articulated best in the words of Cuban theologian Justo González: "It does not rob one of money. Perhaps it even improves one's economic condition. But it is also a form of poverty inasmuch as it deprives one of identity, traditions, roots, dignity, family."[38]

Latin@ Theological Directions

In Latin@ theological and biblical studies, exile functions as hermeneutical lens, vocation, paradigm, and method. Biblical scholar Francisco García-Treto situates himself in the broader centuries-old tradition of Cuban exilic experiences, "not only when I locate myself in the contemporary Cuban diaspora for whom exile from the *patria* (fatherland) is a historical reality, but when I use that location as a standpoint from which to reflect on the biblical exile and its literary products as a target for interpretation."[39] For him exile, with its connotations of expulsion and loss, better expresses his experience than the less specific term immigrant. This experience also brings bilinguality as a constitutive aspect that informs his scholarship and his identity as a biblical hermeneut. He juxtaposes biblical texts—for example, Lamentations—with Cuban exilic texts drawn from the works of other writers of Cuban diasporas, such as José Martí or Daína Chaviano—in order to focus his "emotional resonances with the loss caused by exile from 'the City,' be it Jerusalem or Havana, even to the choice of a victimized and defiled 'Daughter City' as a central figure whose suffering puts into question the fairness or applicability of former values."[40] This interaction of survival literatures across time marks Garcia-Treto's stance in reading "the Hebrew Bible as exilic, not only chronologically (product) but discursively (content)."[41]

Mujerista theologian Ada María Isasi-Díaz uses her exilic experience as a vocation. She recognizes the pain and the tensions between memory and lived reality that characterize exile yet she hopes that this will give birth to new possibilities that require attention to reconciliation. Exile as vocation creates conditions for developing new visions. "The future does not rest with a fractured Cuban community, exile groups against each other, or exiles against those who stayed in Cuba. In order to be a unified country we must forgive even when there is no repentance. . . . But we ourselves must also repent and humbly ask for forgiveness for not understanding from afar, for judging from afar."[42] Reflected in her words is an understanding of an exile, even one who is a naturalized citizen of a new land, as always belonging to one's native land, so much so as to be involved in its future. Isasi-Díaz explains that among the motivations for her work on reconciliation "is my love for Cuba, a love that urges me to find ways of being a faithful daughter of the land where I was born and hope to die."[43]

Theologian Justo González sees exile as a paradigm for how Hispanics in general read and interpret scripture in order to make meaning of their own lives. He perceives exile as the metaphor that resonates with pan-Latin@ experiences and he proposes that the Babylonian exile functions for Latin@'s in ways the exodus does for Latin Americans and African Americans. For González the relationship between exile and the experience of being alien, even in one's own land, is one that crosses intraLatin@ ethnic and national distinctions. At the root of exile, according to González is some fundamental and systemic decay at the center that sets people literally in motion. The factors may vary—politics, socioeconomics, military conquest, oppression—but the result is inevitably exile, "a dislocation of the center, with all the ambiguities and ambivalence of such dislocation."[44] For González what had been the center of one's life is now periphery and often times the move is to a new center—a center of imperial power that pushes home to the edges of empire. "We have come to the center, yet we remain at the periphery. . . . we no longer know where the center is—for that is the very nature of exile, a life in which one is forced to revolve around a center that is not one's own, and that in many ways one does not wish to own."[45]

Fernando Segovia perceives an integral interrelationship between social location and interpretation therefore his experience of exile provides his locus and informs his method for his biblical scholarship and theologizing. Employing an explicitly postcolonial optic, he carves out a "theology of diaspora—a theology born and forged in exile, in displacement and relocation."[46] He describes a context of "double and reinforced otherness" constitutive of Latin@ experiences in the United States no matter the status of their citizenship or the conditions of their migrations. Segovia observes, "In our present, permanent and everyday world, we begin as strangers and remain strangers throughout—the undesirable others, the ones who do not fit."[47] The same holds true in "our former, traditional and distant world, there, we gradually and inevitably become and remain aliens as well—the distant others, the ones who left."[48] Segovia turns this dual belonging/not belonging or perpetual state of otherness into a creative departure point for the formulation of his voice, resistant and even rebellious in response to colonizing forces.[49] This dual "identity of otherness" paradoxically has advantages because the exile is fluent in the ways of the present world and the one left behind. With this "privileged knowledge" of both worlds the diasporic person knows that "all worlds are constructions" and is able not only to recognize and choose what is positive and negative in each but "to offer informed critique of each world—its visions, its values, its traditions."[50] For Segovia, a theological and hermeneutical voice grounded in an identity of otherness would avoid replicating its own experience of being colonized by externally imposed definitions or categories. From this contested experience and embrace of otherness, Segovia derives a reading strategy for engaging difference that in effect "begins with contextualization and aims for contextualization."[51]

Surviving Exile and Beyond

For a number of first generation Cuban immigrant theologians and biblical scholars, the exile metaphor expresses best their diasporic experience. The temptation is to interpret other Latin@' experiences of migrations and/or life in the United States through an exilic lens.[52] Being from two worlds or places literally or figuratively is not limited to experiences of exile. At the same time there are several responses to exile, which are also evident in displaced communities.[53] These include but are not limited to assimilation, socio-economic status that exceeds what was possible in the homeland, accommodation, acquiring new citizenship, embrace of the receiving land. Furthermore, not all exiles are treated in a similar fashion in the receiving land; for example, contrast the U.S. immigration policies for Cuban versus Haitian exiles, or in the 1980s the status of Nicaraguan versus Salvadorian exiles. The exilic experience is further complicated when descendants, born as citizens in the receiving land, do not understand themselves as outsiders nor do they bear animus either to their native land or their ancestral home. While there are indeed intersections, maintaining the distinctiveness of experiences avoids an imposed homogenization that ignores the complexities and particularities that require attention in the drafting of equitable public policies, in the crafting of appropriate pastoral ministries and in the forming/informing of individual and social consciences.

Theological scholarship grounded in exile yields a number of fruitful trajectories. Segovia's strategy has potential beyond its value as an effective hermeneutical approach for engaging texts. Emerging from the margins, there is an embedded and embodied quality to a diasporic theology that seeks to engage others/otherness from a posture of one's own otherness. There is promise in utilizing such a method to read the multidimensional contexts of migrations. What might be the possibilities for engaging the otherness of God? Isasi-Díaz's attention to reconciliation has practical, ethical and eschatological implications. Like Varela, she remains intimately connected to the concerns of her native land. Identifying an exilic commitment *por allá* she appreciates that for whatever reason *allá* is home to those who remained behind and solidarity among Cubans is necessary for an improved future. She draws briefly on Varela, citing his contention that the good of the nation is also connected to the virtuous behavior of its people. What benefits might a more engaged retrieval of the writings of an exilic Varela bring to contemporary theological constructions?

MAPPING COORDINATES: DIASPORA

While exile is understood in diasporic terms, all relocations and dislocations, forced or voluntary, are not necessarily exilic. As employed in Latin@ theologies, especially by diasporic Puerto Ricans, the metaphor of diaspora is less inclined to bear the nostalgic longing and remembering that accompanies exile. The more fluid and idiosyncratic relationship between la Isla and the United States may in part be responsible for that interpretation. In the words of biblical scholar and theologian Jean-Pierre Ruiz, "This experience [*exile*] is not my own, for I am not a member of the Cuban, diaspora, but I am an Antillean cousin, as it were, with a Puerto Rican heritage. Even more specifically, I am a Nuyorican, a member of that peculiar hybrid group that rides the frequent flyer hyphen between San Juan and New York."[54]

Historical Context

In 1898, a "spoil" of the Spanish-American War, Puerto Rico becomes part of the colonial orbit of the United States, the only Spanish possession in las Américas denied independence. While the Jones Act of 1917 conferred U.S. citizenship on all Puerto Ricans, it comes with restrictions that impact those who live on la Isla but not in diaspora.[55] Described in paradoxical terms as "alien-citizen" the reality is a second class citizenship, with obligations such as military service if conscripted, however with limited participation and protections tied to residency in a particular place.[56] Theologian Samuel Solivan tries to make sense out of the impact of these conditions on diasporic Puerto Ricans, who he views as citizen-exiles.[57] In other words, they are afforded the full rights and constitutional protections of citizenship aquí (in the fifty states) but are regarded by their stateside citizen-neighbors as foreign immigrants and they are dislocated as a consequence of the colonized status of their homeland.

Like their Cuban counterparts, nineteenth century Puerto Ricans seeking independence from Spain found refuge in places like New York and Santo Domingo. Prior to 1898 and into the twentieth century, besides artists and intellectuals, migrations and relocations to the city, as well as to parts of Florida like Tampa, included industries and their respective workers—most prominent was the tobacco industry.[58] Internal migrations from Puerto Rico to other states and territories in the U.S. constellation were often driven by socio-economic concerns and later the ease of mobility due to citizen status. This results in waves of migrations from la Isla and the development of Puerto Rican communities from Hawai'i through Chicago to the eastern seaboard. However culture studies scholar Juan Flores suggests, "in the U.S. setting, the community forged of a colonial labor migration stands in greater long-term disadvantage than that which has issued from political exile, or even the more recognizable Third World immigration."[59] According to Flores the colonial dependence of the Island and its internalization in diaspora compound both class and racial subordination in Puerto Rican experience.

Latin@ Theological Directions

In Latin@ theological and biblical studies, the image of diaspora, especially as articulated by diasporic Puerto Ricans, reflects the ambiguities, tensions and multiple layers of complexity associated with possibilities of dislocation, bilocation, relocation and return available to colonized citizens. Complicated by power dimensions with class, racial, gender and geographic overtones, these contested experiences inoculate diasporic interpreters from perceiving identity as fixed or univocal in any text or context. At the same interpreters necessarily situate and localize identities with a specificity that is resistant to hyphenated labels. Obviously Puerto Rican-American is redundant, to be Puerto Rican is to be a U.S. citizen, whether welcome or not, and to be from la Isla or born in diaspora significantly shapes points of view.

For example, Jean-Pierre Ruiz identifies as Nuyorican, in his case a life-long New Yorker born of a Puerto Rican father and a Belgian immigrant mother. This moniker he borrows gained currency in the 1970s as "a response to the derogatory meaning it carried among many people on the Island, especially those of cultural privilege who had a stake in demarcating 'authenticity' in the claim for national identity."[60] Re-signified in a manner that modeled the hybridity of life and language in diasporic New York it also reflected tensions between the Island based and diasporic communities, as well as between the colonizer and the colonized in diaspora. Culture studies scholar Juan Flores explains, "Disdain for what they perceived as the oppressive, racist, crassly materialist nature of U.S. society was generally accompanied by a disdain for the condescending, racist, and self-serving attitude of the Island elite, who were felt to be the beneficiaries in some way of the hardship that the emigrant community was put through over the decades."[61]

In many ways, Ruiz's scholarship embodies these complexities. In his book on biblical interpretation and migrations, he trains his postcolonial optics on a "mildly transgressive agenda" selecting texts "not because they are at the 'heart' of the canon but because reading them from the edges invites us to think differently about people on the move both in the texts and among the specialists and nonspecialists who may read these texts in our own time."[62] He proposes a strategy "of not only reading *about* immigrants but also reading *as* immigrants and reading *with* immigrants."[63] This strategy exposes the multidimensionality of the bible as well as of contexts of migrations and their aftermath. Ruiz remains attentive to multiple perspectives with their "complex harmonies and sometimes with harsh dissonances."[64]

For example, he grapples with economic refugee Abram behaving badly in Genesis 12, a hermeneutical move away from the usual textual focus on his hospitality to the angelic visitors. This re-orientation, while attending to the legitimate fears and dangers associated with migrations, also deals with ethical complications by intentionally addressing the victimization of Sarai, a gendered reality that finds expression in contemporary migrations as well.[65] Such an interpretation challenges pastoral temptations to romanticize or canonize migrants let alone spiritualize migrations. In Ruiz's words,

> The moral clarity of the regulations in the Hebrew Bible regarding the treatment of aliens becomes considerably more muddled as these aliens themselves become implicated in the tension between disclosure and nondisclosure, between the truth and trickery that are essential to survival in the borderlands, the life-and-death tension at the barbed-wire boundary between truth and trickery where the collateral damage is considerable, and where the most vulnerable also become the most expendable.[66]

Ruiz reads with immigrants as a hybrid child of colonial diaspora, therefore he is especially attuned to such byproducts of imperial aspirations and globalization as multiple and fluid identities, hybridity, and assimilation. These offer sites of accommodation, creative survival and resistance especially for those on the move, those generations of the resettled, and those who are in varying degrees of relationship with empires ancient and new.[67]

This openness to multiple interpretations and an appreciation for subtle variations associated with situated perspectives is evident in work of other diasporic Puerto Rican theologians and scholars. Theologian Luis Rivera-Rodríguez self-identifies as a "transnational diasporan," in other words, "one who has come from another country, conditioned by colonial relationships with Spain and the United States, and who has resettled in the United States while keeping real and imaginary relationships and connections to the place of origin."[68] From this vantage point he reads biblical texts and migratory contexts sensitized toward ambiguities and aware of the variety and distinctiveness of migrations and diasporic survival strategies. He urges a cautious and critical retrieval of biblical texts, counteracting naïve interpretations that marshal such texts on behalf of social justice while ignoring inconvenient aspects of non-innocent histories. Rivera-Rodríguez reminds contemporary audiences, "The God of the Deuteronomist is also a god who promotes the conquering of territories, the destitutions of indigenous populations, the genocide of native peoples, the discrimination of foreigners, and allows the subordinate and dependent status of resident aliens."[69]

For Rivera-Rodríguez, theological, ethical and pastoral responses to migrations in all their complexities necessitate a "practice of a political hermeneutics." This entails recognition of differences and commonalities across historical contexts as well as a critical appreciation for and appropriation of "the possibilities, limits, and ambiguities of these traditions as resources."[70] A political hermeneutic acknowledges the interaction between interpretation and the situatedness of hermeneuts especially in terms of "our social locations, ideological commitments, strategic agendas, reading strategies, and religious and ethical options."[71] Rivera-Rodríguez advocates what can be described as an intertextual approach between biblical texts and "contemporary experiences and sources that provide us with visions, values, and options to interpret and deal with migration issues."[72] In this way the integrity of each is preserved yet the justice focus is not lost. Rivera-Rodríguez seeks to avoid imposing anachronistic and shallow correspondences across texts and contexts dealing with people on the move. At the same time he is cognizant of intersections across texts and contexts and finds such connections illuminative. This leads him to posit what he calls "a mediating liberation model of critical correspondence or, in Hispanic/Latino theological lingo, 'reading in Spanish (correspondence) from the diaspora (otherness and engagement) through Hispanic eyes.'"[73]

Complicating Diaspora

The peculiar condition of Puerto Rico vis-à-vis the United States results in complicated, at times contested and often ambiguous relationships on all sides of diaspora. In theological and biblical scholarship by diasporic Puerto Ricans this manifests in a necessary and critical openness to ambiguity in sources, including biblical sources. The elasticity of diasporic Puerto Rican lived experience in terms of daily language, identity construction and embodied hybridity emerges as locus theologicus in considerations of dislocation, bilocation and relocation. This situatedness in multiple places finds expression in a careful identification of the scholar's location with respect to the United States and la Isla. This locating communicates the significance of the particularity of each interpreter's lens, whether Nuyorican Ruiz, transnational diasporan Rivera-Rodríguez, or even Connecticut born and raised "Yankee Puerto Rican" Edwin Aponte.[74] This attention to distinctiveness of circumstance and place fosters a sophisticated, nuanced and complicated exchange among sources and contexts.

The intersections of class, race and political action, while present in the current corpus of diasporic Puerto Rican scholarship, receives laser focus in a new generation of scholars. For example, the nascent work of ethicist Maria Teresa (MT) Davila on the interaction of social mobility, class and immigration sorts through the lived reality of middle class existence for Latin@s too easily classified as the poor.[75] Migrations are often fueled by economic reasons, yet the achievement of socio-economic stability and its implications remain off the radar in theological explorations of im/migration.[76] Davila's attention to race and militarism further demonstrate the complexities that are interwoven in matters of social justice, so much so that it is impossible to speak of migration in isolation.

The work of Elias Ortega-Aponte at the intersections of race and political action uncover acts and movements of diasporic local resistance in his development of a Latino ethics. [77] The relationships of race, language and citizenship are another area where Puerto Rican experiences challenge attempts to homogenize migrations let alone betray the fallacy behind popular national narratives touting "English only" on one side or "post-racialism" on another.

In many ways Puerto Ricans are interstitially situated between the colonial and the post-colonial. Culture studies scholar Juan Flores elaborates, "for the purpose of identifying the conditions faced by Puerto Rican, Mexican American, Dominican and other Latino peoples in the United States, and the economic and political domination of their home countries, the term postcolonial seems to be jumping the gun at best."[78] While a number of diasporic Puerto Rican scholars engage postcolonial optics, they are in a unique position to critique certain assumptions in the field of postcolonial studies from the ambivalence of their colonial-citizen matrix with its specific geographically conditioned limitations/benefits. The possibility of return to la Isla afforded by internal migrations further complicates simplistic understandings of power dynamics and socio-economic, political and cultural exchanges. Juan Flores talks of "Re-asporicans" [79] those diasporic Puerto Ricans who return to la Isla and with their children reshape the daily and the local yet again—only this time when they nostalgically remember "home" it not la Isla but el Bronx, or El Barrio in Spanish Harlem. This too remains an area ripe for intercontextual exploration and engagement across the "charco."

DOCUMENTING DISSIDENT CARTOGRAPHERS[80]

As is evident from this modest exploration of Latin@' biblical interpretation and theological scholarship on migrations, "The contours of this voice can be described in terms of a number of distinctive and recurring concerns and themes that have been articulated through a broad spectrum of dialects and idiolects—each with its own vocabulary, grammar and pronunciation."[81] Situated across a vast spectrum of peoples in motion, these diverse perspectives represent dissident social cartographies mapped from varying coordinates by theologians and scholars subsumed under an umbrella of latinidad. This provisional charting of some of the more prominent coordinates that form and inform the theologizing that arises from these embedded theologians and biblical scholars is not intended to restrict images by ethnicity. Rather it is to document the existence of a rich body of scholarship that is consummately aware of its grounded yet translocal character.

This attempt to document is in no way comprehensive, or exhaustive. The reality of global migrations requires consideration of an array of interrelated challenges. For example, to date Latin@́ reflections tend to be framed almost exclusively in Judaeo-Christian terms. The scholarship developed by many Asian North American theologians on the other hand has been cutting edge in addressing interreligious dimensions with an intentional focus on religious pluralism. Consideration of people on the move need also take into account those among us who have been unceremoniously removed or trampled upon. Theologies from our First Nations, indigenous, and aboriginal peoples offer yet another set of diverse perspectives that cannot be ignored. Whether or not theologians care to admit it, God-talk impacts actions and reactions in the public arena; and quite a lot has been articulated on the politics of migrations.

I return to Matsuoka's profound insight, that the movement of theologies from the wombs of faith communities into the broader arena of public discourse poses unsettling challenges to public and theological credibility.[82] From the perspective of those of us who are among the alternately documented, at times non-referenced scholars, on matters of migrations, theology is not a "disciplinary refugee" that we enter from the outside. For any number of Latin@́ theologians, we enter as socially located, embedded and implicated interpreters. In the words of Ruiz,

> We do so because their stories are our stories as well, stories of our parents and grandparents, stories of the communities with whom we worship and whose struggles we share. We do so because so many of us stand at the intersection of pastoral de conjunto and teología de conjunto, as Latinas/os for whom scholarship and ministry are richly interwoven, for whom scholarship is a matter of engagement with and not flight from lived daily experience.[83]

For any number of Latin@́ theologians this communal accompaniment implies a responsibility to be active participants necessary to any conversation or endeavor dedicated to creating a justly negotiated and peacefully navigated convivencia, a shared living that inevitably begins in a globally connected but particular local context.

NOTES

1. Daniel G. Groody, C.S.C., "Crossing the Divide: Foundations of a Theology of Migration and Refugees," *Theological Studies* 70 (2009): 640.
2. Ibid., 641.
3. This chapter employs Spanglish as both an intentional writing strategy and as a metaphor for the hybridity constituted by the Hispanic presence in the United States. Spanglish is one of many terms used to describe the fusion of Spanish and English in daily communication. It is manifest here through the following conventions. First, words and expressions in Spanish are not italicized or translated unless they appear as such in direct quotations; at times, sentences include both languages. Second, I created @́, the "at" symbol (el arroba) with an accent mark. I borrow the use of @ from others because it conveniently combines the "o" and "a" into one character that is gender inclusive. I add the acute accent (@́) as a reminder of the fluidity of language, culture,

and identity. I develop these themes in my book *Theologizing en Espanglish: Context, Community and Ministry* (Maryknoll, NY: Orbis, 2010).

4. D.N. Premnath, "Margins and Mainstream: An Interview with R.S. Sugirtharajah," in *Border Crossings: Cross-Cultural Hermeneutics*, ed. D.N. Premnath (Maryknoll, NY: Orbis Books, 2007), 158.

5. Ibid., 158.

6. I credit my colleague Gilberto Cavazos-González, O.F.M., for introducing me to this expression. See Gilberto Cavazos-González, "Racism of Omission," March 4, 2011, *Spiritualitas: On the study of Christian Spirituality — sobre el estudio de la espiritualidad cristiana*, http://spiritualitas.edublogs.org.

7. Fumitaka Matsuoka, introduction to *Realizing the America in Our Hearts: Theological Voices of Asian Americans*, eds. Fumitaka Matsuoka and Eleazar S. Fernandez (St. Louis: Chalice Press, 2003), 8.

8. D.N. Premnath, "Margins and Mainstream: An Interview with R.S. Sugirtharajah," in *Border Crossings: Cross-Cultural Hermeneutics*, ed. D.N. Premnath (Maryknoll, NY: Orbis Books, 2007), 158.

9. Nancy E. Bedford, "To Speak of God from More than One Place: Theological Reflections from the Experience of Migration," in *Latin American Liberation Theology: The Next Generation*, ed. Ivan Petrella (Maryknoll, NY: Orbis Books, 2005), 104.

10. Matsuoka, introduction, 8.

11. Greer Anne Wenh-In Ng, "Land of Maple and Lands of Bamboo," in *Realizing the America in Our Hearts*, 99–114.

12. Peter C. Phan, "The Dragon and the Eagle: Toward a Vietnamese American Theology," in *Realizing the America in Our Hearts*, 158–79.

13. This distinctiveness of experience is also respected in Miguel A. De La Torre, Edwin David Aponte, *Introducing Latino/a Theologies* (Maryknoll, NY: Orbis Books, 2001), 46ff. In their book they use exile when speaking of the Cuban experience, alien for the Mexican experience, and outsider for the Puerto Rican experience.

14. Miguel H. Diaz raises this as a critique in his review of *A Promised Land, A Perilous Journey: Theological Perspectives on Migration*, eds. Daniel G. Groody and Gioacchino Campese, *Theological Studies* 70 (2), June 2009: 490–91.

15. Arturo Bañuelas, "U.S. Hispanic Theology," *Missiology: An International Review* 20 (2) April 1992: 294. http://www.strategicnetwork.org/pdf/kb14065.pdf.

16. Nicholas De Genova and Ana Ramos-Zayas, *Latino Crossings: Mexicans, Puerto Ricans, and the Politics of Race and Citizenship* (New York: Routledge, 2003), 3-4. It is estimated that 80,000 to 100,000 Mexican citizens lost their nationality as a result of the 1848 Treaty of Guadalupe Hidalgo following the 1846 war of U.S. aggression (4). For a bilingual copy of the Treaty of Guadalupe Hidalgo go to the Library of Congress "Treaty of Peace, Friendship, Limits, and Settlement with the Republic of Mexico," (February 2, 1848). http://memory.loc.gov/cgi-bin/ampage?collId=llsl&fileName=009/llsl009.db&recNum=975.

17. De Genova and Ramos-Zayas, *Latino Crossings*, 6.

18. See, for example, Virgilio P. Elizondo, *Galilean Journey: The Mexican-American Promise*, revised expanded edition (Maryknoll, NY: Orbis Books, 2000). This seminal work, first published in 1983, grows out of Elizondo's doctoral dissertation at the University of Paris. Virgilio Elizondo, *The Future Is Mestizo: Life Where Cultures Meet*, revised edition (Boulder, CO: University Press of Colorado, 2000).

19. Gloria Anzaldúa, *Borderlands/La Frontera: The New Mestiza* (San Francisco: Aunt Lute Books, 1987, 1999), 25.

20. Anzaldúa, 27.

21. Bañuelas, "U.S. Hispanic Theology," 294.

22. Ibid.

23. For a significant critique of this position, see Jean-Pierre Ruiz, "Good Fences and Good Neighbors? Biblical Scholars and Theologians," in *Readings from the Edges: The Bible and People on the Move* (Maryknoll, NY: Orbis Books, 2011), 13–23. From his review of the biblical and archaeological scholarship he concludes that "the complex-

ity of this body of research itself recommends modesty with respect to affirmations about the first-century economic, political, religious and social context of Jesus, and even greater modesty in bridging the distance between the first and the twenty-first centuries of our era" (145n24).

24. Roberto S. Goizueta, "A Christology for a Global Church," in *Beyond Borders: Writings of Virgilio Elizondo and Friends*, ed. Timothy Matovina (Maryknoll, NY: Orbis Books, 2000), 157.

25. Néstor Medina, *Mestizaje (Re)Mapping Race, Culture, and Faith in Latina/o Catholicism* (Maryknoll, NY: Orbis Books, 2009).

26. Jean-Pierre Ruiz, *Readings from the Edges: The Bible and People on the Move* (Maryknoll, NY: Orbis Books, 2011).

27. "WATER Teleconference with Nancy Pineda Madrid," May 11, 2011, http://fortresspress.com/media/downloads/0800698479Followupnotes.pdf.

28. Nancy Pineda-Madrid, *Suffering and Salvation in Cuidad Juárez* (Minneapolis: Fortress Press, 2011), 1–2.

29. Ibid., 126.

30. Guillermo Gómez-Peña, "An Open Letter from an Artist to a Mexican Crime Cartel Boss," *La Bloga*, November 14, 2010, http://labloga.blogspot.com/2010/11/guillermo-gomez-pena-open-letter-from.html.

31. Fernando Segovia, "Two Places and No Place on Which to Stand: Mixture and Otherness in Hispanic American Theology," in *Mestizo Christianity: Theology from the Latino Perspective*, ed. Arturo J. Bañuelas (Maryknoll, NY: Orbis Books, 1995), 35.

32. Fernando Segovia describes Cuban history in terms of three spheres of colonial power and influence: Spanish (1492–1898); United States (1898–1959); Soviet Union (1959–present). Even after the collapse of the Soviet center, Cuba remains according to Segovia a "committed outpost or redoubt." See Fernando F. Segovia, *Decolonizing Biblical Studies: A View from the Margins* (Maryknoll, NY: Orbis Books, 2000), 5n3.

33. Mike Wallace, "Nueva York: The Back Story" and Lisandro Pérez, "Cubans in Nineteenth Century New York: A Story of Sugar, War and Revolution," in Edward J. Sullivan, ed., *Nueva York 1613–1945* (New York, NY: New York Historical Society with Scala Publishers, 2010), 18–81 and 96–107.

34. Felix Varela y Morales, a Catholic priest, philosopher, educator and a Cuban delegate to the Cortes in Madrid is forced to flee because of his pro-independence and abolitionist stance. He arrives in New York where he founds Spanish-language publications, ministers to Irish immigrants and emerges as an early advocate for immigrant rights against often violent nativist opposition. He dies in exile having served the Catholic Church of New York, rising to the position of vicar general of the diocese. His case for canonization as a Catholic saint is in process. His publications are available primarily in Spanish. See Felipe J. Estévez, STD, ed., *Félix Varela: Letters to Elpidio* (Sources of American Spirituality series) (Mahwah, NJ: Paulist Press, 2002); "Felix Varela: A Cuban for the Irish Immigrant," in *Transfiguration Church: A Church of Immigrants, 1827–1977* (New York: Park Publishing Co., 1977), excerpt available online at *The Félix Varela Foundation, Inc./La Fundacion Félix Varela, Inc.*, accessed July 6, 2011, http://pfvarela.org/English/News/Irish_Immigrant.htm; Félix Varela, *Cartas a Elpidio sobre la Impiedad, la Supersticion, la Fanatismo en sus Relaciones con la Sociedad* (Madrid: Imprenta de D. Leon Amarita, 1836), accessed July 8, 2011, http://books.google.com/books?id=yvUWGG5vctwC&printsec=frontcover&dq=cartas+a+elpidio+f%C3%A9lix+varela&hl=en&ei=2OkWTrSXD4nt0gGA7vBx&sa=X&oi=book_result&ct=result&resnum=1&ved=0CC0Q6AEwAA#v=onepage&q&f=false.

35. Considered the "Father of Cuban Independence," José Martí lived in exile in New York, from 1890 to 1895. A journalist, writer, literary critic he also established a revolutionary movement that solicited financial and moral support from the grassroots, especially emigré workers. He died in 1895 after returning to Cuba to participate in the renewed hostilities against Spanish colonial forces. While the United States provided refuge, he remained suspicious of his exilic land's imperial aspirations.

52 Carmen M. Nanko-Fernández

36. Félix Varela y Morales, *Letters to Elpidio*, volume 1, letter 6, cited in John Paul II, Address at the University of Havana, July 23, 1998, #4, accessed July 8, 2011, http://www.vatican.va/holy_father/john_paul_ii/speeches/1998/january/documents/hf_jp-ii_spe_19980123_lahavana-culture_en.html. The original in Spanish reads "y guiado por la antorcha de la fe camino al sepulcro, en cuyo borde espero con la gracia divina hacer con el último suspiro una protestacion de mi firme creencia, y un voto fervoroso por la prosperidad de mi patria." See Félix Varela, *Cartas a Elpidio*, 221, http://books.google.com/books?id=yvUWGG5vctwC&printsec=frontcover&dq=cartas+a+elpidio+f%C3%A9lix+varela&hl=en&ei=2OkWTrSXD4nt0gGA7vBx&sa=X&oi=book_result&ct=result&resnum=1&ved=0CC0Q6AEwAA#v=onepage&q&f=false.

37. De La Torre, et al, *Introducing Latino/a Theologies*, 47.

38. Justo González, *Santa Biblia: The Bible through Hispanic Eyes* (Nashville: Abingdon Press, 1996), 75.

39. Francisco O. García-Treto, "Exile in the Hebrew Bible: A Postcolonial Look from the Cuban Diaspora," *They Were All Together in One Place? Toward Minority Biblical Criticism*, in Randall C. Bailey, Tat-siong Benny Liew, Fernando F. Segovia, eds. (Atlanta: Society of Biblical Literature, 2009), 72. See also Francisco García-Treto, "Hyphenating Joseph: A View of Genesis 39-41 from the Cuban Diaspora," in *Interpreting beyond Borders*, Fernando F. Segovia, ed. (Sheffield: Sheffield Academic Press, 2000), 134–45.

40. García-Treto, "Exile in the Hebrew Bible," 77.

41. Fernando F. Segovia, "Toward Minority Biblical Criticism: A Reflection on Achievements and Lacunae," in *They Were All Together in One Place?*, 372.

42. Ada María Isasi-Díaz, *Mujerista Theology: A Theology for the Twenty-First Century* (Maryknoll, NY: Orbis Books, 1999), 47.

43. Ada María Isasi-Díaz, "Reconciliation: A Religious, Social, and Civic Virtue," *Journal of Hispanic/Latino Theology* 9 (August 2001): 6n2. Available online at http://latinotheology.org.

44. Justo L González, *Santa Biblia: The Bible Through Hispanic Eyes* (Nashville: Abingdon Press, 1996), 92. See also Justo L González, "Metamodern Aliens in Postmodern Jerusalem," in *Hispanic Latino Theology: Challenge and Promise*, Ada María Isasi-Díaz and Fernando F. Segovia, eds. (Minneapolis: Augsburg Fortress Publishers, 1996), 340–50.

45. González, *Santa Biblia*, 92.

46. Fernando F. Segovia, *Decolonizing Biblical Studies: A View from the Margins* (Maryknoll, NY: Orbis Books, 2000), 122. See also Fernando F. Segovia, "Aliens in the Promised Land: The Manifest Destiny of U.S. Hispanic American Theology," and "In the World but Not of It: Exile as Locus for a Theology of Diasporas," in *Hispanic/Latino Theology: Challenge and Promise*, Ada María Isasi-Díaz and Fernando F. Segovia, eds. (Minneapolis: Augsburg Fortress Publishers, 1996), 15–41 and 195–217; Fernando F. Segovia, "Toward a Hermeneutics of the Diaspora A Hermeneutics of Otherness and Engagement," in *Reading from This Place: Social Location and Biblical Interpretation in the United States*, Fernando F. Segovia and Mary Ann Tolbert, eds. (Minneapolis: Augsburg Fortress Press, 1995), 57–73.

47. Fernando F. Segovia, "The Text as Other: Towards a Hispanic American Hermeneutic," in *Text and Experience: Towards a Cultural Exegesis of the Bible*, Daniel Smith-Christopher, ed. (Sheffield: Sheffield Academic Press, 1995), 288.

48. Ibid., 289.

49. Ibid., 289–90.

50. Ibid., 290.

51. Ibid., 293. For a detailed explication of this reading strategy see pages 292–98.

52. This also occurs with the image of border.

53. For one perspective on adaptation in exile, see Francisco García-Treto, "Hyphenating Joseph: A View of Genesis 39-41 from the Cuban Diaspora," 134–45.

54. Ruiz, *Readings from the Edges*, 72.

55. See H.R. REP. NO. 105-131, pt. 1, at 19 (1997) (statement of Rep. Young),

> It is not equal, permanent, irrevocable citizenship protected by the Fourteenth Amendment. Puerto Ricans lack voting representation in Congress, and lack voting rights in presidential elections. Their rights of equal protection and due process have a different application than in the rest of the U.S., and Congress retains the right to determine the disposition of the territory.

This statement is cited in See Ediberto Róman, "The Alien-Citizen Paradox and Other Consequences of U.S. Colonialism," *Florida State University Law Review* (1998). http://www.law.fsu.edu/journals/lawreview/frames/261/romafram.html. See also Adriel I. Cepeda Derieux, "A Most Insular Minority: Reconsidering Judicial Deference to Unequal Treatment in Light of Puerto Rico's Political Process Failure," *Colombia Law Review* 110 (2010): 797–839. http://www.columbialawreview.org/assets/pdfs/110/3/Cepeda-Derieux.pdf.

56. See Ediberto Róman, "The Alien-Citizen Paradox and Other Consequences of U.S. Colonialism," *Florida State University Law Review* (1998) http://www.law.fsu.edu/journals/lawreview/frames/261/romafram.html.

57. Samuel Solivan, *The Spirit, Pathos and Liberation: Toward an Hispanic Pentecostal Theology* (Sheffield: Sheffield Academic Press, 1998), 137–38.

58. See Virginia Sánchez Korrol, "Puerto Ricans in "Olde" Nueva York: Migrant *Colonias* of the Nineteenth and Twentieth Centuries," in *Nueva York*, 108–20. This occurs for Cubans as well. The tabaqueros and the men and women who were hired to read to these cigar factory workers (lectores/lectoras) are intimately tied to political activism and movements advocating labor rights in the United States and across the Caribbean. It is worth noting that Jean-Pierre Ruiz considers la lectora Luisa Capetillo in his essay, "Reading Between the Lines: Towards a Latino/a (Re)configuration of Scripture and Tradition," in *Futuring Our Past: Explorations in the Theology of Tradition*, Orlando O. Espín and Gary Macy, eds. (Maryknoll, NY: Orbis Books, 2006), 83–111.

59. Juan Flores, *The Diaspora Strikes Back: Caribeño Tales of Learning and Turning* (New York: Routledge, 2009), 66. Flores notes that the significance of the diaspora in terms of volume, that is, "the diaspora stands nearly equal in size to that of the Island population." From 1898 on, migration of contract laborers was encouraged to meet needs. in industries and agriculture in other areas of the United States and its annexed territories. See, for example, the history of the Puerto Rican presence in Hawai'i: Iris López, "Puerto Ricans in Hawaii," in *Latinas in the United States: A Historical Encyclopedia, Volume 1*, Vicki Ruíz, Virginia Sánchez Korrol, eds. (Bloomington, IN: Indiana University Press, 2006), 591–95.

60. Flores, *The Diaspora Strikes Back*, 174. See also Juan Flores, "Nuyorican," in the *International Encyclopedia of the Social Sciences*, William A. Darity, ed. (Detroit: Macmillan Reference USA, 2008), 552–53. http://www.encyclopedia.com/doc/1G2-3045301783.html.

> It signified cultural inauthenticity and evoked a paternalistic sympathy for the cultural loss, or even blame for the betrayal involved in the migrants' adaptation to North America. It also could imply significantly negative qualities in terms of class (usually very poor and lazy), sometimes described with the idea of "lumpen" (proletarian), and race (generally identified as black, perhaps tainted with the proximity of African Americans).

61. Flores, *The Diaspora Strikes Back*, 174.
62. Ruiz, *Reading from the Edges*, 9.
63. Ibid., 64.
64. Ibid., 138.
65. In his reading of Abram's attempt to pass Sarai off as his sister, Ruiz writes:

> Sarai finds herself doubly victimized by powerful males in this story: first by her own husband, whose fear and desire for self-preservation take priority over her welfare, and second by the Pharaoh, the foreign sovereign whose attendants acquire her for their master's house in a transaction in

which—to put it as bluntly as possible—Abram receives far more livestock than he loses by surrendering Sarai. (68)

66. Ibid., 69–70.
67. See for example Ruiz's readings of Ezekiel 12:1–16, Ezekiel 20 and Nehemiah 13 in *Readings from the Edges*, 71–82, 83–99, and 100–14.
68. Luis R. Rivera-Rodríguez, "Immigration and The Bible: Comments by a Diasporic Theologian," *Perspectivas/Occasional Papers* (Fall 2006): 23–24.
69. Ibid., 32.
70. Ibid., 34.
71. Ibid., 34.
72. Ibid., 34.
73. Luis R. Rivera-Rodríguez, "Reading in Spanish from the Diaspora through Hispanic Eyes," *Theology Today* (January 1998). Provided by ProQuest Information and Learning Company at http://findarticles.com/p/articles/mi_qa3664/is_199801/ai_n8787983/pg_6/?tag=mantle_skin;content.
74. Miguel A. De La Torre and Edwin David Aponte, *Introducing Latino/a Theologies*, 2–5.
75. Maria Teresa (MT) Davila, "A Liberation Ethic for the One Third World: The Preferential Option for the Poor and Challenges to Middle-Class Christianity in the United States" (PhD diss., Boston College, 2007).
76. See Carmen Marie Nanko, "Justice Crosses the Border: The Preferential Option for the Poor in the United States," in *A Reader in Latina Feminist Theology: Religion and Justice*, María Pilar Aquino, Daisy L. Machado, and Jeanette Rodríguez, eds. (Austin, TX: University of Texas Press, 2002), 177–203.
77. Elias Ortega-Aponte, "Raised Fist in the Church! Afro-Latino/a Practice Among the Young Lords Party: A Religious Humanist Model for Radical Latino/a Religious Ethics" (PhD diss., Princeton Theological Seminary, 2011).
78. Juan Flores, *From Bomba to Hip-Hop:Puerto Rican Culture and Latino Identity* (New York, NY: Columbia University Press, 2000), 214.
79. Flores, *The Diaspora Strikes Back*.
80. My use of the expression "dissident cartographer" is influenced by and developed in reflection on the book and multi-media project *Dissident Cartographies*, José Miguel G. Cortés, curator (Barcelona: Sociedad Estatal para la Acción Cultural Exterior [SEACEX] 2008).
81. Fernando F. Segovia, "Aliens in the Promised Land: The Manifest Destiny of U.S. Hispanic American Theology," in *Hispanic/Latino Theology: Challenge and Promise*, 18.
82. Matsuoka, *Realizing the America in Our Heart*, 8.
83. Ruiz, *Readings from the Edges*, 2.

SELECTED BIBLIOGRAPHY

De La Torre, Miguel A., and Edwin David Aponte. *Introducing Latino/a Theologies*. Maryknoll, NY: Orbis Books, 2001.
Elizondo, Virgilio. *The Future Is Mestizo: Life Where Cultures Meet*, Revised Edition. Boulder, CO: University Press of Colorado, 2000.
González, Justo. *Santa Biblia: The Bible through Hispanic Eyes*. Nashville: Abingdon Press, 1996.
Petrella, Ivan, ed. *Latin American Liberation Theology: The Next Generation*. Maryknoll, NY: Orbis Books, 2005.
Pineda-Madrid, Nancy. *Suffering and Salvation in Cuidad Juárez*. Minneapolis: Fortress Press, 2011.
Premnath, D.N., ed. *Border Crossings: Cross-Cultural Hermeneutics*. Maryknoll, NY: Orbis Books, 2007.

Ruiz, Jean-Pierre. *Readings from the Edges: The Bible and People on the Move*. Maryknoll, NY: Orbis Books, 2011.
Segovia, Fernando F. *Decolonizing Biblical Studies: A View from the Margins*. Maryknoll, NY: Orbis Books, 2000.

THREE

How to Shape Christian Perspectives on Immigration?

Strategies for Communicating Biblical Teaching

M. Daniel Carroll R.

Immigration takes on significance as it intersects our own stories. Perhaps we are immigrants ourselves or children of immigrants. Maybe we have gotten to know some immigrants personally. The immigration debate no longer is about abstract socio-political and economic issues or about a faceless "horde" that is "invading" our shores. It is about real people and their families. Drawing from my experiences traveling around the country speaking about the Bible and immigration, this chapter outlines three principal audiences I have encountered and suggests constructive ways to engage them with Biblical insights about immigration.

ESTABLISHING A FRAMEWORK

I am the son of a Guatemalan mother and an American father. My brother and I were raised bilingual and bicultural. We had Guatemalan relatives as neighbors for many years in Houston, where we grew up, and we spent many summers in Guatemala with extended family. In Houston my parents' Latin American friends were Cubans, part of the diaspora who fled the island after it fell to Fidel Castro. In time, my brother married someone from that community.

Our contact with the large Mexican immigrant population in Houston, though, was minimal. I remember going to mass at Our Lady of Guadalupe Church a few times, and once my father hired mariachis for my mother's birthday. Our contact with Mexicans was limited to our trips to Guatemala. It was not uncommon for us to drive to Guatemala from Houston. We would cross the border at Matamoros and stop in Tampico, Veracruz, and Tapachula on the way to Guatemala. Once we took a route through the center of Mexico, via Oaxaca and Mexico City. In short, we had seen the country of Mexico, but its immigrants were largely unknown to us.

Years later, as an adult, I moved with my wife to Guatemala, where I was a professor at an international interdenominational seminary for thirteen years. I had students from Mexico and had occasion to visit some theological institutions there for academic matters. We moved back to the United States in 1996, where I took a position at Denver Seminary. It was in Denver that I came into contact with the Mexican immigrant community for the first time.[1] And my entry into the immigration debate came in unexpected fashion.

Jorge, a Peruvian pastor of a local Hispanic congregation, took classes from me at the seminary and encouraged me to start a Spanish-speaking program for lay people. He had come to the United States as an undocumented immigrant many years before, had married an American, and was now a naturalized citizen. His passion touched me, and so, with his help and that of two other Hispanic pastors, in 2004 Denver Seminary launched IDEAL (Instituto para el Desarrollo y Adiestramiento de Líderes). It has grown to more than 100 students—almost all undocumented—and we now have contact with more than sixty Hispanic congregations in the metro-Denver area.

It was in this program that I began to hear the stories of immigrants, so unlike mine as a "half-breed" citizen of this country. Theirs were about the trials of crossing; they shared tales of finding work in order to provide for their families, of the pressures of maintaining a healthy marriage and raising their children in the shadows. They had migrated with the hope of a different life than what they had known in the *ranchos* from where they had come, but instead had encountered many obstacles and unanticipated prejudice. These were Christians, Bible in hand, spending one Saturday morning a month at the seminary, eager to learn more about their faith. We shared food and jokes and prayed together. I taught them the Scripture, but they were educating me in profound ways. I became a part of the Alianza Ministerial Hispana and found an Hispanic church to attend.

I became aware of a reality that was profoundly disturbing. The media often presented false stereotypes of immigrants, especially of the undocumented. The tone could be harsh, the portraits a caricature. Even people I knew would make derogatory comments about those I now embraced as friends and as brothers and sisters in Christ. These conversations with people who professed Christian faith usually were in no way explicitly Christian. There was talk of the economic impact of immigration, possible threats to national identity, pressures on the school system and hospital emergency rooms, border security, Hispanic gangs, the supposed reluctance to learn English, and more. All important topics, but what of the contribution of faith to the discussion?

I began to ask myself, what might an informed Christian perspective on immigration look like? Did the Bible, which Christians hold as a guide for faith and practice, have anything to say? Could the tone of the debate change, at least among majority culture Christians? At the same time, the Bible also is the Scripture of Christians within the immigrant community. Could it offer encouragement and provide direction to them in this new, and sometimes hostile, land?

I began to educate myself about the history of immigration and immigration legislation, and I investigated what the Bible reveals about God's take on immigration. The result of those efforts has been *Christians at the Border: Immigration, the Church, and the Bible* and other publications. That book has generated speaking opportunities across the country and in all sorts of venues—local churches, denominational gatherings, seminaries, and universities—and across the theological spectrum. The challenge I faced was to think through *how* to present this biblical message in an engaging way. What follows describes what shape these presentations take and why.

MATCHING THE MESSAGE WITH THE AUDIENCE

It is not enough to write a book about what the Bible says about immigration and then let it lie. The goal must be larger, to take that material to whomever might listen. Questions now surface, such as, what might be effective ways to communicate scriptural teaching to Christians, no matter their present convictions, to season their understanding, attitudes, and actions? Once Christians begin to rethink their stance on the issue, what impact could their views have on the broader society? The challenge is to formulate a sensible strategy that is sensitive to different positions in order to win hearts and minds.

I have encountered, in very general terms, three basic types of audiences. First, there are audiences who are suspicious of these recently arrived outsiders. They are taken aback by the demographic shifts in their neighborhoods and by the sudden appearance of ethnic restaurants and grocery stores; they hear other languages being spoken in shops and on the radio and television; they see signs and billboards directed at foreigners with words they do not recognize. Their world is changing. This is not only hard to grasp; it is hard to accept. Normal fears and uncertainties can override faith commitments, or those commitments are defined narrowly in patriotic fashion as the obligation to be exemplary law-abiding citizens. Immigrants, especially the undocumented, are perceived as violators of the "rule of law."

A second group is those Christians who seek biblical foundations in support of immigrants. They are found among mainline Protestants, evangelicals, and Roman Catholics, who are coming together for a common cause. This constituency has Christian impulses to reach out to newcomers, but they sense their need for deeper biblical and theological foundations. Some can appeal to a few passages in the Bible in support of immigrants (e.g., Lev. 19:33-34; Matt. 25:31-36), but they are eager to expand the scriptural roots of their convictions.

Third, there is the audience that is scared. These are the immigrants themselves. They worship in Christian churches, often renting space on Sunday afternoons from majority culture congregations that sometimes are ambivalent about their presence. Immigrant churches function as extended family and are an alternative social network to that of the society that marginalizes them. Prayers are offered for those who have been detained or who seek employment; they share funds to pay for medical bills (insurance is not available to them), and they have a meal together after the service to solidify their bonds of friendship and solidarity. Worship times are full of praise, and congregants relish release from the pressures that haunt their daily lives. Rarely does the preaching focus on their immigrant status. The Bible is applied to general human and familial needs, and they are encouraged to celebrate God's the goodness, but there is little teaching about migration in the Bible or about God's commitment to the sojourner. It is ironic that this group, too, is uniformed about what the biblical text says about immigration.

Each of these three audiences has a perspective and experiences to which the Bible can respond. The first group, which is negatively disposed toward immigrants, needs exposure to how much the Old and New Testaments speak to immigration issues. Introduction to this vast material often yields an "Aha!" moment: "Wow! I never knew all that was in the Bible!" As the presenter, my obligation is to offer a gracious invitation to these Christians to ground opinions along biblical lines, as well as give them permission and the freedom to express their concerns. Allegiance to a contrary political stance and untoward attitudes must be reevaluated in the light of Scripture. The aim is not win the biblical argument or berate those who might disagree, but instead to put forward another view in a civil manner and model courteous discourse. On the other hand, as the second group surveys the biblical teaching, they are confirmed and empowered in a fresh way. God is in this! Their efforts are not in vain, even if the wider culture does not agree.

For immigrants, the Bible takes on a new significance. As they encounter narratives of the migrations of the people of God, they find themselves in the pages of Scripture: "¡*Allí estamos nosotros!*" ("There we are!"). It describes similar situations and spurs them to deeper faith in their circumstances today. The Bible also presents case studies of failure of those long ago, who were strangers in strange lands. There they see vignettes of frustration, humiliation, worry, persecution, and triumph. In all of this, *el texto nos acompaña en el camino de migrar y de vivir en tierra ajena* ("the text accompanies us on the immigration journey and as we live in a land not our own"). The Bible can be embraced as a uniquely immigrant book![2]

In sum, the presentation of the biblical material on immigration should have emphases geared to elicit constructive responses from each audience. In what follows I present images that can be effective conversation starters. I then will offer a brief overview of the Bible's teaching on immigration.

MATCHING THE MEDIA WITH THE MESSAGE

In a visually stimulated culture, images can be used to great effect. So, in presentations on immigration I begin with a series of pictures. The choice of pictures has a two-fold purpose. The first is to provide an historical perspective to the current situation. Debates over immigration are not new, and that fact can lower the tension in the room. We have been here before. The second is to demonstrate how caricatures have never been either fair or productive. Some of the images I show are amusing, and that bit of humor can lighten the mood of an audience before I move on to the biblical material. I also combine these with funny stories of my own life as a bicultural person. To get people laughing can result in greater openness to new ideas.

The first four images are scenes of immigrants from the nineteenth century. The first two are drawings of Castle Garden, through which some eight million people came between 1855 and 1890 (Figure 3.1).

Castle Garden was replaced by Ellis Island (1892–1954) as the major port of entry on the East Coast.[3] Some twenty-five million came through the facility there. The next image is a photograph taken of a boat arriving at Ellis Island (Figure 3.2).

What is striking in these two pictures is the sheer number of people. Mass migration is not a recent phenomenon. The third picture is of a poor Italian family. The hardships of poverty always have been major reasons why people migrate. The same is true today.

Another way to provide historical perspective is to read things written by important figures in this country's history. For example, one of the largest populations to migrate to the United States in the first decades of the republic's founding was the Germans. They actually began to arrive earlier, in the seventeenth century, and often were not welcome. These

Figure 3.1. Interior of Castle Garden, *Harper's Magazine 1871*. Picture Collection, New York Public Library, Astor, Lenox and Tilden Foundations.

are Benjamin Franklin's sentiments about their presence in Pennsylvania in 1751:

> Few of their children in the country learn English. . . . The signs in our streets have inscriptions in both languages. . . . Unless the stream of their importation could be turned they will soon so outnumber us that all the advantages we have will not be able to preserve our language, and even our government will become precarious.

He goes on, "Why should Pennsylvania, founded by the English , become a Colony of Aliens, who will shortly be so numerous as to Germanize us instead of our Anglifying them, and will never adopt our Language or Customs, any more than they can acquire our Complexion."[4] He complains that the Germans have their own schools, stores, churches, and newspapers. These words find an echo in contemporary rhetoric.

This country's history is strewn with suspicions about immigrants. When the Irish began to arrive, as they fled the Great Potato Famine (1845–1852), the Know Nothing Party sprang up to preserve what was felt to be the Protestant heritage of this country and to protect it from Catholicism. Prejudice against the Irish continued through the early twentieth century, when it was coupled with intolerance toward the Ital-

Figure 3.2. Immigrants on an Atlantic Liner, December 1906. Photo by Edwin Levick (1869–1929). Courtesy of the Library of Congress.

ians—again, largely for religious reasons—and led to the establishment of quota systems. Another dark story is the history of Chinese immigration. Brought in for labor needs connected with the California Gold Rush to help build the railroads that were coming West, they soon faced a backlash that culminated in the Chinese Exclusion Act (1882), which effectively barred any Chinese from entering the country until its repeal in 1943. Figure 3.4 is a political cartoon from *Harper's Weekly* in the 1880s. Note the image of a wall to keep the Chinese out! Today the wall is a reality, not a metaphor.

The emotional level in the national discussion means that those with different opinions usually talk past each other. Historically, as in the present, little listening or thoughtful exchanges occur. A line from a telephone provider is apropos: "Can you hear me now?" The answer most of the time would be "no!" In such a climate it is easy for stereotypes to flourish. Indeed, foreigners have been caricatured for over a century. These representations reveal nativist antagonistic feelings, but they also express fears about the other. A cartoon from 1899 is illuminating (Figure 3.5).

It exemplifies the coexisting contradictory stances toward the immigrant presence. In this drawing, Uncle Sam stands at a gate that announces "Admittance Free," "Walk In," and "Welcome." At the same

Figure 3.3. Italian Immigrant Family at Ellis Island, circa 1910. Courtesy of the Library of Congress.

time, paradoxically, Uncle Sam holds his nose, as he looks disdainfully at the immigrant. This ragged newcomer holds bags labeled "poverty" and "disease," and on his back carries barrels of "Sabbath desecration" and "anarchy." Whereas the barrels reflect the late nineteenth-century context, immigrants have always been accused of bringing in those two bags.

Figure 3.4. Throwing down the ladder by which they rose. *Harper's Weekly: A Journal of Civilization 1870*. Picture Collection, New York Public Library, Astor, Lenox and Tilden Foundations.

Sometimes the caricatures are tongue-and-cheek critiques of this dread. Some worry that newcomers, if they have come in large numbers, will radically change the (idealized) character of the majority culture. One of the enduring images of Americana is Grant Wood's 1930 portrait of a farming couple from Iowa. *American Gothic* is one of this country's most famous paintings, and over the years it has been spoofed many times. A recent twist shows the couple wearing ponchos and Mexican sombreros. The man (now with a mustache) has a guitar in his hand, instead of a pitchfork. This is a humorous warning of where the country might be headed as the deluge of Hispanic immigrants continues unabated!

Figure 3.5. Stranger at the Gate by Frank Beard 1896. The Ohio State University Billy Ireland Cartoon Library & Museum.

A patent illustration of unfortunate generalizations of the "other" is the term "Hispanic." It came into common parlance via the U.S. Census Bureau, which created this catch-all category to refer to the broad swath of groups from Spanish-speaking nations. Anyone with basic knowledge about Latin America and the Caribbean, however, is aware of just how inadequate the label is. There are around thirty countries, with a range of ethnicities, which fit under this rubric. The label covers, for instance, the indigenous descendents of the pre-Columbian civilizations, the *mestizo* (or *ladino*) mixtures of their intermarriage with the Spanish, blacks descended from slaves brought from Africa by Spain and Portugal, and immigrant populations from Europe and Asia (Figure 3.6).

These images can help people to recognize that the immigration debate is more complex than most realize. Interspersing a little humor also lowers the emotional quotient. These images also serve as a transition to the biblical survey. If this is how this country has reacted to the millions of immigrants in the past and today, what might the Bible teach us about the topic?

INSIGHTS FROM THE SCRIPTURES ABOUT IMMIGRATION

All Christians claim that the Bible should inform their lives. There are differences of opinion as to which parts might be relevant and about how to apply the Scripture to the modern world, but this general agreement opens a door to present the material on immigration that is found in its pages.

Figure 3.6. Which Hispanics? Jeff Parker, *Florida Today*, January 31, 2003.

The Hebrew Bible/The Old Testament

It is crucial to appreciate the importance of the proper place to start the biblical discussion. Where the presentation begins determines the direction that the conversation will go and its tenor. Christians, who take a suspicious view of immigrants, default to Romans 13 and its call to submit to the governing authorities. This limits the discussion to matters of legality. Either someone has legal status and proper documentation or they do not; either someone has followed established laws for entry or they have not. This black-and-white view does not allow for more nuanced positions conversant with the history of immigration and of immigration law. Worse, it is only one passage among many in the Bible that can be brought to bear and ignores the fact that more than a thousand pages of text precede it!

Where then do we start the conversation? I always say, "Let us go to chapter one, page one." That is, the presentation should begin at the beginning, in Genesis 1. There we find the creation of humanity (1:26-28) and are told that every person, male and female, is created in the image of God.

The image of God has been understood in several ways in Christian theology. I mention two. First, the image of God can be taken to refer to what humans possess in a unique way among all creatures. Humans have a will, emotions, and an intellect—things that are shared in some measure with others—but they also have a spiritual dimension, which Christians and other religions would call a soul. These features give everyone special worth. The fact that in the Christian faith, God became flesh in Jesus Christ and sacrificed himself for humanity demonstrates that each person has infinite value. This, of course, includes immigrants! They are not some faceless mass of "aliens" coming across a border; they are human beings made in the image of God. They are of inestimable importance in God's sight and also should be in the sight of all.

A second interpretation concentrates on the words that humans are to "subdue" and "rule" the earth, which leads to a more functional view of the image. In the ancient world kings set up images of themselves in distant parts of their territory to communicate that their reign was present there. In the Genesis account humans are that living image in God's land, the earth. As God's representatives, they are given the privilege of participating in the divine administration. In the second chapter of Genesis, humanity is called to work and take care of God's creation and name the animals (2:15, 18). These mandates speak to the potential and giftedness of all persons. This truth has significant implications for attitudes toward immigrants. The majority culture should appreciate their talents, which can contribute to the common good, and recognize their incalculable promise for the country. This is a far cry from decrying immigrants as a burden.

The image of God also speaks to immigrants. They need to understand that they are not inferior because of where they come from, their race, educational level, or socio-economic status. They have worth before God, no matter what others might think. They have the potential to accomplish great things, as they grow into what God has designed them to be and do. It also means that they should live responsibly as God's representatives in their new land.

We begin the biblical discussion on immigration on page one, with the fundamental conviction that we are dealing with people wonderfully made in the image of God, who are capable of amazing things. This is a constructive and respectful starting point. Once the groundwork of the image of God is established, what I then do is present some of the narratives of migration in the Bible. Some of the great characters of the Hebrew Bible/Old Testament were forced to migrate and live in foreign lands.

Abram, for example, appears in Genesis as a migrant. He and his extended family travel from Ur in Mesopotamia to Haran, close to the modern border of modern Syria and Turkey (11:31). There he receives the call to go to Canaan and moves in obedience to that command (12:1-5). Soon afterward, there is a famine in the land, and his family travels to Egypt for food. Abram migrates to feed his extended family. As they approach the border, out of fear, he and his wife Sarai come up with a scheme. They are willing to lie to get across the border. She is to say she is Abram's sister (she actually was a relative, so this is a half-truth; 20:12). Sarai is put at tremendous risk, so that all can be spared. Desperate actions in desperate situations—similar motivations and perils of migration that we see today, and women continue to be those whose lot is the most precarious. They are in danger of physical abuse and rape, as they cross the borderlands to save their families. Abram continued to wander his entire life. The only property he owns is what he buys to bury his wife (Gen. 23). Abram, the father of the faith (Romans 4; Galatians 3), was a migrant!

Later Joseph is sold into slavery by his brothers and is taken to Egypt (Gen. 37). There he is put to work in Potiphar's household. He earns the Egyptian's trust and becomes head of that estate (Gen. 39). When Potiphar's wife tries to seduce him, he runs away but is taken and put into prison. Whom would the authorities to believe, the Egyptian woman or the foreigner? Eventually he is released after deciphering Pharaoh's dream and is made second in command in the country. Joseph assimilates to the host culture: he is given an Egyptian name, marries an Egyptian, and has children with her, although he gives his children Israelite names (Gen. 40-41). He would have been fluent in Egyptian.

Years afterward his father Jacob sends his brothers to Egypt to buy food (Gen. 42). Although Joseph recognizes them, they cannot identify him. How can that be? In Egyptian culture, men of his status would have been clean-shaven and painted their faces. He probably wore a headpiece commensurate with his station. That is why they cannot recognize him. He uses an interpreter (42:23), but it is a ruse. Joseph understands what his brothers are saying. This immigrant had not forgotten his mother tongue, his family, or his homeland. Assimilated, yes, but still with ties to his roots. This immigrant had a major impact on his adopted country: he saved it from famine (Gen. 47).

The book of Exodus begins with the Israelites suffering under the rule of the Egyptians. What triggers the fear of the Egyptians is the growing number of this foreign work force. This is a common phenomenon: a numerical threshold triggers the anxiety of the majority culture. What it was for the Egyptians, we do not know, but they legislate draconian measures to control the Israelite population (Exodus 1-2) and then make it harder for them to make bricks (Exodus 5). These are irrational and contradictory actions. The Egyptians try to diminish the immigrant population and make their lives miserable, but they still want them to work! This nativist reaction has played itself out throughout history. Immigration is largely about labor, but host cultures get nervous when there are too many foreigners in their midst. Constraints are placed on the immigrant population, even as its labor continues to be exploited. Legislation reflects this incongruity between nativist feelings and labor needs.

Ruth is a wonderful book to explore the assimilation process. It begins with Noemi and her family moving to Moab, because there is hunger in Bethlehem. Ruth, a Moabitess, marries one of these immigrants. Noemi's husband and sons die, so she wants to return to her hometown. One daughter-in-law stays behind, but Ruth decides to accompany Noemi. Now, the one who had married an immigrant becomes an immigrant. The rest of the book describes how this widowed outsider tries to gain her mother-in-law's approval (note that Ruth is ignored when they arrive in Bethlehem), provide for them both in that patriarchal world, and gain the acceptance of the townspeople. She is perceived as a foreigner by the reapers in Boaz's fields, though they appreciate her hard work (2:5-7). Is this not how many immigrants are valued today, as nameless hard workers? And, women are conspicuous in their efforts to feed their families by pursuing menial labor jobs. By the end of the tale, she is praised by the elders as equal to heroines of the past, marries Boaz, and is blessed by the other women (Ruth 4). The child she bears is handed to Noemi, who takes the baby in her arms. Is this the moment that she finally accepts her immigrant daughter-in-law? One thing is for sure: her son would not have to go through what his mother did to become part of that community. The book closes with the genealogy of David. The story of this immigrant woman in a small village in Judah was part of a bigger story she could never have imagined!

There are accounts of people in exile, living in Babylon after the fall of Judah. Each depicts different levels of assimilation and how these persons' integrity played itself out in their particular circumstances. Daniel and his friends are given new names and a first-rate education, so that they might serve the empire (Daniel 1). They are the best of the lot, but they decide to maintain their own diet. Food, then and now, is a foundational cultural marker. We are what we eat! You can spot immigration neighborhoods by the restaurants, and one of the first things immigrants will do to those who befriend them is to invite them over for a meal. Daniel and his friends serve the empire, but they are still Israelites who refuse to abandon totally their heritage.

Ezra does not want to integrate at all. This teacher-leader returns to the land to set up a community that will follow the letter of the Law (Ezra 7-10). Nehemiah, on the other hand, works in the royal court. Even so, he is attentive to news from home (Nehemiah 1). He is loyal to the Persian king. He must be as his cupbearer. At every meal his life, literally, was on the line, because he would taste things to make sure nothing was poisoned. In an amusing scene, the king wonders why Nehemiah's face is sad. The last thing he wants to see is an unhappy face on his cupbearer. *This food and drink are OK, aren't they?* Nehemiah is so trusted by the Persians that he is allowed to go back to Jerusalem with royal help and rebuild the city walls, with the proviso that he return (2:1-6). Esther, in contrast, is very assimilated. She has both an Israelite and Persian name (Esther 2:7) and must be prodded by her relative Mordecai to use her position as queen to save her people. Hers is a growing awareness of her roots and responsibilities.[5]

Each of these stories is a window into the immigrant experience. Majority culture audiences can begin to read them with new eyes. They can see that many of their biblical heroes were immigrants, some out of need and others forcefully deported by an occupying army. They learn that these individuals' faith in God was shaped in the cauldron of their status as foreigners. At the same time, immigrants can read these accounts as their own stories. What those in the Bible went through is what they now experience. They too endure marginalization, even persecution, but they can learn to rise above these obstacles, as they watch those migrants from centuries ago respond with trust in God.

Biblical Legislation on Immigration

Immigration is not only about the life stories of immigrants. It also is about legislation. Host countries must make decisions concerning access across borders, eligibility for work and community benefits, and availability of legal status. Laws help organize a country. Legislation decrees what should be done with property, crime and criminals, commerce, transit, personal matters (like marriage, the registration of newborns, and death), and much more. Every sphere of life is regulated to some degree and defined by legislation. For those in any given setting, these laws seem "natural" and "normal." They represent what life should be like and how society must function. In other words, legislation reflects, generates, and preserves cultures. It shapes humanity's social constructions of reality. Everything makes sense and has its place, and all this is institutionalized and sanctioned in language, family traditions, community rituals and rites of passage, certain foods, societal celebrations and allegiances (national holidays, parades, anthems). This frame of reference for life is context specific. This explains why we feel "culture shock" when we go somewhere else. We do not recognize the different cultural cues and feel out of place.

In immigration discussions today one often hears that this country follows "the rule of law." In light of the preceding paragraph, this is a truism. Since the dawn of human civilization every society has had its "rule of law"; every society has had its own legislation. What differs is what that looks like. The United States simply has a certain kind of rule of law. What is key for our purposes is not the *existence* of law, but rather its *moral core*. A society's values are expressed in law codes, but fundamental is the importance placed on vulnerable groups, such as children, widows, orphans, single parents, the sick and disabled, the poor... and immigrants. What is legislated in regard to these people speaks volumes about the heart of a culture. It is not just an issue of *order* and *legality* (which, are important); it is a question of *compassion* and *charity* towards the needy.

The Two Challenges and the Law's Provisions

How does Israel's Law respond to immigrants? In the ancient world, immigrants were particularly deprived. On the one hand, there were no government welfare programs to offer aid to the disadvantaged. While temples at times functioned as distribution centers of food and offered work, most help came through extended family. When crops were bad, people were sick, or at childbirth and death, family members were present to lend a hand. The majority of Israel's population lived in villages made up of extended family. Outsiders, however, had no kin to turn to. Immigrants would have been at the mercy of the Israelites for provision and protection.

On the other hand, in that agrarian peasant economy land was crucial for survival. Ownership of property, however, was passed down through the male heir. Once more, foreigners were at a loss. Land to own would have been hard to come by, so they would have had to look for employment on others' farms. Immigrants also were at the mercy of the Israelites for work.

The Law responded to the needs of immigrants in several ways.[6] They were given opportunities to acquire food. They were to be allowed to work the edges of the fields at harvest time (Lev. 19:9-10; Deut. 24:19-22; cf. Ruth). There was a special tithe of produce every three years for the needy (Deut. 14:28-29; 26:12-13). Ideally, immigrants could expect impartial treatment in legal proceedings (Deut. 1:16-17; 24:17-18; 27:19). They also were to receive a fair wage, be paid on time (Exod. 23:12; Deut. 24:14-15), and enjoy rest from their labor on the Sabbath (Exod. 20:10; Deut. 5:14). The Law, in other words, was structured to prevent the exploitation of immigrants.

Even the most precious part of Israel's life and the core of its cultural identity—its religion—was mostly open to the sojourner. In addition to the Sabbath, foreigners could participate in the Day of Atonement (Lev. 16:29), the Passover (Exod. 12:45-49; Num. 9:14), the Feast of Weeks (Deut. 16:11), the Feast of Tabernacles (Deut. 16:14), and Firstfruits (Deut. 26:11). The command to love the neighbor (Lev. 19:18), which Jesus later cites (Matt. 19:16-19 and par.), is connected to the love of the sojourner (Lev. 19:33-34). The love of the outsider is the true test of the love of neighbor. It is also a criterion for acceptable worship of God (Isa. 58:7).

This openness likely carried with it expectations of the sojourner. Foreigners, who lived among the Israelites, would have had to learn the language to work and to take part in these religious rituals. There was to be a periodic public reading of the Law, which would have helped these outsiders to understand and to accommodate themselves to their new milieu (Deut. 31:8-13; cf. Neh. 8). Integration then (and now) was a process of mutual learning and acceptance.

Why would Israelites do these things for immigrants? Did the Law threaten them with sanctions, if they did not show hospitality to outsiders? What reasons were given for them to obey these commands? The first is the appeal to historical memory. Israel once had been immigrants in Egypt (Exod. 22:21; 23:9; Lev. 19:34; Deut. 24:17-18). Israel must never forget the socio-economic, racial, and political oppression they had suffered. If and when they did, they would replicate that treatment with those who had come to live among them. Israel would become like the repressive people from whom they had been liberated. The second motivation is even more important. They were to love the sojourner, because God does (Deut. 10:12-22; cf. 24:14-15). His love for immigrants was concrete, too, providing them with food and clothing. This tangible expression of his care, of course, would have to come through the actions of his people. It would be difficult indeed to evade that moral obligation.[7]

There is much to learn here. The United States, whose history is one of immigration, has historical amnesia. Forgotten are the hardships faced by earlier generations, the suspicions of the Germans, the racial and religious marginalization of the Chinese, the ghettoes of the Irish and Italians, the struggles with learning English, and more. The very things God told the Israelites not to forget—the socio-economic, racial, and political—are not remembered, so the ill treatment of newcomers of yesteryear is repeated today. Whatever immigrant memories many have are minimal. Often they are nothing more than culinary (a favorite family recipe from the "old country") or festive (St. Patrick's Day or Oktoberfest). What of the second motivation? Why should the majority culture love the immigrant? Because God does.

Immigrants can take heart. Their God loves them and calls those of faith of the host culture to put hands and feet to that love. Fair legislation is possible, and the laws of ancient Israel may be a pointer to a more just future. This is a long and complicated process, but the Law can be a helpful guide to how to approach immigration through our legislation.

The New Testament

The New Testament continues the concern for the outsider. Jesus himself began life as a refugee, fleeing as a baby with his family to Egypt to escape Herod's troops (Matt. 2:13-18). In other words, the Messiah knows what it means to live in a foreign land. How can majority culture Christians turn their back on immigrants today, when the Savior himself experienced that journey? And, immigrants can freely ask for help and guidance, confident that God understands their plight in a personal way.

Learning from Jesus's Teaching

Jesus does not teach directly on immigration. But, his constant contact with outcasts powerfully implies the need to engage immigrants. His interaction with the Samaritans, a group despised by the Jews (these feelings were mutual), is instructive. He speaks with a Samaritan woman at the well (John 4), heals a Samaritan of leprosy (Lk. 17:11-19), and uses a Samaritan as the example of what it means to be a good neighbor, the one whom the Jews were to love (Lk. 10:25-37). Perhaps Matthew 25:31-46 applies to the sojourner (vv. 35, 38, 43-44), yet there is debate about whether "the least of these" and "brothers" refer to Jesus' disciples or to all strangers more broadly. Be that as it may, there is no doubt that Jesus sets the example to reach out to those others reject. In our day, this clearly includes immigrants.

All Christians Are Sojourners

The epistles tell us that all Christians are sojourners on earth, citizens of another kingdom (Phil. 3:20; Heb. 13:14; 1 Pet. 1:1; 2:11). These verses teach that the experience of being a stranger in a strange land is so illuminating and so fundamental that it is a central metaphor of what it means to be a Christian! It would not be farfetched to suggest, therefore, that we may actually get a better sense of what it means to be a Christian as we engage immigrants. Immigrants can appreciate their own lives as special windows into the faith and as helpful to fellow Christians in the majority culture to grow in their relationship with God.

In addition, Christians are to be hospitable (Lk. 14:12-14; Rom. 12:13; 1 Pet. 4:9). This is a distinguishing mark of being a follower of Jesus and is expected especially of church leaders (1 Tim. 3:2; Titus 1:8). To entertain a stranger, the author of the letter to the Hebrews tells us, may be to host an angel unawares (13:2)!

Romans 13

I leave this passage for last, and I do not spend much time on it. The preceding summary of biblical teaching alters the perspective on 13:1-5. One can no longer say cavalierly, "Obey the laws of the land." One has to ask if the laws are just and to what extent they reflect the heart of God. If these are not good laws, then it is the responsibility of Christians to work to change them. It is also the responsibility of the church to reflect on its appropriate role in the present climate.

The United Nations estimates that over 210 million people are migrating around the globe, looking for food, fleeing armed conflicts, and seeking employment. Immigration is not just a U.S. problem. The reality of this massive movement of peoples changes the direction of the discussion. Issues related to the mission of the church come to the fore. Now the questions are, "In a world, where over 210 million people are on the move, what does it mean to be a Christian? What does it mean to be the church?"

The place to begin the reading of Romans 13:1-5 is not at 13:1, but at 12:1. Christians are exhorted not be molded by the values and views of the culture. Sadly, this is what has happened on immigration. Political parties and prejudices define the stance of many Christians. Romans 12 also commands Christians to be hospitable and to feed our enemies and give them drink. This is where I give the very hard challenge: Even if you consider immigrants to be enemies of this country, as a follower of Jesus you are commanded to give them food and drink.

WHERE DO WE GO FROM HERE?

I close my presentations with this final thought. As Christians, we stand before two borders, one physical, one metaphorical. There is the physical, national border to the south. There socio-economic, political, and security issues must be handled. These matters need to be rethought to move to a viable solution to the immigration situation. For Christians, there is another border, or line, before which we stand: the biblical teaching on immigration. What are we to do with that? How can we relate it to our political views? Are we willing to accept it and make a decision of faith to let the Scripture establish our commitments and values? That is a hard choice that each Christian must face.

The logic of my presentations on immigration is to move audiences from an expansion of their understanding of the immigration debate through a brief look at history, with the help of images, to a reconsideration of the relationship of their faith to the topic by surveying the Bible's teaching. The goal is to inform and to reform the opinions of the majority culture in a constructive fashion and to encourage the hearts of immigrants.

My hope for this essay is that perhaps something that has been offered by way of strategy or content might be of help to others, who speak up for immigrants and reach out to them in their need. By God's grace and by the prayers and actions of the Christian church this country might become a more welcoming place to the sojourner.

NOTES

1. I will focus on the Mexican immigrant community. In metro-Denver the overwhelming majority of immigrants from Latin America are Mexican.
2. The American Bible Society has published a special edition of the Reina Valera 1960 version of the Bible called *Dios Camina con el Inmigrante*.
3. On the West Coast the major entry point was at Angel Island in San Francisco harbor (1910–1940).
4. *The Papers of Benjamin Franklin*, vol. 4, ed. Leonard W. Labaree (New Haven: Yale University Press, 1959), 234.
5. These three books do not appear as welcoming of the "other." Note Ezra's and Nehemiah's rejection of intermarriage (Ezra 9-10; Nehemiah 13). Conflicted feelings hold true for both host and immigrant cultures. This discussion lies beyond the purview of this essay.
6. In *The Immigration Crisis*, Hoffmeier argues that these laws applied only to legal immigrants. I do not find his hypothesis convincing.
7. This passage alludes as well to their time in Egypt, and so combines both motivations.

SELECTED BIBLIOGRAPHY

Carroll R., M. Daniel. *Christians at the Border: Immigration, the Church, and the Bible*. Grand Rapids, MI: Baker Academic, 2008. Spanish: *Cristianos en la frontera: La inmigración, la iglesia y la biblia*. Transl. L. H. Sáez. Lake Mary, FL: Nueva Creación, 2009.

———. *Immigration and the Bible*. Missio Dei 19. Elkhart, IN: Mennonite Mission Network, 2010. Spanish: *La inmigración y la Biblia*. Transl. M. Rindzinski. Elkhart, IN: Red Menonita de Misión, 2010.

———. "Aliens, Immigration, and Refugees." In *Dictionary of Scripture and Ethics*, ed. J. Green et al, 53–58. Grand Rapids: Baker, 2011.

———. "Reading the Bible through Other Lenses: New Vistas from a Hispanic Diaspora Perspective." In *Global Voices: Reading the Bible in the Majority World*, ed. C. S. Keener and M. Daniel Carroll R., 5–26. Peabody: Hendrickson, 2012.

Daniel, Ben. *Neighbor: Christian Encounters With "Illegal" Immigration*. Louisville: Westminster John Knox, 2010.

González, Justo L. *Santa Biblia: The Bible through Hispanic Eyes*. Nashville, TN: Abingdon, 1996.

Groody, Daniel G., and Gioacchino Campese, eds. *A Promised Land, A Perilous Journey: Theological Perspectives on Migration*. South Bend: University of Notre Dame Press, 2008.

Hoffmeier, James K. *The Immigration Crisis: Immigrants, Aliens, and the Bible*. Wheaton: Crossway, 2009.

Myers, Ched and Matthew Colwell. *Our God Is Undocumented: Biblical Faith and Immigrant Justice*. Maryknoll: Orbis, 2012.

Rivera Rodríguez, Luis R. "Toward a Diaspora Hermeneutics (Hispanic North America)." In *Character Ethics and the Old Testament*, eds. M. Daniel Carroll R. and J. E. Lapsley, 169–90. Louisville: Westminster John Knox, 2007.

Ruiz, Jean-Pierre. *Readings from the Edges: The Bible and People on the Move*. Studies in Latino/a Catholicism. Maryknoll: Orbis, 2011.

II

The Borderlands as a Political and Religious Reality

FOUR
Borderlife and the Religious Imagination

Daisy L. Machado

The U.S./Mexico border has been and continues to be contested space, a place of conquest, re-conquest, and colonization where human bodies are at the core of both experience and history. In the borderlands the people who lived in the northern Mexican territory of *Tejas/Coahuila* experienced a second colonization (the first being the sixteenth-century Spanish Conquest) that began with the creation of the Republic of Texas in 1836 and was completed with the Mexican-American War of 1848. Today's borderlands don't have to be geographically located in the southwestern United States. The twenty-first-century Latino borderlands are understood as those places where culture, race, identity, politics, and religion intersect in complicated and even violent ways whether in El Paso, in the South Texas Valley, in the mushroom farms of southern New Jersey, in the desert of Arizona, or in the meat packing plants in Iowa, East Los Angeles, the Bronx, and New York. In the borderlands the international processes of economic, political and social globalization happen every day in the midst of terrible poverty, overt and often violent racism, a rising xenophobia and fear. In the borderlands of the United States, you find a *mestizo* people who daily encounter "dominant paradigms, predefined concepts that exist as unquestionable, unchallengeable."[1] Chief among these is the paradigm of nationhood where citizenship has become so "increasingly conceptualized primarily in judicial terms in relation to non-citizens and (im)migrants" that it is now common practice to criminalize immigrants living in the United States who do not have documents.[2] The clearest example is found in the Mexican U.S. experience which is "distinguished by a seeming paradox that is seldom examined: while no other country has supplied nearly as many immigrants to the United States as Mexico has since 1965, virtually all major changes in U.S. immigration law during this period have created ever more severe restraints on the conditions of 'legal' migration from Mexico."[3]

A recent example is the passage of immigration bill SB1070 by Arizona Governor Jan Brewer who signed it into law Friday, April 23, 2010, in Phoenix. According to newspaper reports,

> The new law makes it a crime under state law to be in the country illegally. Immigrants unable to produce documents showing they are to be allowed to be in the U.S. could be arrested, jailed for up to six months and fined $2,500. It also allows lawsuits against government that hinder enforcement of immigration laws and toughens restrictions on hiring illegal immigrants for day labor and knowingly transporting them.[4]

The passage of this law in Arizona continues the trend around the country in legislative activity at the state and country level to restrict or halt immigration. State laws related to immigration have increased dramatically in recent years:

- In 2006, 570 bills were introduced; 84 laws were enacted and resolutions adopted.
- In 2007, activity tripled: 1,562 bills were introduced and 240 laws were enacted and 50 resolutions adopted.
- In 2008, activity remained consistent: 1,305 bills were introduced; 206 laws were enacted and 64 resolutions adopted.
- In 2009, activity again remained consistent: More than 1,500 were introduced; 222 laws were enacted and 131 resolutions adopted.[5]

This kind of legal construction of citizenship that is given to some and denied others, or that is held out as a reward for military service, makes it very easy to connect the idea of a non-citizen with a non-person and therefore the non-citizen in this country can be easily denied access to basic governmental services. This was the case with Arizona Proposition 200 (passed in 2004) that requires individuals to produce citizenship documents when voting or receiving government social services. (The law also says that government employees that provide services to undocumented individuals could face misdemeanor charges.) Thus, it is in the view of this contemporary dialectic that the relevance of citizenship as a possible restraint on globalized racism and economic pillage can be discussed.[6] As a result the push for the comprehensive reform of immigration policies becomes even more urgent; but this is only one of the many realities of borderlands life.

The U.S. borderlands "cannot be understood without reference to the history of race relations and discrimination against nonwhite people that has long structured political and social relations in U.S. society."[7] In this history it has been race that has been used as the exclusionary category "in the differentiated daily-life realities and expectations of this society's members."[8] And what is becoming more clear in the Latino borderlands experience is that the popular long held notion that immigrants come to feel a part of the United States over time as they and their families assimilate and as these new arrivals increasingly identify with the dominant cultural practices and identify with the country as "Americans," no longer applies. Because the borderlands reality for Latinos has always been about otherness—because of race and especially because of the racial hybridity or *mestizaje* born of the encounters between Indian, African and European—more and more research shows that a sense of belonging for many Latinos comes "as they learn and share their experiences of exclusion."[9] What happens in this process is very important for our analysis of borderlands life because this new and more broader way of understanding citizenship forces the expansion of the more narrow legal definition from one of legal equality to one of social equality so that "citizenship [is understood] as a lived experience . . . [that is the] need for an ongoing process of participation in a movement that continuously generates and reaffirms individuals' self-respect, and hence creates the conditions to experience belonging to a community of equals."[10] This was the power behind the activism of César Chávez and the great emotion that accompanies the cry of "*Sí Se Puede*" (Yes, We Can!) that continues to be heard as Latinas/os call out for their rights across the country.

This more visible activism and participation of Latinas/os, documented and undocumented, in the struggle for immigration reform particularly enhances "their sense of well-being in material, lived, and symbolic ways even while their juridical status remains unchanged" yet it also expands the definition and understandings of what it means to live in a nation-state.[11] In the context of the borderlands this civic activism reaffirms identity, individual worth, and self-respect. And directly connected to this civic engagement is the religiosity of borderlands people, that "complex of practices, beliefs, devotions, and modes of social organization and relations [which then becomes] a vector for collective and individual transformation."[12] Borderlands religiosity cannot be disconnected from the reality of the historical forces that have shaped borderlands life. This is a *lived* religion, a powerful "religious imagination" which is a way of understanding and interpreting the world in light of the Divine. What gives this lived religion, this religious imagination, its power is that it is forged in the context of racism, rejection, poverty, and exploitation, which is why it has been able to sustain these borderlands communities and continues to sustain them today as these communities are being reshaped by the daily arrival of Spanish-speaking immigrants that continue to enter our borders. In order to examine what I am calling "the religious imagination of the borderlands" we will look at beliefs, practices, practitioners, sacred space, and images. Fully aware of the great diversity of this lived religion that includes African and indigenous identities, I will limit my analysis of the religious imagination of border life by keeping my focus on the Mexican and Mexican-American reality.

THE BODY IN THE BORDERLANDS: THE NAHUAS

Scholarly works on the sources that help us to better understand Mesoamerican life tell of a people with a "highly developed complex of ideas and beliefs that constituted the dominant epistemological framework among the Nahuas [and] Mayas."[13] Sylvia Marcos, Mexican social scientist, who has specialized in Mesoamerican spirituality and is currently working with indigenous women's spirituality in Chiapas, presents the importance of the concept of duality for Mesoamerican thought. For example, *Ometeotl*, the supreme creator who lives beyond the thirteen heavens of the Mesoamerican cosmology is thought of as a masculine-feminine pair, *Omecihuatl/Ometecutli*. This cosmic duality was also found in corn, basic key nourishment for Mesoamericans, which was in turn feminine (*Xilonen-Chicomeocoatl*) and masculine (*Cinteotle-Itzlacoliuhqui*).

Time was also dual in nature since the Mexicans kept two calendars.[14] One is a ritual calendar of 260 days (which some believe is linked to the gestation calendar), and the second is an agricultural calendar of 360 days to which 5 days were added in order to adjust it to the astronomical calendar.[15] However, what needs to be noted when speaking of this duality is its fluid nature—the masculine and the feminine flow in and out of each other. As a result, Marcos tells us, "in a cosmos so constructed, there would be little space for pyramid-like 'hierarchical' ordering and stratification" making the "the only essential configuration . . . the mutual necessity to interrelate and interconnect."[16] And the importance of this interconnection was to achieve balance or equilibrium. In this worldview there is an understanding that each individual needs to seek a balance with the forces of nature and with the universe so as to promote stability and balance for the entire cosmos. In order to do this, opposites must be embraced and integrated: cold and hot, night and day, feminine and masculine, sacred and profane. And it is the sense of a collective responsibility for maintaining balance that produced the moral codes found in the *Códice Florentino: Historia General de las Cosas de Nueva España* containing writings and drawings by Nahuas written in Nahuatl and which were supervised by Fray Bernardino de Sahagún (1575–1577).

As a result of this fluid interrelationality it would follow that for the Nahuas the body's immersion in the cosmos was total, meaning that there could not be a body/mind split. The realm of the material and the realm of the immaterial were intrinsically integrated, which again has to do with this sense of balance needed for both realms to exist and which stands in opposition to the mind/body duality the Spaniards brought with them to the Americas. But it wasn't just that the body and mind are interconnected or that the external world and the body are in constant relation and flux. For the Nahuas the skin itself was not an hermetic barrier so therefore there was a continuous exchange between what is inside the body and what is outside the body. Sylvia Marcos explains it this way:

> Material and immaterial, external and internal are all in permanent interaction while the skin is constantly crossed by all kinds of entities. Everything leads toward a concept of corporeality in which the body is open to all dimensions of the cosmos: a body, both single and dual, incorporates solids and fluids in permanent flux, generally immaterial "airs" or volatile emanations as well as "juices" and solid matter. . . . The head corresponded to the heavens, the heart as the vital center corresponded to the earth, and the liver to the underworld.[17]

The closest the Nahuas come to the idea of a "soul" in the Christian sense can be found in three entities: the *tonalli*, the *teyolia*, and the *ihiyotl*.[18] The *tonalli* resided in the head and travels at night during sleep. The *teyolia* resides in the heart and was understood to be the center for memory, knowledge, and intelligence. And when the *ihiyotl*, considered breath or "soplo," leaves the body, then death occurs. The *ihiyotl* also associated with the liver can produce emanations that harm others and is the center of passion and feeling.[19] Because of the permeability of the skin and because of the fluidity of movement between the immaterial and the material realms in Mesoamerican cosmology, external entities could enter the human body from both the divine realm or from the spirit world. This makes spirit possession, sacred or not, an accepted reality and helps to shape the understanding of sickness as an external force/energy that could enter a body and when expelled could take on a physical form. An example of this is can be found in the current practice by many Mexican Americans who go to get a *limpia* or cleansing that is done with an egg. If there is a disease (a sign of imbalance or evil), when cracked open, the egg is filled with blood, a physical manifestation of the disease or evil.

The body is therefore part of the continual flux between the immaterial and the material and as such is never ignored nor pushed aside. This is important for us to note because while the borderlands experience is often described as a circuitous flow of commerce and culture, the reality of this religious cosmovision created and nurtured centuries ago by the Nahuas of Mesoamerica and still present today in a variety of ways is not so readily included in this description. Religion in the borderlands is often seen in terms of the context of colonization, that is first the Roman Catholicism the Spaniards brought in the colonization that took place in the sixteenth century followed by the Protestantism the Anglo-Americans brought in the second colonization that took place in the nineteenth century. The unspoken assumption is that at the arrival of both expressions of Christianity, the Roman Catholic and the Protestant, this earlier indigenous religion had virtually disappeared and lost meaning so that it has become little more than the feather-adorned dancers who entertain at cultural festivals; however history tells us otherwise.

As we look back and try to identify the religious imagination of the borderlands we find that the U.S./Mexico borderlands continues to be a place of great fluidity resembling the cosmovision of the Nahuas; a space where boundaries of religious belief and practice are fluid. And perhaps it is this very fluidity that helps to maintain this resiliency where despite the bloody encounters between colonizer and colonized that led to the death of so many, and despite the assimilation, forced and organic, that has taken place, borderlands people still seek the sacred and do so by merging the religious understandings of the past with their present. And I return to the example of the *limpia* using the egg as not only a physical manifestation of that which can permeate and harm the human body but as a way of merging a religious past with a religious present. I have a very good friend who is an ordained Assemblies of God minister born and raised in Texas. She and her family are very active Pentecostals who celebrate their faith yet she tells me how when she was a child her mother had no problems taking her or any of her siblings to a *curandero* for a *limpia* when any of them were sick. This is the fluidity of religious practice I am talking about—an important characteristic of borderlands religiosity.

That is why *curanderismo* and its "underlying worldview are useful in negotiating institutions and positioned identity, in order for individuals to both accommodate a necessary acculturated existence along with cultural lives defined by non-mainstream traditions and practices."[20] To take from what is part of one's collective memory as *Mexicano/a* and merge that with the reality of present life is in many ways a subversive act because this is a way to create an authentic identity, a self-understanding, in the face of racism and rejection while reclaiming a tradition that has deep roots not only in one's family but also in the community. This fluidity and how it contributes to the creation of identity and self-understanding is a key component of the religious imagination found in the borderlands.

CURANDERISMO IN THE BORDERLANDS

Before continuing any further let me define the term *curandero* so we can see how the term itself, though shaped by a Mesoamerican worldview, plays itself out in the context of the borderlands. In a position paper presented to the University of New Mexico, Eliseo Torres gave this definition of *curandero/a*:

> He or she is a folk healer who heals in the material level with herbs, amulets, etc. and/or in the spiritual level using religion, God, saints, prayers, and petitions to heal a patient. The word curandero comes from the word *curar*, which means to heal. The curandero practices the art of folk healing and uses religion and the supernatural. The belief that all healing comes from God makes it religious as does the concept that a curandero can only bring God's will. The belief that certain rituals and practices can effect a certain outcome makes it supernatural. A person can receive a God-given gift or *don* to become a curandero or the gift can be accomplished through an apprenticeship.[21]

Note how Torres says that the healing done by the curandero/a is done on two levels—the supernatural and the divine. Like the Nahuas before him, today's curandero maintains this fluidity of movement between realms that is not only evident but also expected. This is about the human and divine working together, this is the Nahua concept of interrelations and interconnections where a balance is struck between both realms. This is not about medical school nor scientific training and knowledge where human knowledge and training are core. Instead this is about a human body, and the curandero/a, who mediates between the divine and the supernatural.

Torres says that the first curandero of the Americas was Alvar Nuñez Cabeza de Vaca, Spanish explorer who arrives in 1527, seven years after the great destruction by Cortés and his men of the grand city of Tenochtitlan, destroying in the process some "three thousand distinct medicinal plants utilized by the natives."[22] But what is interesting to note is how Cabeza de Vaca is transformed from conquistador to curandero. We know that Cabeza de Vaca is part of the Narvaez expedition and he comes from an aristocratic Spanish family. The expedition wrecks off the coast of Florida and in the nine years of wandering, with an ever-decreasing number of survivors, Cabeza de Vaca manages to arrive to Mexico's interior but in the long process, was "a slave, healer, and a trader. His life among the indigenous people changed him profoundly. He became a marginalized person; he learned what it was like not to be in the majority, the one with power or hegemonic rule. He survived this by adapting and negotiating a new identity. . . . He became a bordercrosser."[23] So Cabeza de Vaca did more than just "blend indigenous cultural material with European ideology"[24]—he also learned to navigate the fluid religious borders of the Nahua and Spanish worlds. Eliseo Torres reminds us, "Religion and faith play an important role in curanderismo or the folk healing process and is based on the patient's faith. Not being of [the] Christian faith, the Indians may not have believed in Cabeza de Vaca's God but they believed in a spiritual being; therefore, the praying and sign of the cross was part of the healing process as it has been for years in curanderismo."[25]

Three of the best-known borderlands curanderas/os are Teresa Urrea (1873–1906), Don Pedro Jaramillo (1850–1907), and el Niño Fidencio (1898–1938). According to Eliseo Torres there are five main characteristics these modern figures share with one another and also with Cabeza the Vaca: First, these curanderos, though not accepted nor canonized by the Catholic Church, were considered folk saints recognized by the common people. Second, these traditional curanderos used a series of rituals in order to heal the sick. Third, all were charismatic leaders and healers. Fourth, all believed they had a gift or *don* from God to heal. They all gave credit to God for their healing gift and prayed including "laying of the hands" on their patients. Fifth, all these curanderos performed miracles and possessed extraordinary powers.[26]

Now let's turn our attention to Teresa Urrea and examine how as a curandera she not only worked in healing bodies but also worked to transform social realities as she crossed the borders of race and class. Teresita, as she is commonly known, was born of a relation between a middle class dairy farmer and an Indian woman in the state of Sinaloa, Mexico, in 1873. Raised by her mother, it was her arrival in her father's estate in Cabora upon the death of her mother when she was sixteen years old that changed her life. During these years Teresita developed a relationship with a local curandera named Huila who treated patients with herbals and massages.

> [Teresita] became her apprentice through the fall of 1889. On October 28, 1889, she lapsed into the first of a series of trancelike comas that lasted two weeks. After regaining consciousness, she displayed bizarre behavior; she frequently experienced seizures and catatonic states and began exuding a heavy perfumed odor. Moreover, in exchange for renewed health, [Teresita] promised the Virgin Mary that she would be devoted to "healing humanity." By December 1889 she had amassed a considerable local, regional, and national following. Her adherents dubbed her *la Santa de Cabora,* an unrecognized folk saint, which provoked skepticism from the Catholic Church.[27]

While Teresa Urrea's development as a curandera is noteworthy in itself, I am most interested in how she was seen by the Mexican government and by the communities in the southwestern United States including Anglos Americans. The changes in Mexican politics in the late 1800s to the early 1900s meant tremendous social upheaval for the country. Because the Yaqui and Tarahumara Indians sought Teresita's counsel in their continuing resistance to the federal government in Mexico City, the Porfirio government had her under surveillance and in mid-1892 she and her father were briefly arrested and then sent into exile in Nogales, Arizona. A border incident involving an attack on a border customs house by a group calling themselves "*teresistas*" led the Mexican government to lodge a formal complaint to the U.S. government and she was asked by the State Department to move to the mining town of Clifton, Arizona where she began to work with the Anglo American community: "One of the families she helped was that of a local banker, Charles Rosencrans, whose young child she treated. The Rosencranses persuaded Teresa to go to California to help the small daughter of a friend in San Jose, a Mrs. A. C. Fessler."[28]

In 1900, Teresita began touring the major metropolitan areas around the country as a healer, a tour financed by a medical company. As she began to question the motives behind the tour, she began to exert her own autonomy. "When she discovered that patients had indeed been asked to pay to see 'Santa Teresa,' she successfully sued the company for the remainder of her contract" and moved to Los Angeles in 1902.[29] At that time Los Angeles itself was attracting a large number of Mexican immigrants from Sonora, her home state, who came to work at Pacific Electric Railway. Finding themselves exploited and living in great poverty, these Sonorans found in Teresita a beacon of hope since she not only continued to heal their bodies but now began to raise her voice against the terrible labor conditions of her countrymen. In 1904, Teresita returned to Clifton, Arizona, where she built a home for herself and her children, perhaps seeking some refuge from the harsh conditions in Los Angeles. In Clifton, she continued her healing activities, bore a second daughter in 1904, and died of tuberculosis in 1906 at the age of thirty-two; such a short life yet one of great influence for borderlands people. Teresa Urrea was able to embody not only the work of a healer of the body but also someone the people trusted enough that they sought her counsel for dealing with social problems and they found in her a source of wisdom that would help them fight for their rights.

Teresita, as curandera, did not see the body disconnected from the social realities that caused the bodies of her community hunger and loneliness. She understood the toll harsh work conditions took on the workers' bodies and she was willing to work on behalf of both realms on a variety of levels, the human and the divine, the individual and the community, seeking a balance that would ease the physical and social pain of her community. This explains the vigilance of the Porfirio government in Mexico over her activities and once in exile, their pressure on the U.S. government to force her to move inland away from the border.

What is interesting is that when she moved away from the border to a town with a larger Anglo American population, Teresita was also embraced for her healing abilities by a community not her own. Here we see how for Teresita the idea of curandera becomes a fluid category or border that she can easily cross, for she not only heals the bodies of poor Anglo Americans, as she did poor Mexicans, but she also heals the body of the child of a local banker. Again, like the cosmovision of the Nahuas that understands the fluidity of any border, Teresita as curandera manages to cross the dangerous borders of race and class in the borderlands of the early 1900s. It is also important to point out Teresita's own empowerment when she confronts the medical company sponsoring her healing tour for making money from her healings by charging people, something she did not want, and successfully sues them and is released from her contract. Here is a woman from rural Mexico, a *curandera del pueblo* (a healer of the people), who will not allow her gifts and her image as a *santa* to be manipulated for monetary gain; given the time and context of her lawsuit this is indeed an unexpected outcome.

THE RELIGIOUS IMAGINATION AND SACRED SPACE

Let us now move to examine the intersection of the religious imagination and sacred space. Most sacred spaces are places where ritual and ceremony help to create a sense of connection with the divine and with others forming a community. One such very prominent and important sacred space in the borderlands, which houses a very important religious image, is the Basilica of Our Lady of San Juan del Valle. The Basilica, located in San Juan, Texas, houses a statue of the *Virgen de San Juan del Valle* and has become a pilgrimage site visited by an average of 20,000 faithful every weekend. While the origins for the devotion to Our Lady of San Juan can be found near Guadalajara, Mexico the Basilica in the south Texas Valley has become one of the most visited shrines in the U.S. borderlands. Characteristics of this site show clearly why it has become such an important religious location for borderlands people. We begin with its history.

According to legend it was the resurrection of a young child in 1623 by *La Virgen de San Juan de los Lagos* in Mexico that made that site one of great devotion and it was the desire to inspire this same kind of devotion in his small parish in San Juan, Texas that led Father José Maria Azpiazu, O.M.I., to order a replica of the statue in Mexico be brought to the borderlands. An eyewitness relates that in 1949 as he was driving with Father Azpiazu to Mexico to pick up the statue, their car went off the road and they were rescued by a family from a nearby ranch. This family not only got their car out of the ditch, but also gave them some gas and a small donation for the church in Texas. Upon the return drive to Texas it was discovered that no such ranch ever existed, which confirmed Father Azpiazu's belief that he should construct a shrine in San Juan, Texas.

The parish grew quickly and a new church was built by 1954 and by 1965 the shrine expanded to include a convent, a school, a pilgrim house, a retreat house, and by 1964 a nursing home. In the midst of such a thriving religious community, on the morning of October 23, 1970, a small-engine pilot

> reportedly radioed a warning that all Methodist and Catholic churches in the lower Rio Grande Valley should be evacuated, then twenty minutes later struck the shrine, which at the time was occupied by more

than 130 people [plus one hundred children in the nearby cafeteria]. The pilot [Francis B. Alexander] was the only fatality. Two priests were able to save the statue of the Virgin, but damages to the shrine were estimated at $1.5 million and were a devastating blow to the community.[30]

It took ten years for the current shrine to be built and it was finally dedicated on April 19, 1980. However, there are a few parts of this history that tell a uniquely borderlands story. The destruction of the shrine in 1970 by someone who intentionally wanted to destroy a religious site that was home to a vibrant Mexican American religious community raises many questions. This terrorist act—for that is what it was, an unmerited attack on an innocent civilian population—is very telling of the racial politics and the tensions that abound in the Texas borderlands to this very day. In a sad and frightening prelude to today's Minute Men and others who perpetrate border violence, Francis Alexander's intentional crash into this church community is but another expression of the ways in which Latinos in the borderlands are still denied their place in a geography that has been Mexican and Spanish-speaking for centuries. Yet despite the destruction that took place on that October morning, Our Lady of San Juan del Valle stands on the side of the innocent and the perceived protection she provided to the Mexican American community is but another sign of her love and solidarity with her people.

This shrine today resonates with a sense of awe, not only for its lovely thirty-three acre campus, but also for the way it welcomes the pilgrim and provides a space for a people to come and not only remember how Our Lady was with her children on a day of great violence, but to see themselves reflected in the brown faces of both the Virgen and the enormous mosaic of Jesus that covers one of the exterior walls of the shrine. In the outdoor mosaic Jesus and Our Lady align themselves over the fertile south Texas Valley, home to the largest population of farm workers in all the country and also home to the four poorest counties in all of the United States. The south Texas Valley, like all borderlands spaces, is a place of great contradictions, as it also the home of the famed "winter Texans" those thousands of retirees from northern states who spend their winters in the warm Texas Valley. Many of these retirees own expensive homes and many live in gated golf communities that cater to their leisure activities all of which stands in contrast to the 850,000 *colonia* dwellers who live in unincorporated communities that lack basic services such as clean drinking water, sewers, street lights, sidewalks, school-bus stops, and garbage pick-up. And these *colonia* dwellers are not undocumented, the overwhelming majority are farm workers or day laborers, many second and third-generation borderlands residents and U.S. citizens.

In the mosaic Our Lady of San Juan and Jesus stand looking over this lush fertile valley of south Texas, Mother and Son, united in their love for the poor and ignored. And so it is no wonder that so many come as pilgrims to pray and ask Our Lady to intercede on their behalf. There is a large miracle room to the side of the main altar where there are hundreds of artifacts that give witness to the care Our Lady and Jesus show the community. There are many crutches, wedding veils, snippets of hair from newborns, pictures, and letters expressing gratitude for bodies healed, longed-for babies born, new jobs found, and above all, hope regained. Standing in that miracle room, which contains a life-size statue of Jesus after he was taken down from the cross, one cannot help but be moved. The wounded Christ figure lying in that room is a visual and powerful reminder to all who come in prayer. There is Christ, in human form, able to understand the hurts and pains of humanity, but because we know that the resurrection will come, the wounded figure is also about hope and the possibility of a miracle. Very near to this "miracle room" is another space that houses the thousands of candles lit by those who come to the Basilica to pray. As one gazes into the windows that protect from the great heat given off by so many candles, one is again reminded of the power of prayer as a religious ritual in a place where violence has occurred. The words of the supplicant may have been lost but each candle is a reminder that these prayers are not lost to God nor are they forgotten. Like the Christ figure which is not meant to hang in a lofty, elaborate, and inaccessible altar, and instead lies at precisely eye level, in a glass case that any woman, man, or child can approach and kneel by, so too the candle room with its thousands of candles reminds the worshipper that God is close by and accessible through prayer.

    This sacred space is about the community and the community's access to the divine. In the mosaic as Our Lady and Christ look down upon the river we have a sense that it represents not only the specific Río Grande border but also the many other borders of race, unequal opportunity, inferior public education, and invisibility, that keep this area of the country entrenched in overwhelming poverty. These communities may be ignored by politicians and by the rest of the nation, but this mosaic is the reminder to the community of the continued presence of Our Lady and her Son who never abandon the people of the south Texas Valley.

OUR LADY OF GUADALUPE: ACTIVIST AND BORDER CROSSER

One cannot speak of the religious imagination of the U.S. borderlands and not speak about Our Lady of Guadalupe. I want to place this very powerful religious image in the context of a particular borderlands location that is about two thousand miles north of the South Texas valley in the Bronx, New York. There in Our Lady of the Rosary Parish we find a Shrine to Our Lady of Guadalupe and a very active *comité guadalupano* or Guadalupan Committee that belongs to a much larger network called

Asociación Tepeyac de New York. The borough of the Bronx has undergone unexpected changes in its demographics in the last ten years and it is now the borough in New York City "with the third largest population of Mexicans, after Brooklyn and Queens, [and] it is one that has experienced the steepest growth in its Mexican population in recent years, 92.5 percent since 2000 . . . versus an average of 33.5 per cent for the other four boroughs this decade."[31] And this population comes together around veneration to *la Virgen de Guadalupe,* which in this parish is directly tied to a form of civic engagement sponsored by the *comité guadalupano.*

What is very important in this expression of religious faith and practice is that "[i]n a decade in which an average of 500 migrants per year have died crossing the border, Democratic and Republican members of the U.S. Congress have voted overwhelmingly in favor of the construction of a border fence . . . undocumented immigrants do not have the luxury" of being silent and inactive.[32] Being excluded from the rights and privileges of "first class citizenship" these women and men can be understood to come under the heading of "cultural citizens" a category that broadens the strict legal definition of a citizen so that it can now include the "moral and performative dimensions of membership that define meanings and practices of belonging in a society."[33] In other words cultural citizenship encompasses "a broad range of activities of everyday life through which Latinos and other groups claim space in society and eventually claim rights."[34] By their membership in the *comités guadalupanos* and the Asociación Tepeyac's activities, immigrants find very compelling ways to insert their own, often harrowing, migration stories, into a context which acknowledges their sacrifice and challenges, and offers tools and support for building a new life in New York. . . . In these sites, faith in Our Lady of Guadalupe, undocumented immigration status, and Mexican nationality constitute primary modes of identification and offer a frame for making meaning out of personal experience.[35]

For the Mexican parishioners of the Bronx there are two main ways that their participation through religious action becomes political activism. One is the Guadalupan Torch Run, a binational torch run that begins at the Basilica of Our Lady of Guadalupe in Mexico City and concludes at St. Patrick's Cathedral in New York City. The other is *"el viacrucis del inmigrante,"* the Way of the Cross of the Immigrant organized annually by the Asociación Tepeyac. The first *Carrera Internacional de la Antorcha Guadalupana* took place on October 29, 2002, and it was "one of the first activities innovated by the Asociación Tepeyac to draw together members of comités guadalupanos from all over New York City, and it would become the most spectacular."[36] Torch running dates back to pre-Columbian times when the emperor would commonly use relay-runners to keep his kingdom informed. Today in the "La Mixteca region of Mexico, *carreras de antorchas*, torch runs, are a common way for young people to celebrate the feast day of the Virgen of Guadalupe. Torch runs are also used by social movements to create a sense of community."[37] The torch, which is carried for sixty-nine days through nine states in Mexico and thirteen in the United States for a distance of three thousand miles, is carried by both Mexican nationals and Mexican immigrants who keep the focus on the realties on both sides of the border. For the Mexican torch runners the call is for the Mexican government to support programs that provide employment for those deported from the United States or returning on their own as a result of the economic crisis, as well as to aide families in the integration of family members who were gone for long periods while working in the United States. For the migrant torch runners from the United States the focus was on migrant rights, a call for the reformation of U.S. immigration laws, a remembering of the many border crossers who have died, and a symbolic union of the many families divided by the border. In 2009, the run attracted twenty-five thousand runners from both countries.

As we examine the use of religious symbol in the very physical act of running over not only a very long geographical area but across a militarized and racially politicized border, there are two important aspects of the Guadalupan Torch Run that need to be highlighted. The first is that any migration that is undertaken is a life-changing experience for that migrant and her/his family. While some social scientists have begun to talk of border crossing as a rite of passage as defined by anthropologist Victor Turner where there are three distinct phases—separation, liminality, and being "fashioned anew," there are some who are critical of this model. Some are against it because it fits too neatly within the "hegemonic liberal nationalistic mythologies of assimilation."[38] However I think the work of cultural anthropologist Alyshia Gálvez offers another interpretation of the rite of passage model that is more helpful. She says,

> To acknowledge that migrants undergo life altering transformations is not to assume that this transformation makes them more palatable to the nation-state as citizens or that their transformation entails erasure of what they were before. I would also argue that the rite of passage metaphor is especially applicable to religious identity in the sense that while migrants do not leave behind their religious selves, neither do they carry them over the border intact.[39]

While preserving the traditional veneration of Our Lady of Guadalupe found in Mexico, the *comités guadalupanos* are also creating a new expression of that devotion. Migrants are now remaking their time-honored traditions so that they answer the problems and questions of the new nation in which they live. Their devotion to Guadalupe in Mexico is transformed in New York City into an activism that provides them with self-respect, with a sense of personhood that gives them agency in their own struggle to become legal citizens. Membership in these *comités* is also an important process that creates community, in this case a religious community. In this way, national identity, migration status, and the experience of migration as well as devotion to Guadalupe, reinforce one another and produce the conditions for the formation of immigrant communities among people who did not previous know each other or consider themselves to share much in common.[40]

Chicana artists have often used the image of Our Lady of Guadalupe to express what Chela Sandoval has called an *oppositional consciousness,* which is strategy whereby "the trans-cultural, trans-gendered, transsexual, and transnational are activated with the aim of equalizing power on behalf of the colonized."[41] This idea is made clear and embodied in the work of Chicana artist Esther Hernández. In her drawing titled "La Virgen de Guadalupe defiendo los derechos de los Xicanos" (1975) Hernández takes the traditional well-known image of Guadalupe and instead of a woman holding her hands in prayer surrounded by an aura, Hernandez's Guadalupe is that of a woman in a kick-boxing stance surrounded by an aura, with Asian features, similarly shared by the figure that holds up the Virgin. Here the artist emphasizes the mixing of races, in this case Indo-Asian-Hispanic-American as a rejection of the racial binary (black/white) that still dominates racial discourse in the United States.

> Likewise, the female body in movement, extending beyond the frame of the aura, signifies resistance to the patriarchal ideology, sustained in part by forced female passivity. The stars in the rebozo—which in the original icon referred to the "luminous skirt wrapped about the feminine aspect of Ometeotl," the Aztec divinity that reunited the feminine and masculine principles of the universe—point to the American flag, as if reclaiming the right to the nation.[42]

A second painting by Hernández shows both the particularity of the Guadalupe symbol and its universality. In this painting the female figure, Guadalupe, is dressed as a day laborer selling flowers. The "jeans, a sweatshirt and tennis shoes—signify the spread of cultural homogeneity throughout the globe, while her *rebozo*—with the stars and colors of the Mexican flag—points once again to the local, the Virgin of Guadalupe. Her brownness marks the flesh of the Chicana mestiza, whereas the flowers point to the miracle of Tepeyac—the roses in the hill and in Juan Diego's *tilma*—now for sale."[43] The artists says this about the painting:

> postmodern with her sweat shirt, athletic shoes and denim pants, creatively and independently making a living for herself, living her life in two worlds—traversing the traditional as well as the contemporary—neither here nor there but somewhere in between, a new reality. She presents an image of someone who has traversed many translucent borders and has recreated herself in the mode of "Do or Die." She has left her family, her home, her country, her language. She has adapted

in her role as a woman. This image also celebrates an entrepreneurial spirit in so many immigrant women to survive with dignity.[44]

In Esther Hernández's use Our Lady of Guadalupe she maintains the importance of female religious imagery for borderlands life, reworking the traditional to point to the tensions between the transnational and the local, as well as to reject the dominant culture's racial hierarchies. For Hernández Guadalupe does not stand as an isolated religious icon but must be in "connection with social movements and subjects experiencing serious historical transformations."[45]

CONCLUSION

The contradictions found in the borderlands are not limited to its history but can still be found in its religious imagination. The religious life of border people is diverse, vibrant, life-affirming, and one that provides hope for the transformation of laws that continue to exclude those non-citizens who are also seen as non-persons. Through the religious practices of the *comités guadalupanos* and organizations like the Asociación Tepeyac we find the creation of "dispositions that transform the posture of immigrants and their interactions with others. [And it] is a stance that makes exploitation less feasible at the same time that it has the snowball effect of leading to every larger and more public assertions of rights and cultural expressions."[46] In many very profound ways, the illegal status of these immigrants is truly transformed to one of undocumented as they engage U.S. society and the nation as cultural citizens whose moral actions cannot be easily dismissed. In this we see how religious devotion and practice are transformed into agency, which has a very distinct spiritual identity quite different from the one these immigrants had in Mexico.

In a similar manner the devotion to and the interpretations given to symbols like Our Lady of San Juan or Our Lady of Guadalupe are also transformed by crossing the border. The Holy Mother is now a survivor of terrorist attacks, of immigration raids; she has survived the crossing of a militarized border and she stands with her communities around the nation. Once she arrives to *el norte* she dons jeans and a sweat shirt to sell roses in order to feed her families and she stands in a shrine in an inner city street of the Bronx looking upon her neighbors with eyes that speak of change and transformation that can happen when her children join efforts to seek social reform and justice. There is, of course, so much more to this story of the religious imagination of the borderland because the Protestant story has not been told with its charismatic fervor and prophetic use of the Bible. This story is beautiful and complex, but for now we will acknowledge the wisdom of the Nahuas, the strength and faith of Teresita Urrea, and the hard work and hope that embody the many *comit-*

és guadalupanos that join hands to create a new United States, one filled with less fear and rejection of the immigrant. Surely in the borderlands of this nation the religious imagination of its people has indeed been shaped, expanded, challenged, and transformed by this large and creative cloud of witnesses that bring together past and present in the hopes of transforming the future.

NOTES

1. Gloria Anzaldúa, *The Bridge Called My Back*, first edition (San Francisco: Aunte Lute Books, 1987), 16.
2. Suzanne Oboler, "Redefining Citizenship as Lived Experience," in *Latinos and Citizenship: The Dilemma of Belonging*, ed. Suzanne Oboler (New York: Palgrave Macmillan, 2006), 7.
3. Nicholas De Genova, "The Legal Production of Mexican/Migrant 'Illegality,'" in *Latinos and Citizenship, The Dilemma of Belonging*, ed. Suzanne Oboler (New York: Palgrave Macmillan, 2006), 61.
4. Jonathan J. Cooper, "Advocates Vow Challenges to Arizona Law," *Connecticut Post*, April 23, 2010, http://www.ctpost.com/news/article/US-governor-signs-immigration-enforcement-bill-458888.php#page-2 (accessed April 24, 2010).
5. Immigration Policy Project, http://www.ncsl.org/portals/1/documents/immig/immigration_report_april2010.pdf (accessed April 23, 2010).
6. Oboler, "Redefining Citizenship as Lived Experience," 9.
7. Ibid.
8. Ibid.
9. Kathleen Coll, "*Necesidades y Problemas*: Immigrant Latina Vernaculars of Belonging, Coalition Building, and Citizenship in San Francisco, California," in *Latinos and Citizenship, The Dilemma of Belonging*, 213.
10. Oboler, "Redefining Citizenship as Lived Experience," 7.
11. Alyshia Gálvez, *Guadalupe in New York: Devotion and the Struggle for Citizenship Rights among Mexican Americans* (New York: New York University Press, 2010), 4.
12. Ibid., 5.
13. Sylvia Marcos, "Embodied Religious Thought: Gender Categories in Mesoamerica," in *Gender/Bodies/Religion*, ed. Sylvia Marcos (Cuernavaca, Mexico: ALER Publications, 2000), 94.
14. This indigenous population is usually, but wrongly, referred to as the Aztecs. The Mexicas had conquered much of what is now modern-day Mexico by the time the Spaniards arrived, and many of those conquered people spoke their language, Nahuatl. All those who were not Mexica but used Nahuatl are correctly referred to as Nahuas. See Nancy Fitch, American Historical Association, http://www.historians.org/tl/LessonPlans/ca/Fitch/conquestbib.htm (accessed on June 14, 2011).
15. Marcos, "Embodied Religious Thought," 96.
16. Ibid.
17. Ibid., 101.
18. Ibid., 102.
19. Ibid.
20. Elizabeth De La Portilla, *They All Want Magic, Curanderas and Folk Healing* (College Station: Texas A&M University Press, 2009), 25.
21. Eliseo Torres, "Curanderos and Shamans in the Southwest," University of New Mexico, Position Paper, November 1996, http://www.hartford-hwp.com/archives/41/251.html (accessed April 19, 2010).
22. Ibid.
23. De La Portilla, *They All Want Magic, Curanderas and Folk Healing*, 21.

24. Ibid., 20.
25. Torres, "Curanderos and Shamans in the Southwest."
26. Ibid.
27. "Teresa Urrea" in *Latinas in the United States, A Historical Encyclopedia*, eds. Vicki Ruíz and Virginia Sánchez Korrol (2006), cited in The Latino Experience, http://lae.greenwood.com/doc (accessed April 20, 2010).
28. "Teresa Urrea," in *Notable Latino Americans, A Biographical Dictionary*, eds. Matt S. Meier, Conchita Franco Serri, and Richard A. Garcia (1997), cited in *The Latino Experience*.
29. "Teresa Urrea," in *The Borderlands, An Encyclopedia of Culture and Politics on the U.S.-Mexico Divide*, Andrew. G. Wood (2008), cited in *The Latino Experience*.
30. "Plane Crashes into Religious Site," *Texas Day by Day*, October 23, 1970, Texas State Historical Association Online, http://www.tshaonline.org/daybyday/10-23-003.html (accessed April 19, 2010).
31. Alyshia Gálvez, *Guadalupe in New York: Devotion and the Struggle for Citizenship Rights among Mexican Americans* (New York: New York University Press, 2010), 12.
32. Ibid., 17.
33. Ibid., 18.
34. Ibid., 19.
35. Ibid., 25.
36. Ibid., 143.
37. Ibid., 142.
38. Ibid., 86.
39. Ibid.
40. Ibid., 89.
41. Chela Sandoval, *Methodology of the Oppressed* (Minneapolis: Minnesota University Press, 2000), 63.
42. Clara Román-Odio, "Transnational Alliances, US Third World Feminism, and Chicana *Mestizaje* in Ester Hernández's Visual Art," *Latino Studies* http://www.palgrave-journals.com/lst/journal/v7/n3/full/lst200925a.html (accessed April 21, 2010).
43. Ibid.
44. Hernández, quoted in Román-Odio, "Transnational Alliances."
45. Román-Odio, "Transnational Alliances."
46. Gálvez, *Guadalupe in New York*, 187.

SELECTED BIBLIOGRAPHY

De La Portilla, Elizabeth. *They All Want Magic, Curanderas and Folk Healing*. College Station: Texas A&M University Press, 2009.
Gálvez, Alyshia. *Guadalupe in New York: Devotion and the Struggle for Citizenship Rights among Mexican Americans*. New York: New York University Press, 2010.
Marcos, Sylvia, ed. *Gender/Bodies/Religion*. Cuernavaca, Mexico: ALER Publications, 2000.
Oboler, Suzanne, ed. *Latinos and Citizenship, The Dilemma of Belonging*. New York: Palgrave Macmillan, 2006.
Román-Odio, Clara. "Transnational Alliances, US Third World Feminism, and Chicana *Mestizaje* in Ester Hernández's Visual Art." *Latino Studies* 7, no. 3 (Autumn 2009): 317–35.
Sandoval, Chela. *Methodology of the Oppressed*. Minneapolis, MN: Minnesota University Press, 2000.

FIVE
A Tour of the Border in San Diego

Militarization of the Line and Criminalization of Immigrants

Pedro Rios

The narrator of Robert Frost's poem "The Mending Wall" casts doubt on the rationale for building a wall. Responding to what appears to be a truism, that "good fences make good neighbors," the speaker playfully suggests that the wall does not serve even the most mundane purpose of walling in or out cows. In fact, the narrator has an aversion to walls, because they keep people in as much as keep people out. Ironically, anti-immigrant organizations use this poem—in particular, the line "good fences make good neighbors"—to justify walling off the U.S.-Mexico border.[1] The appropriation of this line by border wall enthusiasts reaffirms the need to complicate the symbolism of border walls, and border enforcement in general, along the U.S.-Mexico border. For many engaged in the debate to reform immigration policies, a common denominator is to accept that increased border security needs to occur before any reform is possible. Not only do misguided patriots maintain this rationale, but for political convenience, strategic alliance, or simply because of ignorance, this "close the border" attitude prevails in immigration debates regardless of party affiliation and often even by those who advocate on behalf of migrant communities.

The building of fencing structures along border communities is a minor piece of the enforcement regime that more broadly has come to define immigration reform. In border communities, security framed through immigration enforcement has become synonymous with heavy-handed policies that are an affront to human rights and civil liberties. Border communities bear the brunt of detrimental policies that have escalated violence without relief or redress to complaints.

At the American Friends Service Committee's (AFSC) U.S.-Mexico Border Program in San Diego part of our work includes conducting border tours to groups interested in learning more about how border militarization has evolved over recent decades. The border tour has been an integral part of the work of the AFSC's work and builds on our expertise of documenting civil and human rights abuses along the border since 1977. The border tour typically visits three or four areas of the United States side of the U.S.-Mexico border, including Friendship Park, the western-most part of the U.S.-Mexico border. While these visits provide only a glimpse of a more complicated and politicized terrain, the purpose of the border tour is to interrogate a simplified understanding for what border militarization has become as symbolized through border wall infrastructure and the violence it connotes. More than a reality tour for border residents and non-border residents alike, it is an opportunity for participants to learn about the tensions that have defined the complexities of border life. Indeed, it is an introduction into a dynamic political, economic, social, and cultural landscape that has become the focal point for how immigration and border policies are reproduced in interior communities throughout the United States. This essay leads the reader on a virtual border tour and incorporates themes from discussions and conversations that have taken place during actual tours.

BORDER VIOLENCE INSTITUTIONALIZED

To begin each tour, I share my background to put my point of view in context and to explain why I am an advocate for human rights in border communities. I grew up in the South San Diego community of Otay Mesa, a five-minute drive to the San Ysidro border crossing. From our backyard I could see Tijuana. At night the Tijuana Valley glowed from so many lights that spotted its mountainsides, and from the distance of my home it seemed as though the starry night from above dropped onto the Tijuana Valley. On weekends I crossed the border regularly to visit family in Tijuana. As a child I was acutely aware that I could cross to Tijuana, but that family members who resided there could not visit me in San Diego. I must have been five years old when my father explained to me what the Border Patrol was, when innocently I confused them with local police officers. In his explanation, he described how their function was to stop people *sin papeles* from crossing from Mexico into the United States. This seemed strange to me, almost unnatural. I comprehended almost immediately that a function of the Border Patrol would be to stop my relatives from crossing into the United States because they didn't have "papers." I thought of my adopted cousin Margarita, who was my age, but she was never able to attend my birthday parties in San Diego. She regularly stayed behind while some of her siblings would visit. From my young perspective, it was an unfair predicament.

As the years passed I believe I fell victim to the "normalization of violence" that is part of the border landscape.[2] This normalization includes the constant presence of Border Patrol vehicles in my community, being asked to state where I was born, the steady flow of migrants who crossed by the side of my grandparent's home in the border town of San Ysidro, some thinking they had made it to Los Angeles, but really they had been walking in circles in the eastern San Diego mountains only to find themselves again a mile north of the San Ysidro Port-of-Entry. I remember in high school how the grisly news of another person being run over by cars on Interstate 5 trying to make it into San Diego communities became so commonplace that it no longer made the evening news. During those years, bonsai and soccer runs were popular ways of crossing into the United States. These would entail creating a distraction for Border Patrol agents, so that a large group of people would run into the urban areas of south San Diego. Some people would get caught by the Border Patrol, while most would not. Politicians running on anti-immigrant policy platforms continue to use the dated images of entire families running in between cars into the United States at the San Ysidro Port-of-Entry to depict an "out-of-control" border.

The border tour's first stop is five miles east of the Pacific Ocean, behind a water treatment plant off of Monument Road where many of these bonsai and soccer runs took place. The landscape is much more tranquil now, enough so that Army Corps of Engineers have regularly used the area as a staging ground for large fencing projects. Experimentation with bollard-style and mesh fencing went on for several years, as a way to test efficiency when migrants attempted to make their way into the United States. On tours it is commonplace for Border Patrol agents to approach and ask the purpose of our visit to the area. On one occasion, Border Patrol agents threatened to arrest me if I did not leave the area, despite it being a San Diego County access road. They said I was not permitted to photograph the border wall, though when I pressed them on about this, they could not cite any legal reference, but insisted that they had the authority to remove me from the area.

In the late 1980s and early 1990, this was a site of nightly chaos. Just on the opposite side of the primary fence, made of rusty landing mats recycled from the Vietnam War, there was a more festive air, with food carts stationed across the side of the road leading towards *Playas de Tijuana*. Hundreds of nervous migrants and their *coyote* guides waited for sundown, when darkness would provide an extra layer of cover. This was a spectacular, but also dangerous, nightly occurrence; migrants would risk apprehension or death in crossing the freeway on foot.

But violence associated with the border is nothing new. The U.S.-Mexico border is a product of military aggression that was propelled by the ideological concept of Manifest Destiny.[3] After the U.S.-led war against Mexico, Mexico was forced to cede nearly half of its territory in 1848 after the signing of the Treaty of Guadalupe Hidalgo; the 1853 Gadsden Purchase further demarcated the current U.S.-Mexico boundary. For many living in the Southwest, both Mexico and the United States have not clearly acknowledged the implications this war had on the living history of the descendants of those lands. It is important to place contemporary border dynamics within this history during border tours. It helps create a more complete understanding of tensions that exist between border residents and how they respond to violence perpetuated by the state. Of this period in U.S.-Mexican history, the historian Tomás Almaguer has written, "[t]he United States' incursion into sovereign Mexican territory in the war of 1846-48 was only the most explicit political expression of this notion of 'manifest destiny'."[4] In turn, a legacy of violence has marked the borderlands, as violent episodes have continued to define past and present relationships between migrants, borderland residents, and the U.S. and Mexican governments. Hence, a collective healing for border residents is nearly impossible when present incidents of violence are connected to a past that goes largely uninterrogated.

POLICES OF WAR DEFINE BORDER PRIORITIES

Behind the water treatment plant sit dozens of camouflaged trucks, many dismembered, parts left to rust just like the landing mats they helped place on the international border. Belonging to the Army Corps of Engineers, the trucks are vestiges of militarism that litter the border. The militarization of the border has involved a process that is an accumulative effect of policies that promote increased enforcement resources for border control. Often, these resources are organized in response to a co-called "war," where the borderlands are identified as primary lines of defense that require control and manipulation.

On border tours led by Border Patrol officials, a description of their "Theater of Operations" adopts militaristic attributes for how they view their mandate of border control.[5] The framework of "war" allows policy makers to address summarily issues as diverse as drug enforcement and work visas. This war framework has guided policy structures in the borderlands for the past three decades, under Presidents Ronald Reagan, George H. W. Bush, Bill Clinton, and George W. Bush.

President Barack Obama distanced himself from his predecessors' rhetoric on border enforcement, but has not taken measures to alleviate some of the more serious problems associated with border enforcement and has promoted the same types of ill-conceived polices. In fact, under the Obama Administration record deportations have already distinguished his record on immigration.[6] And while deportations occur as a result of apprehensions that take place throughout the country, the deportees return to their place of origin by crossing the border. The border becomes a metaphor for failure, and also the precise physical location where families are separated indefinitely and where violence is embedded into the practice of forcibly removing people from one country to another.

President Obama's border enforcement and immigration policies resemble those advanced over the last thirty years. The so-called War on Drugs that President Ronald Reagan declared in the early 1980s meshed together drug interdiction programs with border enforcement operations. Significant policy changes in the Posse Comitatus statute of 1879, which prevents the deputizing of U.S. military personnel to carry out domestic law enforcement operations, created a precedent-setting trend for increasing military-style operations and personnel for use in border enforcement activities. According to the sociologist Timothy Dunn, changes that were included in the Defense Authorization Act of 1982 "allowed the U.S. military to become involved at least indirectly in various types of civilian law enforcement—most notably, immigration enforcement."[7] Dunn explains that changing policy on the U.S. border with Mexico with respect to the Posse Comitatus statute of 1879 resembled and incorporated a low-intensity conflict framework. More intensive and purposeful operations involved multi-agency collaborations that included formal agreements between local and federal law enforcement agencies, focused primarily on drug interdiction programs but that also included enforcement of immigration laws.[8] Policy changes in Department of Defense bills in the late 1980s further violated the spirit of the Posse Comitatus statute and expanded the role of the U.S. military in domestic affairs. These included the Defense Authorization Acts of 1990 and 1991 that "specifically mandated that the military conduct training exercises 'to the maximum extent possible' in drug-interdiction areas" as well as allowing for "transfer surplus military supplies, including small arms and ammunition, to federal and state agencies for their use in counterdrug activities."[9] The border line itself has become the object of military technology, including magnetic ground sensors, infrared night-vision scopes, Javelin missile sights, unmanned Predator drones used in Iraq and Afghanistan, as well as Black Hawk and Huey helicopters, and humvees.[10] The people who cross the border have also become targets of increasingly strict laws. Border and immigration policies should be considered in tandem, because border and immigration enforcement are connected.

Reagan is often lauded for signing the Immigration Reform and Control Act (IRCA), or Amnesty bill as it became known, because it provided people who had lived in the United States a means to become permanent residents. However, the law set into motion a trend that would seek to criminalize the right to work by requiring documentation validating one's eligibility for employment. The I-9 forms required for employment, along with proof of proper work authorization, pushed the undocumented labor force further underground and subjected workers to unscrupulous employers who would regularly violate their labor rights. Employers could easily threaten to fire someone or report workers to immigration authorities for demanding better working conditions. As a compromise bill, IRCA was meant to appease immigrant rights organizations because it would have adjusted the status of approximately three million previously undocumented people. An unfortunate trade-off in IRCA was its implications to border communities; it "called for the appropriation of $35 million for the establishment of an 'Immigration Emergency Fund' to be made available for border patrolling and other enforcement activities."[11] On the implications of the emergency fund on the U.S.-Mexico border, Dunn states,

> the formulation of contingency plans for dealing with "immigration emergencies" and "alien terrorists and undesirables" indicates that immigration enforcement efforts were conceived of in broad and at times severe terms by Reagan administration officials, potentially involving the use of repressive police-state tactics in both the U.S.-Mexico border region and other areas.[12]

The dangerous trend of militarizing the U.S.-Mexico border became a much more public affair on May 20, 1997, when a platoon of U.S. Marines patrolling the U.S.-Mexico border in Texas under a Joint Task Force 6 operation shot and killed eighteen-year-old Esequiel Hernández from Redford, Texas. As Hernández was tending to his family's goats approximately one mile from the U.S.-Mexico border, Marines involved in the War on Drugs claim to have mistaken him for a drug runner and shot him after pursing him for twenty minutes. Hernández became the first U.S. citizen to be killed by active duty U.S. soldiers since the Kent State University student massacre in 1970.[13] Though the incident led to a temporary suspension of U.S.-military involvement in operations on the U.S.-Mexico border, the four U.S. Marines involved in the tragedy were never indicted for possible criminal conduct.[14]

CRIMINALIZING IMMIGRANTS

In the 1990s, border and immigration policies capitalized on the War on Drugs by changing course and targeting lower-income communities in a "tough on crime" approach to social policy. While statistics indicate that overall crime rates were down in the 1990s, reforms of the criminal justice system became increasingly punitive and tended to promote a "war on crime" outlook for dealing with immigration issues.[15] A recent study by the Brookings Institution shows that despite assumptions in the 1990s that crime rate would soar in relation to increased migration to the United States, in fact, the "association between crime and community characteristics—like the proportion of the population that is black, Hispanic, poor, or foreign-born—diminished considerably over time."[16] In addition, "the association between the share of Hispanic residents and violent crime all but disappeared."[17] A similar pattern was apparent in border communities, where "[b]etween 1991 and 2000, the median border county crime rate fell 34 percent while the U.S. crime rate fell 30 percent."[18] Though this latter study concludes that violent crime did not drop in border communities at the same pace as the rest of the country, "increases in border enforcement in one sector have had spillover effects that have led to higher violent crime rates in neighboring sectors."[19]

In spite of these trends, immigration policy became more punitive in the 1990s in California's electoral cycles, beginning in 1994 with California's Proposition 187, a state ballot initiative that sought to deny social, health, and educational services to persons "suspected" of being undocumented. In 1994, the incumbent Republican Governor Pete Wilson was behind Democratic State Treasurer Kathleen Brown in the polls. Wilson turned to burgeoning anti-immigrant public sentiment to buoy his campaign. As reporter Steven Scott put it, "While Brown was stumbling, Wilson was playing to his strength, jamming his fingers down on the hot buttons of crime and immigration. Operating with a single, consistent message—'tough governor for tough times.'"[20]

At the border, in the early 1990s it was common to see "Light Up the Border" gatherings in San Diego where those who advocated for restrictive immigration policies held events to dramatize the need for "order to the border."[21] The actions, held in the area adjacent to the water treatment plant on the first stop of the border tour, helped popularize a growing but misguided sentiment that more needed to be done to "secure" the border. During my time in high school, groups of youth associated with white supremacist organizations, and many of whom were part of the local Marion High School Reserve Officers' Training Corps (ROTC) program in Imperial Beach, would dress in fatigues and carry their pellet guns in "hunts for illegals." The Tijuana Estuary and its marshy lands along the western side of the border south of Imperial Beach provided perfect cover for those involved in vigilante behavior. Though vigilantism has been part of the border landscape for many years, these anti-immigrant campaigns became the precursors of contemporary and hostile vigilante movement that in recent years has successfully influenced policy circles in state and federal governments.[22] In one border tour I led for an AFSC-affiliated group, a member of the local San Diego Minutemen, an anti-immigrant group that regularly "patrolled" the border, accosted us and asked us questions about our immigration status. He insisted to know if we all had our "papers" in order. When no one responded, he made a phone call and within minutes Border Patrol vehicles approached our group and questioned us about our presence in the area.

The same bitter sentiments against migrant communities that the members of the San Diego Minutemen have displayed through their actions in recent years created a foundation for opportunistic politicians to use for their personal gain in the early 1990s when other anti-immigrant groups supported Proposition 187.[23] Unfortunately, other California propositions have also targeted the civil rights and liberties of migrant communities. In 1996, Proposition 209 had the intention of prohibiting public institutions from considering affirmative action standards for eligibility opportunities in public education, public employment, and public contracting. In 1998, promoted by a 1994 Republican gubernatorial nominee, Proposition 227 severely limited and constrained bilingual education programs. In 1999, then former Governor Pete Wilson, who was considering a presidential bid, led the campaign to qualify Proposition 21 to the 2000 statewide ballot. The proposition intended to criminalize youth by imposing harsher sentencing standards, such as trying fourteen-year-olds as adults.

The virulent politics that fueled Proposition 187 catapulted anti-immigrant fervor to a national level. In 1996, President Bill Clinton signed the Illegal Immigration Reform and Immigrant Responsibility Act (IIRIRA), which made minor crimes deportable offenses and implemented retroactive components that permitted the then Immigration and Naturalization Service (INS) to deport persons convicted of minor crimes prior to the enactment of the legislation in 1996. Political analyst Tom Barry explains that "[r]ising immigration flows in the early and mid-1990s drew increasing attention from politicians in Washington and immigration restrictionist organizations like the Federation for American Immigration Reform."[24] The passage of the IIRIRA followed the passage of another Act, the Anti-Terrorism and Effective Death Penalty Act (AEDPA), which placed greater restrictions on political asylum claims and created grounds for indefinite detention of immigrants.[25]

Also in 1996, President Clinton signed the Personal Responsibility and Work Opportunity Reconciliation Act, better known as the Welfare Reform law, which changed the federal government's approach to how it managed public benefits by placing more stringent requirements on welfare recipients. According to Bill Ong Hing "the structure of the bill and the resulting political fallout revealed, however, that a fundamental reason for the legislative choice was economic: eliminating coverage for immigrants saved an estimated $23.7 billion over the first six years, and constituted 44% of the total $53.4 billion savings package."[26] Immigrants became economic scapegoats under the Welfare Reform law, which was passed partly as a result of pressure from political organizations that connected immigrants to dependency on social services. In 1993 Newsweek held a poll in which 59 percent of its respondents held the perception that "many immigrants wind up on welfare."[27] In San Francisco, where I worked with elderly immigrants from Latin American countries from 1995 to 2002, many who survived on fixed-incomes suddenly had their public benefits reduced or cut altogether. The Welfare Reform legislation placed the burden of the social safety net on states and local municipalities that were already struggling with budgetary constraints. Cases were recorded of elderly immigrants committing suicide as a desperate measure when they became aware that they would lose their only source of income as a consequence to the restrictions in changes to welfare laws.[28]

The economics of migration is a principal theme on every border tour in response to questions related to "why" people migrant. Coincident with "war on crime" legislation on the state level were changes to economic agreements that directly dealt with U.S.-Mexico border policies. In 1994, the North American Free Trade Agreement (NAFTA) went into effect. A neoliberal economic agreement between the United States, Canada, and Mexico, NAFTA liberalized trade by eliminating barriers to trade and commerce. After years of negotiation between the three governments that began under Reagan, Clinton promised NAFTA would create jobs in Mexico and reduce income disparities between the United States and Mexico. Labor activist David Bacon has described the border in relation to economic treaties in this way, "the border symbolizes the nature of the new economic reality. Production and jobs can move across it easily, but the people who perform those jobs cannot. The border, an imaginary line in the sand for most of its two-thousand-mile length, enforces vast differences in both standards of living and social and political rights."[29]

NAFTA has transformed the Mexican side of the border. On the eastern edges of Tijuana along the U.S.-Mexico border, dozens of *maquiladoras*, or assembly-line factories, mass produce television sets and have made Tijuana the TV-producing capital of the world. In spite of progressive labor laws that were instituted during Mexico's struggle for agrarian reform after the Mexican Revolution of 1910, and reinforced during 1930s, many organized workers remain disempowered at *maquiladoras* because of grotesque labor practices.[30]

OPERATION GATEKEEPER AND DETERRENCE

In 1993, INS Commissioner Doris Meissner forecasted the likely expected increase NAFTA would cause on migration trends, when in Congressional testimony she stated, "Responding to the likely short-to-medium-term impacts of NAFTA will require strengthening our enforcement efforts along the border, both at and between ports of entry."[31] Indeed in the same year that NAFTA was ratified, the United States introduced the Southwest Border Enforcement Strategy that included a series of land and technological operations across the border with Mexico, and which were a logical extension of the trend in the 1980s on focusing resources for border enforcement. In Texas, Operation Hold-the-Line was initially introduced in 1993 as Operation Blockade, Operation Gatekeeper was implemented on October 1, 1994, along the California border, Operation Safeguard was put into practice shortly thereafter in the State of Arizona, followed in 1997 by Operation Rio Grande in South Texas. These operations set the pace for what would become a human rights nightmare on desert, rural, and mountainous terrain throughout the U.S. borderlands. The purported intention of the operations was to close off migration corridors in urban centers, such as San Diego, by saturating the areas with personnel and technology, and to push the migration flows into less populated and more rugged terrain. The theory was that the harsh landscape itself would become a natural deterrent for would-be migrants attempting to cross into the United States, and over time, migration would lessen.[32] The border tour witnesses the jeeps that patrol between the border walls—the increase in personnel and the growing infrastructure such as the layers of wall, stadium lighting and constant surveillance have indeed deterred crossings in San Diego.

But at the border in San Diego, it is difficult to see the disastrous outcome of these operations: since 1994, an estimated 6,400 migrants have been found dead along the U.S. side of the border with Mexico. An untold number of migrants have also perished on Mexican soil in their attempts to cross through vast regions of Sonoran desert. These are much more difficult to tabulate, because U.S. authorities do not classify Mexicans dying on Mexican soil as migrants. More recently, Border Patrol has not classified unidentified human remains found along the Arizona border deserts as migrant deaths because they cannot verify with absolute certainty whether the person was a migrant or not.[33]

INS and Border Patrol officials anticipated that death would result from the changing border operations that would push migrants into harsher terrain. In an INS press release Border Czar Alan Bersin expected that migrants "would be forced to enter into a much more inhospitable terrain, i.e., the Tecate Mountains."[34] To further this point, each of the three successive phases of Operation Gatekeeper pushed the migration flow into remote areas along the border, as had been contemplated in the *Border Patrol Strategic Plan 1994 and Beyond*, wherein it recognized that "'illegal entrants crossing through remote, uninhabited expanses . . . can find themselves in mortal danger' and assumes that the 'influx will adjust to Border Patrol changing tactics.'"[35] The traffic fatalities that I came to know as almost nightly occurrences in my youth quickly dissipated, and in effect, Operation Gatekeeper disappeared the migrant death toll from urban areas. In place of those, migrant deaths became less real and less present, having been pushed out of the public eye, where hypothermia and dehydration have taken their toll. In line with the pattern of normalizing violence, it is much more difficult to accuse someone of having committed murder when the scene of the crime is less traceable. Following this logic, if someone dies in the desert or drowns in a canal, it is difficult to pinpoint an assailant when one cannot be immediately defined. State violence became less accountable with the new strategic plan for border enforcement. This is apparent now on border tours, where human rights claims for border justice run counter to what seemingly appears as uneventful border landscape, with only Border Patrol vehicles patrolling the hills west of the San Ysidro Port-of-Entry.

In a well-documented report, long-time human rights advocate María Jiménez qualifies the border as undergoing a humanitarian crisis. She concludes that border enforcement strategies since the mid-1990s have utterly failed to prevent migrant deaths.[36] Jiménez charges that U.S. authorities consider migrant deaths an acceptable consequence for national security, and that in spite of the increased death toll since the implementation of Operation Gatekeeper, restraints put in place to purportedly prevent migrant deaths "have not precluded the U.S. government from deploying deadly border enforcement policies and practices that, by design and by default, lead to at least one death every day of a migrant crossing the border."[37]

In addition to deaths along the border, border enforcement operations implemented in the mid-1990s have sorely reduced the quality-of-life of border residents. Civil and human rights violations that already appeared as predominant complaints since the 1970s about Border Patrol and INS abuse of power have not diminished, and appear to have been exacerbated by increased border enforcement measures.[38] In March 1997, two months before the killing of Esequiel Hernández, the Arizona, California, New Mexico, and Texas Advisory Committees to the United States Commission on Civil Rights presented its fact-finding report titled *Federal Immigration Law Enforcement in the Southwest: Civil Rights Impacts on Border Communities* based on meetings held in 1992 and 1993 which concluded that "border communities in the Southwest are uniquely impacted by the presence of large-scale Federal immigration law enforcement activity and oftentimes, this serves to diminish civil rights protections, especially for Hispanics."[39] The report also found "possible pattern of abusive practice," a deficient complaint process, no mechanisms for independent oversight, and "severe mismanagement" within the immigration agencies.[40] In his analysis of abusive practices by Border Patrol Agents of hundreds of documented cases,[41] law professor Jorge A. Vargas concluded:

> The most egregious abuses and violations committed by the U.S. Border Patrol agents usually take place in isolated or remote areas where

no witnesses are present.... Once an abuse or violation is committed upon an undocumented person by a U.S. Border Patrol agent, generally the same agent becomes directly involved in deporting to Mexico (or voluntarily sending back to that country) any incriminating witnesses.... The U.S. Border Patrol protects the individual members of the force by applying the "Green Code" (or Code of Silence).... In the overwhelming majority of incidents involving abuses or violations inflicted by the U.S. Border Patrol agents upon undocumented persons, the victims of these abuses do not file any complaint against the U.S. Border Patrol.[42]

In the 2000s, charting patterns of abuse and calling for accountability and transparency became much more complicated. After the attacks on September 11, 2001, immigration enforcement became a central component of the "War on Terror," and as such, border policies and immigration matters fell under this new rubric for national security. As early as October 2001, President George Bush issued the *Homeland Security Presidential Directive 2: Combating Terrorism through Immigration Policies*, which linked immigration matters with terrorism.[43] In 2003 the primary mandate for border and immigration enforcement shifted from the Department of Justice to the newly created Department of Homeland Security, which focused on preventing terrorism in the United States. Border Patrol agents were quoted in local and national press describing immigrants as potential terrorists. If, before September 11, policies surrounding border issues were a mess, now it was much more difficult to address concerns as incidents of violence and abuse were veiled under a pretext of national security.

THE RISE OF CONFUSION AND IMPUNITY DURING THE "WAR ON TERROR"

Since the Department of Homeland Security has managed immigration control, the AFSC office has noted an increase in confusion about who is carrying out immigration enforcement, thus, an increase also in the risk of impunity, which describes the inability or failure to bring human rights violations to justice. In late 2003, the AFSC office began receiving numerous complaints of home raids of undocumented people. At the time, it was difficult to assess what government agency was involved in these operations.[44] Follow a series of home raids in 2004, AFSC met with Immigration and Customs Enforcement (ICE) officials to get answers about why the raids were taking place and who was carrying them out. ICE officials addressed the new operations and admitted that they did not have sufficient agents to fully carry out their operations. They had to borrow agents from the Border Patrol and from other agencies within the DHS matrix, which created confusion for family members whose relatives were detained as the result of a raid. Suppression of information has become much easier for DHS when it can appeal to "national security" as a reason.

In 2005, AFSC prepared "San Diego: A Case Study on the Impact of Enforcement on Border Communities," a report that highlights an incident which occurred on August 6, 2003 in which Border Patrol Agents shot and killed someone who purportedly was wielding a knife in an area west of the San Ysidro Port-of-Entry, along Virginia Street. This 100-yard long street was commonly referred to as "the 100-yard dash" in the years leading up to Operation Gatekeeper, because migrants would jump the primary fence and make their way into the shopping mall just in front of it.

This stop on the tour gives us an opportunity to discuss impunity in incidents involving Border Patrol agents using firearms in incidents that result in death. Before 2003, there were complaints about abuse of power by INS agents, but information on incidents where Border Patrol used a firearm was released to the general public. After the shift of immigration control to DHS, information has been much more difficult to come by. In the aforementioned case, Border Patrol officials did not address questions brought to them by media or human rights organizations. While the name of the individual shot and names of witnesses were finally acquired through secondary sources, the Border Patrol never confirmed that they had detained a companion of the man killed.[45]

A similar situation occurred on May 17, 2005, at the Park Haven Apartments in San Ysidro, about a five-minute walk from Virginia Street. Residents called the AFSC to report a brutal beating that took place inside the apartment complex courtyard. According to witnesses, Border Patrol agents were chasing two men and caught up to one as he attempted to climb a fence within the courtyard area. Upon reaching him, the agents beat and kicked the man, who was already on the ground. A witness detailed how Border Patrol agents hit the man over the head with a flashlight. The man was bleeding and unconscious, and he was dragged from one side of the courtyard to the parking lot area, a distance of about 200 yards. He was left on the asphalt for thirty minutes before Border Patrol medics arrived. Witnesses were sure that the man had died. When I arrived to the area with co-workers, we took photographs of a blood trail beginning from the area where he had been beaten, which led to a small puddle of blood on the parking lot area where he was left to wait for medical personnel. The Border Patrol would not release information about the location of the beaten man, except to say that he had fallen while in custody. Though residents contradicted Border Patrol's statements with their own eyewitness accounts, Border Patrol spokespersons, citing national security concerns, would not provide any information about the incident.

Beatings and tasings of migrants by Border Patrol agents are not uncommon. A recent case involved Anastasio Hernández Rojas, a father of five and a twenty-seven-year resident of San Diego. In June 2010, a San Diego police officer turned Rojas over to ICE. The San Diego Police Department does not openly collaborate with immigration authorities for minor crimes, but Rojas was booked and his information was automatically sent to DHS through one of several ICE ACCESS programs operating in the County of San Diego.[46] He was subsequently transferred to ICE custody and then removed from the country. In his attempt to return through the mountains of eastern San Diego County, he was apprehended by a Border Patrol agent and injured in the process. He insisted on having medical attention, but was not provided with any; he declined to sign for a voluntary departure. It is not known why the Border Patrol decided to deport him even though he had not requested removal from the country, but at the moment he was taken to the San Ysidro Port-of-Entry's deportation area, an altercation occurred when, according to witnesses, Rojas was beaten and tasered by twenty agents of unknown border enforcement agencies. One witness who recorded part of the incident stated that Rojas was handcuffed and on the ground while agents were beating him.[47] Rojas was taken to a local hospital where he was pronounced brain dead, and died three days later.[48]

Rojas's death was ruled a homicide by the San Diego County Coroner's Office, and the U.S. Attorney's Office turned the case over to the Department of Justice, who has since held a grand jury hearing on the case. While much of the focus surrounding Rojas's death has centered on the troubling incident at the border, the incident should be viewed more comprehensively, taking into consideration that as an undocumented migrant, Rojas did not have a right to certain benefits in the country, despite being a long-term resident of the United States. A comprehensive perspective would also review the programs in place that were quick to remove Rojas from the country. Like Rojas, many face a quick deportation in spite of having extensive family ties in the United States in ways that are indistinguishable from a United States citizen. Since the death of Rojas, there have been at least eighteen other serious incidents involving questionable and excessive use of force by Border Patrol agents, including four deaths.[49] Over the last three years, there have been at least thirty-five Mexican migrants who have died at the hands of Border Patrol agents.[50]

FRIENDSHIP AND FENCES

The border tour typically ends at Friendship Park. In San Diego, the most noticeable public outcry on fencing matters arose with the walling off of Friendship Park situated in the western-most part of the U.S.-Mexico border. In late 2008, advocates began negotiations with Border Patrol officials to regain access to the Monument Mesa, where the historic border marker was placed in 1880 to identify the border between the United States and Mexico.[51] Negotiations with local and D.C.-based Border Patrol officials often ended with little reconciliation. A local minister, the Reverend John Fanestil, began weekly communion services, breaking bread on the United States side to serve to people on both sides of the fence, as a demonstration of his Christian faith that does not recognize borders.[52] The communion service, an act of worship, suddenly became an act of resistance. Reverend Fanestil was deeply involved in negotiations with the Border Patrol, he understood the symbolism of the border wall, and his communion service was instrumental in re-imagining a hostile terrain as one worthy of being sanctified. Where the border fence both physically and figuratively constructs a state of illegality of those without proper documentation, the communion service, much like the annual *Posada Sin Fronteras*[53] held at Friendship Park, assert the need to affirm the humanity of those on either side separated by the physical barrier.

With some success in 2010, the group Friends of Friendship Park has advocated for architectural modifications to the original plans in revamping the park. Despite the fact that in 1971, Pat Nixon, the wife of President Richard Nixon, commemorated the historic Monument Mesa as Friendship Park or *Parque de la Amistad* and remarked "I hope there won't be a fence here too long," secondary fencing structures have created a cage-like feeling to the area around Monument Mesa.[54] At the *Posada Sin Fronteras* of 2009, my seven-year old son commented that it felt like a prison.[55] To enter the Monument area, one had to show identification and be chaperoned by Border Patrol Agents who were taking photographs of those attending the event.

During the "War on Terror," border enforcement has become a lucrative business and private companies have competed for public monies for enforcement projects. The Secure Borders Initiative (SBInet), which initiated in 2006, was a privately managed multi-billion dollar program riddled with problems from the beginning. Initially awarded to Boeing Co., the one-size-fits-all program was supposed to integrate a sophisticated system of operations "to transform border control technology and infrastructure" and create a virtual fence of the more than 6,000 miles of border with Mexico and Canada.[56] It called for the construction of 850 layers of double fencing along the U.S.-Mexico border. The program was cancelled in January 2010 after the Government Accountability Office (GAO) identified significant problems with its administration, systemic and quality-control defects, and for poor management.[57] In a more recent report, the GAO found that DHS paid $750 million to Boeing Co. for SBInet without providing sufficient details on what the agency was purchasing.[58] For instance, the GAO found that travel costs for the surveillance system designated for the border were paid without important information on the purpose for the travel.[59] In addition, labor costs invoices did not include hours worked or labor rates.[60] In spite of these problems, private contractors are already gearing up for prospective opportunities on programs that partially mimic SBInet. The director of homeland security solutions at Lockheed Martin has stated, "[t]he remake of the project gives us another opportunity to put an offer or offers forward," citing "Lockheed surveillance technologies used more recently in Iraq and Afghanistan that could be applicable" for the U.S.-Mexico border.[61]

Border fencing has repeatedly caused environmental and social problems throughout the border. In August of 2008, environmentalists blamed border fencing that was built too quickly as having caused flooding in southern Arizona.[62] Later in 2008, similar problems arose in San Diego's Tijuana River Valley, where significant erosion resulting from massive fencing construction in the Smuggler's Gulch area caused flooding of local farms.[63] In Brownsville, Texas, proposed plans for border wall construction would have placed portions of the University of Texas and Texas Southmost College into inaccessible terrain, ceding some of the land to Mexico.[64] In the Texas Rio Grande Valley, Lipan Apache residents with historic claims to the land had to forfeit their property in order to allow border wall construction.[65] In 2010, in El Paso, President Obama sent a contradictory message about border enforcement by lauding the completion of the border wall structures while at the same time making fun of proponents of more border walls. Many attendees booed the "accomplishment" and audience members called for Obama to "tear down that wall," reminiscent of President Reagan's call to tear down the Berlin Wall twenty-two years before. Neither the supposed accomplishment of existing border wall infrastructure nor the calls for more walls are solutions to the immigration dilemma in the United States. While Obama's speech was a balancing act to appeal to Latino voters, it represented a disquieting disconnect between beltway politics and border realities. President Obama's move away from the War On Terror language seems to be merely a semantic difference from the policies of his predecessors, since Obama's policies continue their failed enforcement strategies.

A NEW DECADE, A NEW WAR

The trend more recently for border enforcement has been to respond to a supposed "spill-over" effect of warring drug cartels along border cities in Mexico. Despite recent indicators that border cities along the United States are safer than interior urban areas, calls for beefing up security along the border even more seem to perpetuate a myth about how violence is generated in border communities.[66] In addition to the lack of accountability and the failure for the DHS to prioritize transparency, internal reviews of corruption on the part of the Border Patrol and Customs agents are lagging in examination. According to border czar Alan Bersin, since 2004, "authorities have made 127 arrests or indictments against border employees for acts of corruption 'including drug smuggling, alien smuggling, money laundering, and conspiracy.'"[67] Even more incredible is the program "Fast and Furious," an operation that funneled assault weapons into the hands of the drug cartels in Mexico in an effort to "track" their use.[68] Two of these weapons were used in the violent incidents that ended the lives of ICE Agent Zapata in San Luis Potosí, Mexico, and Border Patrol agent Brian Terry in southern Arizona. Under the Obama Administration, it appears that we have entered a new decade where violence reigns again on the border.

For border communities, it is imperative that residents have an opportunity to participate in conversations about how they wish to live a qualitative life, one that is not organized around war. Effective dialogue is necessary in order to overturn the culture of violence that gets replicated with every new administration. In spite of this, border communities continue to organize for justice and dignity in their communities. That story is a rich and dynamic history deserving of its own space. It is a story that must be honored and celebrated. In a world of sound bytes, the hope is that the border tour becomes a vehicle to begin a dialogue about how to bring justice and dignity to a border region that is in need of healing.

NOTES

1. For an example of the use of this phrase by anti-immigrant organizations, please refer to the following websites: http://www.indianamilitia.org/MM_Project.html and http://webcache.googleusercontent.com/search?q=cache:23gcMnJChtIJ:www.minutemanhq.com/hq/article.php%3Fsid%3D219+good+fences+make+good+neighbors+minutemen&cd=9&hl=en&ct=clnk&gl=us&source=www.google.com.

2. I use the phrase "normalization of violence" to describe what I believe occurs to longtime border residents, when they are exposed to an unusual level of violence and they stop questioning its abnormality. The sociologist Timothy J. Dunn suggests that this process is a key component of the social control needed to exert a level of repression consistent with a low-intensity conflict doctrine. See, Timothy J. Dunn, *The Militarization of the U.S.-Mexico Border 1978–1992: Low-intensity Conflict Doctrine Comes Home* (Austin, TX: University of Texas Press, 1996), 154–56. Roberto Hernández describes how "normalization of violence" gets reproduced through public interpretations of violent episodes, specifically to a massacre in San Ysidro, CA in 1986, but also more generally throughout border communities, in Roberto Hernández, "McDonald's, Memorials, Murders, and Militarization: The Normalization of Violence Beyond Borders," presented at the "Crossing Borders Conference," Department of Ethnic Studies, University of California, San Diego, March 5–6, 2004.

3. As the historian Tomás Almaguer describes, "European Americans saw it as their providential mission to settle the entire North American continent with a homogenous white population, bringing with them their superior political institutions, notions of progress, and democracy, and economic system," in Tomás Almaguer, *Racial Fault Lines: The Historical Origins of White Supremacy in California* (Berkeley: University of California Press, 1994), 32.

4. Almaguer, *Racial Fault Lines*, 33.

5. At several meetings with high-ranking officials of the Border Patrol San Diego Sector, Border Patrol Agents have described their work as operating under a "Theater of Operations," a military concept used in field manuals to describe a multi-faceted plan of control and action. See http://history.amedd.army.mil/booksdocs/wwii/orgadmin/org_admin_wwii_chpt7.htm.

6. Peter Slevin, "Deportation of illegal immigrants increases under Obama administration," *The Washington Post*, July 26, 2010: A01.

7. Dunn, *The Militarization of the U.S. - Mexico Border*, 106–7.

8. Ibid., 112–13.

9. Ibid., 119.

10. Stuart Magnuson, "Border Patrol Receives Unexpected Technology Boost," *National Defense* (August 2007), 64–65; and Tony Payan, *The Three US-Mexico Border Wars: Drugs, Immigration, and Homeland Security* (Westport, CT: Praeger, 2006), 114.

11. Dunn, *The Militarization of the U.S.-Mexico Border*, 57.

12. Ibid., 59.

13. Monte Paulsen, "Fatal Error: The Pentagon's War on Drugs Takes a Toll on the Innocent," *Austin Chronicle*, December 25, 1998. http://www.dpft.org/hernandez/paulsen.htm. A documentary about the incident produced by PBS on this case can be found here: http://www.pbs.org/pov/ballad/.

14. Joseph Nevins, *Operation Gatekeeper and Beyond: The War on "Illegals" and the Remaking of the U.S.-Mexico Boundary*, second ed. (New York, NY: Routledge, 2010), 170–71.

15. Kenneth E. Fernandez, "Crime Policy in the New Millennium: The End of the 'Tough on Crime' Era?" A paper prepared for the annual meeting of the State Politics and Policy Conference, Hanover, NH, June 3: 6. http://www.sppc2011.org/Papers/Fernandez.pdf.

16. Elizabeth Kneebone and Steven Raphael, "City and Suburban Crime Trends in Metropolitan America," Metropolitan Policy Program, The Brookings Institution, May 2011http://www.brookings.edu/~/media/Files/rc/papers/2011/0526_metropolitan_crime_kneebone_raphael/0526_metropolitan_crime_kneebone_raphael.pdf, 1 (accessed June 3, 2011).

17. Ibid.

18. Pia M. Orrenius and Roberto Coronado, "The Effect of Illegal Immigration and Border Enforcement on Crime Rates along the U.S.-Mexico Border," The Center for Comparative Immigration Studies, University of California, San Diego, Working Paper 131, December 2005: 2.

19. Ibid., 12. This raises questions related to the correlation between increased enforcement measures and their impacts on increased crime rates, suggesting that perhaps border enforcement measures have actually produced a culture of more crime in certain border towns.

20. Steve Scott, "The Race for Governor: Can Pete Wilson be California's 'Comeback Kid'?" *California Journal*, 1994.

21. Patrick McDonnell, "Light-Up-the-Border Drive Turned Off as Officials Pledge Action," *Los Angeles Times*, June 23, 1990.

22. On a brief article on the KKK's border vigilantism, see Susy Buchanan and David Holdhouse, "The Franchise," *Intelligence Report* 119 (Fall 2005). http://www.splcenter.org/get-informed/intelligence-report/browse-all-issues/2005/fall/playing-rough/the-franchise.

23. Though the San Diego Minutemen have been embroiled in internal domestic and legal disputes, they continue to have a marginal presence in San Diego. See http://sandiegominutemen.com/sdmm/index.php.

24. Tom Barry, "'War on Crime' Targets Immigrants," CIP Americas Program, August 5, 2009. http://www.cipamericas.org/archives/1684 (accessed June 3, 2011).

25. By beginning to apply anti-terrorism measures to immigrants, AEDPA also foreshadowed what would later become the "War on Terror" decade following the attacks on the United States on September 11, 2001.

26. Bill Ong Hing, "Don't Give Me Your Tired, Your Poor: Conflicted Immigrant Stories and Welfare Reform," *Harvard Civil Rights-Civil Liberties Law Review* 33 (Winter 1998).

27. Tom Morganthau, "America: Still Melting Pot?" *Newsweek*, August 9, 1993: 18.

28. Susan Ferriss, "Panic sets in over severing of benefits: Welfare reform proves frightening for legal immigrants who have worked in U.S. for years," *San Francisco Chronicle*, April 27, 1997. http://www.sfgate.com/cgi-bin/article.cgi?f=/e/a/1997/04/27/METRO11506.dtl.

29. David Bacon, *The Children of NAFTA: Labor Wars on the U.S./Mexico Border* (Berkeley: University of California Press), 43.

30. For a collection of essays that detail workplace violations and unfair labor practices, see Rachael Kamel and Anya Hoffman, eds.,*The Maquiladora Reader: Cross-border Organizing Since NAFTA* (Philadelphia: American Friends Service Committee, 1999).

31. As quoted in Joseph Nevins, *Operation Gatekeeper and Beyond: The War on "Illegals" and the Remaking of the U.S.-Mexico Boundary*, second edition (New York: Routledge, 2010), 168.

32. Though some scholars and advocates might suggest that the rerouting of migrant corridors was for the purpose of selecting stronger workers while doing away with migrants who would be more likely to use social services. On this analysis, see Michael Huspeck, "Production of State and Citizen: The Case of Operation Gatekeeper" (California State University, San Marcos: 1997). For an intriguing analysis on the impact to immigrant women and their vulnerability to potential increased harm resulting from changes in the migration flow, see Fernando A. Lozano and Mary Lopez, "Border Enforcement and Selection of Mexican Immigrants in the United States," IZA Discussion Paper No. 4898, (April 2010). http://ssrn.com/abstract=1595539.

33. Discrepancies in counting migrant deaths has always been a point of contention between both U.S.-based and Mexican human rights organizations and federal authorities. Mexican authorities often will minimize counting non-Mexican deaths, or will not correctly classify Mexicans who die on Mexican land as migrants, and U.S. authorities will purposefully undercount migrant deaths in order to make their operations more "successful" to the general public. In addition, as a result of migrants traveling longer distances in order to avoid fencing structures, migrant deaths that occur on non-border counties in border states are often not included in official statistics. In addition, many migrants' remains are unidentified and many more are reported as missing, and never to be found. For more information on undercounting of migrant deaths, see Maria Jimenez, "Humanitarian Crisis: Migrant Deaths at the U.S.-Mexico Border," (San Diego: American Civil Liberties Union, October 1, 2009), http://www.aclu.org/files/pdfs/immigrants/humanitariancrisisreport.pdf.

34. From INS Press Release on Operation Lifesaver, Aug. 24, 1998, as quoted in Jorge A. Vargas, "U.S. Border Patrol Abuses, Undocumented Mexican Workers, and International Human Rights," *San Diego International Journal*, Volume 2 (University of San Diego, School of Law, 2001): 67.

35. Ibid., 68n196.

36. Maria Jimenez, "Humanitarian Crisis: Migrant Deaths at the U.S.-Mexico Border," (San Diego, CA: American Civil Liberties Union, October 1, 2009), available at: http://www.aclu.org/files/pdfs/immigrants/humanitariancrisisreport.pdf.

37. Ibid., 3.

38. In 1980, the U. S. Commission on Civil Rights issued a scathing report on INS practices and procedures on apprehensions, deportations, and on its flawed complaint process. U.S. Commission on Civil Rights, *The Tarnished Golden Door, Civil Rights Issues in Immigration* (September 1980).

39. Arizona, California, New Mexico, and Texas Advisory Committees to the United States Commission on Civil Rights, "Federal Immigration Law Enforcement in the

Southwest: Civil Rights Impacts on Border Communities," (U.S. Commission on Civil Rights, March 1997), Letter of Transmittal.

40. Ibid., 85–97.

41. Professor Vargas credits the following organizations with having compiled hundreds of documented cases of alleged abuse: 1) the American Friends Service Committee, 2) Amnesty International, and 3) Human Rights Watch/Americas. Jorge A. Vargas, "U.S. Border Patrol Abuses, Undocumented Mexican Workers, and International Human Rights," *San Diego International Journal*, Volume 2 (University of San Diego, School of Law, 2001): 61.

42. Ibid., 61–64.

43. George Bush, *Homeland Security Presidential Directive 2: Combating Terrorism Through Immigration Policies* (Washington, The White House: October 2001). http://www.dhs.gov/xabout/laws/gc_1214333907791.shtm (accessed June 4, 2011).

44. For a composite description of this type of home raid, and other types of problems associated with the new enforcement patterns under the newly created Department of Homeland Security, see American Friends Service Committee (AFSC), "San Diego: A Case Study on the Impact of Enforcement on Border Communities," (San Diego: February 2005).

45. American Friends Service Committee (AFSC), "San Diego: A Case Study on the Impact of Enforcement on Border Communities," (San Diego: February 2005): 4–5.

46. For an overview of ICE ACCESS programs, see http://www.ice.gov/access/.

47. A video posting of the witness' recording can be found here: http://www.youtube.com/watch?v=S8AH1bNe3kg.

48. Attorneys for Rojas's widow and children held a press conference on June 10, 2010. A video posting of their attorney's statements can be viewed here: http://immigrantsandiego.org/2010/06/11/anastasio-tased-up-to-5-times-constituting-a-form-of-torture/.

49. Elizabeth Aguilera, "Border deaths concern immigrant advocates," *San Diego Union-Tribune*, June 4, 2011. http://www.signonsandiego.com/news/2011/jun/04/border-shootings-raise-concern-among-immigrant-adv/. Also see www.soboco.org for an updated list of recent deaths involving Border Patrol excessive use of force.

50. Gardenia Mendoza Aguilar, "Asesinatos en la Frontera," *La Opinion*, January 7, 2011.

51. For advocacy work related to Friendship Park, see http://friendshippark.org/html/About%20Us.html.

52. John Fanestil, "Border Crossing: Communion at Friendship Park," *Christian Century* 125, no. 20 (October 7, 2008): 22–25.

53. *La Posada Sin Fronteras*, or Posada Without Borders, is a bi-national event first organized in 1994 by ecumenical organizations on both sides of the border. The *Posada Sin Fronteras* is a celebration of the hospitality and welcoming of the stranger found in the original posada story, where Mary and Joseph search for shelter in Bethlehem, in anticipation of the birth of Jesus. The event draws comparisons between Mary and Joseph's search for shelter, with the journey that migrants make in search of a better life in the United States. Organizers of the event seek to bring greater attention to the predicaments facing migrants as their migration progresses into the United States. In recent years, Border Patrol officials have placed physical and time limitations on how participants can engage with each other at the event.

54. Nevins, *Operation Gatekeeper and Beyond*, 190.

55. For a short piece on how Friendship Park represents a public space where detention is replicated, see http://detentionwatchnetwork.wordpress.com/2010/03/22/containment-society-reproducing-detention-at-friendship-park/#comments.

56. U.S. Department of Homeland Security, U.S. Customs and Border Protection, "Fact Sheet: SBInet: Securing U.S. Borders" (September 2006). http://www.dhs.gov/xlibrary/assets/sbinetfactsheet.pdf (accessed June 10, 2011).

57. United States Government Accountability Office, "Secure Border Initiative: Testing and Problem Resolution Challenges Put Delivery of Technology Program at

Risk," Statement of Randolph C. Hite, Director Information Technology Architecture and System Issues (March 18, 2010). http://www.gao.gov/new.items/d10511t.pdf (accessed June 10, 2011).

58. United States Government Accountability Office, "Secure Border Initiative: Controls over Contractor Payments for the Technology Component Need Improvement," (May 2011). http://www.gao.gov/new.items/d1168.pdf (accessed June 10, 2011).

59. Ibid.

60. Ibid.

61. Marjorie Censer, "After major program is canceled, contractors see opportunity," *The Washington Post*, May 22, 2011, Capital Business. http://www.washingtonpost.com/business/capitalbusiness/after-major-program-is-canceled-contractors-see-opportunity/2011/05/16/AF0UXF9G_story.html.

62. Arthur H. Rotstein, "Border fence design blasted as causing flooding," *USA Today*, August 8, 2008, News Section. http://www.usatoday.com/news/nation/2008-08-25-3901692727_x.htm.

63. Janine Zúñiga and Leslie Berestein, "Flooded with questions: Land owners say garbage in gulch could be a factor," *San Diego Union-Tribune*, December 2, 2008. http://wwww.signonsandiego.com/news/2008/dec/02/120208-flooded-questions/.

64. Ralph Blumenthal, "Some Texans Fear Border Fence Will Sever Routine of Daily Life," *The New York Times*, June 20, 2007, U.S. section. http://www.nytimes.com/2007/06/20/us/20border.html.

65. Melissa del Bosque, "All Walled Up: How Brownsville's battle against the federal government's border fence ended in defeat and disillusionment," *Texas Observer*, January 20, 2010, cover story. http://www.texasobserver.org/cover-story/all-walled-up/.

66. Martha Mendoza, "Border cities among safest in U.S., report says," *Associated Press*, June 4, 2010. http://articles.sfgate.com/2010-06-04/news/21656731_1_border-patrol-border-security-lloyd-easterling.

67. Daniel Hernández, "Cartel corruption reaches into the ranks of the U.S. border agents, officials say," *Los Angeles Times*, June 13, 2011, La Plaza. http://latimesblogs.latimes.com/laplaza/2011/06/border-customs-hearing-corruption-agents.html?track=rss.

68. Ibid.

SELECTED BIBLIOGRAPHY

Almaguer, Tomás. *Racial Fault Lines: The Historical Origins of White Supremacy in California*. Berkeley: University of California Press, 1994.

Dunn, Timothy J. *The Militarization of the U.S.-Mexico Border 1978–1992: Low-intensity Conflict Doctrine Comes Home*. Austin: University of Texas Press, 1996.

Fanestil, John. "Border Crossing: Communion at Friendship Park." *Christian Century* 125, no. 20 (October 7, 2008): 22–25.

Hing, Bill Ong. "Don't Give Me Your Tired, Your Poor: Conflicted Immigrant Stories and Welfare Reform." *Harvard Civil Rights-Civil Liberties Law Review* 33, no. 1 (Winter 1998): 159–82.

Kamel, Rachael, and Anya Hoffman, eds. *The Maquiladora Reader: Cross-border Organizing Since NAFTA*. Philadelphia: American Friends Service Committee, 1999.

Nevins, Joseph. *Operation Gatekeeper and Beyond: The War on "Illegals" and the Remaking of the U.S.-Mexico Boundary*. Second Edition. New York: Routledge, 2010.

Payan, Tony. *The Three US-Mexico Border Wars: Drugs, Immigration, and Homeland Security*. Westport, CT: Praeger, 2006.

SIX

Spiritualities of Social Engagement

Women Resisting Violence in Mexico and Honduras

Monica A. Maher

My pastoral and academic work over the past twenty years has focused on women's rights in Latin America, specifically women's faith-based responses to feminicide. In the past decade, I have become intrigued by public expressions of traditional religious practices to protest gender violence, exploring this within northern Mexico and Honduras.[1]

Violence against women is defined by the United Nations as "any act that results in, or is likely to result in, physical, sexual or mental harm or suffering to women, including threats of such acts, coercion or arbitrary deprivation of liberty, whether occurring in public or private life."[2] Public health experts describe violence against women as "gender-based" because it "evolves in part from women's subordinate status in society."[3] It is based on unequal gender relationships of power.[4] I approach gender violence as physical, sexual and mental, as well as structural—emerging from inequalities of power evident in social, political and economic systems. I also address the symbolic aspects of violence, including religious, cultural, and spiritual. The interpersonal, structural and symbolic dimensions of gender violence are inter-related and inseparable, creating a dynamic in which the harming of women is seen as a "normal" part of "everyday" life. My lens is multidisciplinary, based in feminist liberation theologies, political science, legal theory, investigative journalism, and social anthropology.

This chapter is divided into three parts. The first section describes the current situations of violence in northern Mexico and Honduras, highlighting not just the mass murders of women, but also the broader transnational dynamics of structural violence as expressed in militarization, neoliberal economic globalization, forced migration, drug/sex trafficking and gang warfare. The second section addresses responses to gender violence on the institutional levels of Church and State, in light of the pressure of civil society and international organizations. The third section explores actions of local women's groups focusing on their faith, strength and resiliency.

The chapter highlights the ways women are using religion, spirituality and the arts as key aspects of organizing, thereby galvanizing international attention. Their spiritualities of resistance to violence, spiritualities of love and resolve, emerge not out of formal religious institutions but out of a deep human religious impulse of empathy and care. The women offer a model of community that embraces the transcendent dimension of human kindness, which forms the basis of human dignity, rights and solidarity. These are political practices of "living religion" within communities who have faith in the human spirit, and call it forth with incredible courage, compassion and creativity in vibrant spiritualities of social resistance and engagement. The chapter demonstrates that while extreme violence has increased in Mexico and Honduras so too has women's collective spiritual-political action, grounded in a religious imagination which reformulates traditional symbols, practices and beliefs to support the struggle for life. In the face of violence, women are moving forward quite fearlessly armed with the strength of their utopias.

CONTEXT: GENDER VIOLENCE IN NORTHERN MEXICO AND HONDURAS

Extreme gender violence, in the form of the murder of women, is a crisis today in Mexico and Central America. In Ciudad Juárez[5] and the neighboring City of Chihuahua in the northern State of Chihuahua, Mexico, it is estimated that more than 500 women have been killed and 1,000 disappeared since 1993. Gender violence has been steadily increasing in the State of Chihuahua: in 2010, a woman was killed every day,[6] whereas in 1993, a woman was killed every twelve days.[7] In Honduras, the rate of feminicide is also alarming. In the two-year period from 2003 to 2004, at least 300 women were murdered.[8] In 2008 alone, 312 women were murdered. After the coup d'état of June 28, 2009, the rate of feminicide increased again, by at least 60 percent.[9] Feminicide is not contained within Mexico and Honduras but has also affected Guatemala and El Salvador.[10]

These murders have been committed in private and public, by intimate partners and strangers, by persons and groups, serially and individually. Before being killed, women are often subjected to torture, sometimes over several days, in the form of sexual violence (including gang rape), burning, strangling and multiple stabbing and shooting. After being killed, their bodies are often further mutilated, dismembered and discarded in public places, like garbage dumps, deserts or neighborhood streets. Given the level of cruelty involved, these murders are often described as "hate crimes" against women.[11] Still, it is important to recognize that not only is gender a risk factor, but also age, class, and race; the majority of victims are poor, young women of color.[12]

Discussing violence against women in Mexico and Honduras sometimes provokes a question from U.S. audiences: What does this have to do with us? Honduras and Mexico are important cases for analysis of the borderlands in that they clearly represent trans-national structural forces, and the underlining pushes and pulls of migration. Therefore, let us place the problem within a transnational context, emphasizing connections to U.S. policy.

The economic, political, cultural, military realities of all the Americas are tightly interwoven. The United States, in fact, annexed almost half of Mexico at the signing of the Treaty of Guadalupe-Hidalgo in 1848, ending the Mexican-American War; large parts of the current Southwest were previously the United States of Mexico. The present day crisis of feminicide is occurring within a transnational context of neoliberal economic globalization marked by structural violence and great social dislocation. There is a growing gap between rich and poor, decreasing social services, increasing urbanization, migration, trafficking of persons, forced prostitution, narco-trafficking, organized crime, and internal armed conflict.

Ciudad Juárez has been a model city for testing the neoliberal approach to economic development based on low-cost labor and free trade. Today the city has over 300 export-assembly plants or "maquilas," the majority owned by U.S. corporations who can pay workers much less than in the United States, under $50 per week, a wage competitive by Mexican standards (double the minimum wage) yet still not enough to support a family.[13] As political scientists Kathleen Staudt and Irasema Coronado point out, "on a daily basis, residents in the mainstream United States may be wearing clothes assembled in a maquiladora, driving a car partly assembled in a maquiladora, opening garage doors, turning on electronic equipment, and consuming medical supplies all assembled in maquiladoras."[14] When this model of economic development began to be tested in the 1960s as part of the Border Industrialization Program in Mexico, a large majority of the workers in the maquilas were young men; by 2004, women made up over half of the working force.[15] NAFTA (North American Free Trade Agreement), ratified in 1994, has assured continuing subsidies and incentives for multinational investment in Mexico. The borderlands are thus critical to the economic lives of U.S. citizens, although many may not know it. Borderlands here describes the regions that straddle the U.S.-Mexico border. Yet, as this chapter indicates in my discussion of feminicide in Honduras, the policies and social realities that shape life in the borderlands have long-ranging effects thousands of miles away.

The year NAFTA began saw a steep rise in drug cartels in Mexico and in the flow of illegal drugs to the United States. Drug trafficking currently generates $35 to $45 billion per year for Mexico, and the United States is its largest market.[16] At the same time, the large majority of guns flowing into Mexico have originated in the United States.[17] Experts from Honduras, Guatemala, and Mexico have noted that feminicides occur in greatest number in areas where drug cartels are concentrated, in the highway of narco-trafficking from Colombia up through Central America and Mexico into the United States.[18] It appears that women's bodies are being used as fodder to mark drug cartel territories and as part of initiation rituals to seal pacts of fidelity.[19] Many women killed are victims of market profiteering and sex trafficking marked by extreme ritualized violence in the drug wars.

The United States is carrying out a multibillion dollar Mérida Initiative to combat drug trafficking in Mexico and Central America.[20] Critics contend the program is based on policies doomed to fail due to a focus on militarization and security rather than on the social and economic roots of the crisis.[21] They urge the U.S. Administration to distinguish the War on Drugs from a war on the poor, who are fleeing the violence of economic policies. Among the effects of trade policies has been increasing abandonment of agricultural lands by peasants in favor of migration north for work. Since NAFTA, poverty levels have increased in Mexico, a full 50 percent for women headed–households.[22] Reports indicate that the majority of those captured at the Mexico-U.S. border have in fact been economic refugees from Mexico and Central America, not drug-traffickers.

A large part of Mexico's revenue, as well as that of Central America, is in fact the remittances of Latina/o workers in the United States who make huge sacrifices to send economic support back home to their families. Though maquilas are praised as a source of income and job creation for Central America and Mexico, foreign remittances make up a major and more substantial form of national income.[23] Remittances of Hondurans living in the United States are attributed to be the major source of foreign currency in Honduras and the best distributed.[24]

Although Honduras does not border the United States, U.S. involvement in the country, past and present, is still unmistakable. As Gloria Anzaldúa states, "the borderlands are physically present wherever two or more cultures edge each other."[25] The original "banana republic," Honduras has a banana industry dominated since the late 1800s by United Fruit (Chiquita) and Standard Fruit (Dole).[26]

In 1984 during the Reagan administration, military aid to Honduras mushroomed in the form of $77.4 million as part of a regional anti-Communist policy to eliminate dissidents. The aid supported contras to destabilize the Sandinista government in Nicaragua, government forces against the FMLN in El Salvador, and the elite Battalion 316 "death squad" in Honduras.[27] The largest U.S. military base in Central America is Soto Cano (Palmerola) in Honduras, a training site of these armed forces in the 1980's.

On June 28, 2009, a coup d'etat in Honduras ousted the constitutionally elected President, Manuel Zelaya Rosales, forcing him onto a plane to Costa Rica which stopped first at Palmerola. Honduran military leaders involved in the coup, including chief of the armed forces, Vásquez Velázquez, and chief of the air force, Luis Prince Suazo, received training at the U.S. Army's School of the Americas.[28] Billy Joya, the security advisor to de facto President Roberto Micheletti, was the author of the 1980s death squads.

Zelaya's populist polices, "including his alliance with the Bolivarian Alternative (Trade Agreement) for the People of the Americas (ALBA), his attempt to convert Palmerola to a civilian airport, and his increase of the minimum wage by 60 percent, created fear among the Honduran elite that he was trying to establish twenty-first-century Communism."[29] The day of the coup, the military interrupted a national referendum taken place on a possible ballot in the November elections to create a Constituent Assembly in 2010 to rewrite the constitution. The Congress, Supreme Court and many business leaders had opposed this non-binding referendum as unconstitutional, charging Zelaya only intended to extend his four-year term.[30]

The coup and its aftermath strengthened U.S. regional strategies of neoliberal economic development, bolstered by military force, and undermined citizens' movements for participatory democracy. There have been flagrant violations of human rights post-coup, increasing appropriation of indigenous lands and broad-based privatization.[31] The breakdown of democratic institutions has brought widespread impunity, repression and severe civil insecurity. Violence in Honduras has spiked so sharply that by 2010 the country had world's highest homicide rate.[32] That year, U.S. Ambassador to Honduras celebrated with the Honduran, the opening of a new American naval base in la Mosquitia, an indigenous municipality rich in natural resources, justified as part of the war on drugs.

U.S. military-economic interests have a solid historical foundation in the region. During the 1980s, in addition to increasing military aid to Central America, Ronald Reagan spearheaded the Caribbean Basin Initiative, a private sector project which included military assistance, $10 million to Honduras, and fostered the growth, beginning in 1987, of Industrial Processing Zones, offering exemptions to U.S. corporations for establishing export assembly plants. Between 1989 and 1998, the number of workers in the maquilas (primarily the garment industry) grew from 8,000 to 100,000, largely in northern Honduras in the area of San Pedro

Sula. According to anthropologist Adrienne Pine, "the growth of the maquiladora industry in Honduras is indebted to the same forces that fostered growth of the death squads."[33] Neoliberal economic policies have continued with CAFTA, the Central America Free Trade Agreement that began in 2004.

Significantly, feminicide in Honduras is concentrated in the Northern zone in and around San Pedro Sula, where, like in Ciudad Juárez, multinational factories that employ young women proliferate. In 2003, 70 percent of maquila workers in Honduras were women, often functioning as sole heads of household of extended families.[34] The gender balance between ages fifteen and thirty-five in the San Pedro Sula area has shifted as a result of the internal migration of women, and in some factory towns, there has been a tripling of the population in just one decade.[35] When they are far from traditional social ties, women are vulnerable to male violence, especially as a large visible pool of new workers with purchasing power that men increasingly don't have. In the face of rapid economic changes, traditional male identity as the head of household and primary breadwinner can be threatened. Increasing numbers of disenfranchised young men have turned to organized crime and gangs for an income and sense of identity. In the midst of rising absolute poverty in Mexico and Honduras gang violence has skyrocketed, both as part of international criminal networks as well as less powerful local groups.

Mexico and Honduras have both hired former New York Mayor Giuliani as an expert consultant to help curb crime rates. The outcome has been a policy of "mano dura" (hard fist) and zero tolerance, marked by an environment of violent repression, known popularly as "social cleansing" where "unwanted elements" of society are eliminated.[36] A UN Special Rapporteur assessed the situation in 2002 as the "criminalization of poverty" in Honduras.[37]

The current crisis of violence against women in Mexico and Honduras exists then within a context of structural violence impacted profoundly by rapid economic changes. Experts observe an increase in gender violence often accompanies neoliberal economic globalization.[38] The gender violence is occurring within a complex situation of interlocking systems of injustice, economic, military, political, with deep relationships to U.S. policies.

The overall context for the majority of Mexicans and Hondurans is that of fear and the struggle to survive in a world of the "disposable." Certain lives don't matter, and therefore, neither do their deaths. The most disposable are poor, young, women, migrants and indigenous. A prayer for the borderlands of the Presbyterian Churches of the United States and Mexico in 2005 stated: "We confess to you that we have created societies of disposable people, in a world too swift to violence, too prone to fear, too short on compassion. Then, when the suffering of others is too much to bear, we turn way to other distractions."[39]

The cases of Honduras and Mexico underscore that the United States has crossed the borderlands into Mesoamerica over generations in the form of multinational corporations and military forces out of interest to defend U.S. national and economic security. When discussing individual crossing at the borderlands, it is highly critical to place the issue within this wider context and to highlight the deep structural causes of borderland dynamics that transcend national identity and geographic location. United States citizens may react when Mexicans and Central Americans migrate across the border, labeling them criminals, when they themselves have crossed American borders many times in belonging to a country deeply involved in long-term military and economic interventions in the region. These are critical theo-ethical issues requiring serious examination in the United States.

Who has crossed what border when? Who is the stranger in a strange land? Who is the alien and unwanted visitor? Who is the uninvited guest? As Miguel De La Torre emphasizes in discussing U.S. immigration from Mexico, we need to shift from a Christian theology based on the "virtue of hospitality" to one focused on the "responsibility of restitution."[40] Given the history of U.S. colonialism and neocolonialism in the region, it is urgent to expand from a theology of welcoming the "stranger" to developing a theology of reparations.

We need to build a transnational force for just peace across the Americas founded in a new prophetic religious leadership, a renewed sense of theological creativity and artistic risk. Honduran and Mexican women leaders can be our guides, showing us how to respond with courage and imagination in the midst of violence and militarized repression, reformulating theological understandings to address the challenges of the historical moment. Before examining local women's initiatives, let us focus attention on the institutional responses of Church and State.

OF CRIME AND COMPLICITY: CHURCH AND STATE

We now address responses of church and state in light of civil society and international action. It is important to affirm that some individuals at all levels of church and state in Honduras and Mexico have responded with genuine and committed concern. At the same time, institutional actions initiated and implemented by church or state have been lacking at all levels.

Marisela Ortiz, founder of the organization, Nuestras Hijas de Regreso a Casa (Our Daughters Return Home) in Ciudad Juárez, describes overall responses to feminicide in this way: "either people are dead or silent."[41] A climate of terror reigns, a climate of impunity. Mexican anthropologist and parliamentarian, Marcela Lagarde, has highlighted the "silence, omission, negligence and collusion" of official authorities in charge of violence prevention and eradication in her definition of feminicide as a "crime of the State." Lagarde coined the term, feminicide, to underscore that the violence is not random but reflects a social phenomenon akin to genocide, made possible by political, cultural and legal structures that support the violence and assure the impunity of perpetrators. She describes the "social and ideological environment (as one) of machismo and misogyny, of *normalized violence* against women."[42]

Political scientist Kathleen Staudt explains feminicide as part of a continuum of gender violence, emphasizing its connection to domestic violence, which may result in murder as its extreme expression.[43] In Honduras, of the 300 women killed from 2003 to 2004, 30 percent of the homicides occurred at home and 20 percent were committed by intimate partners.[44] Statistics are similar in Mexico where an estimated 25 percent of the murders are the result of domestic or intimate partner violence.

Compounding the problem to address gender violence is a weak political, legal, and judicial system in Mexico and Honduras. There is widespread distrust of public officials, including police, at federal, state, and local levels. This can result in crimes not being reported. Victims' families who do report crimes face being intimidated, threatened, harassed or ignored. When asked about the police's role in responding to violence against women, the municipal police chief in Ciudad Juárez said, "It's not a police problem; it's a social problem."[45]

In both Honduras and Mexico, local, state and national officials have all tended to disregard crimes of gender violence as ordinary or overstated. When these murders began to escalate in San Pedro Sula in 2004, a police chief stated to the media that these were not serious crimes. The initial reaction of the Governor of the State of Chihuahua, Mexico, was minimization, attributing the problem to certain people in certain places, at certain times with certain associations. In both Ciudad Juárez and Chihuahua City, local officials first asserted the women were prostitutes.[46] There has been a pattern of blaming the victims and trivializing the crisis, and a serious lack of political will to investigate, prosecute, and prevent the problem.[47]

This reaction reflects what legal scholar Catherine McKinnon describes as the "double-edged denial" of violence against women: "if it's happening, it's not so bad; if it's really bad, it's not happening." As philosopher Martha Nussbaum explains, "the abuse is either too extraordinary to be believed or too ordinary to constitute a major human rights violation . . . What this lack of recognition has meant is that women have not yet become fully human in the legal and political sense, bearers of equal, enforceable human rights."[48] Thus, the provocative interrogation: "Are Women Human?" is the title of McKinnon's recent book.[49]

In the face of this inaction, "women organizing through the informal social networks of nongovernmental organizations . . . have pressured states and the international community to act." According to MacKinnon,

"Women's resistance to their status and treatment" is "the cutting edge of change in international human rights."[50] This has been true of women in Mexico and Honduras as much as anywhere in the world. State action, if any, has resulted largely from the pressure exerted by local women leaders backed by an international network of support.

Women in the Ciudad Juárez area have set an amazing example of courage, resiliency, and ingenuity in combating the tremendous environment of hatred, violence, and brutality. In fact, Juárez has become a famous microcosm for the opportunities and problems women face in the age of globalization, placed on the map of international human rights struggles. Juárez has generated global attention on feminicide, with highly visible events in 2003 to 2004, including visits of Hollywood stars Jane Fonda and Sally Fields (2004), a report of Amnesty International (2003) and a visit by the Special Rapporteur of the Inter American Commission on Human Rights (2003). As a result, the Mexican government moved to form investigative commissions at the federal and state levels in 2004. Attention on Juárez continued with visits by representatives of U.S. Congress (2006), the UN Rapporteur Against Violence Against Women (2005), and a special hearing on feminicide of the Inter American Commission on Human Rights (2006).

One concrete legislative success has been Mexico's "General Law on Women's Access to a Life Free From Violence." Still, upon the second anniversary of this federal law in January 2009, Amnesty International reported, "the law has had no impact" due to a "clear and deplorable lack of state-level commitment."[51]

Many scholars and activists see State actions as largely superficial, since the overall environment of impunity remains unchanged. In both Mexico and Honduras, there has been little investigation, prosecution or prevention. Corruption remains widespread in police departments and government agencies. In the absence of the necessary intention and infrastructure, the human rights and security crisis has escalated.

Clearly, laws are necessary but not enough. A deeper social change is in order, and this is where religious, spiritual and ethical leaders can play a fundamental role. What have been the institutional responses of the Church in Mexico and Honduras? By institutional Church, I am referring to the Roman Catholic hierarchy, mainstream Protestant churches, and the growing number of evangelical and Pentecostal churches.

When asked what had been the churches' response, a women's rights defender in Juárez, who has received death threats, took a long pause. That, she said, has been the response, "nada," nothing.[52] In fact, there has been a lethal silence on the part of churches, in the face of the horrifying violence toward women, reflecting a global religious trend. According to a 2004 declaration of international peacemakers and women's rights advocates, "religions have been silent when patriarchal systems have legitimated the violence, abuse and exploitation of women by men. This silence has been deafening in the face of atrocities."[53]

In Honduras, the official leadership of both the Catholic Church and most evangelical churches publicly supported the coup; convergence of ecclesial, military, and economic forces made it possible. The Catholic Cardinal Oscar Rodriguez, formerly known as an advocate for the poor, plummeted in public popularity. If ecclesial leaders did not speak out against feminicide before the coup, they did not denounce increased violence post-coup and with few exceptions, were silent about vagrant human rights violations generally.

In Ciudad Juárez, the women's group, Justice for Our Daughters, wrote a prayer of petition to church leaders:

> Dear Brothers, Priests and Bishops: Because we love you profoundly, we want to invite you to reflect . . . your silence wounds us deeply . . . you cannot be the voice of the voiceless if you (don't speak), you cannot ask your people to struggle for human rights and awaken if you yourselves remain asleep, you have to overcome your fear and be courageous, even when the cost is to disobey the civil and ecclesial authority, as Jesus did in his time. The mothers of the girls and women assassinated have cried justice and not heard the echo of their demands in the churches. . . . Daily the system crucifies Jesus in the feminicides, your voices remain silent while the assassinations of women continue, you have disincarnated the gospel . . . you have abandoned us.[54]

Why are institutional churches so hesitant to recognize "Christ crucified" in the deaths of women? Why so hesitant to recognize women as part of the community of faith, as part of the human community? "Are women human?" is the question McKinnon asserts is lingering beneath international human rights discourses. It is a question that indeed lingers beneath official Christian theologies and practices as well. The churches, like the state, are implicated in these crimes due to the institutional sins of silence, omission, negligence and complicity.

In her work on violence in Honduras, anthropologist Adrienne Pine describes the blaming of victims as "symbolic violence," a legacy of neocolonial ideologies of ethnic and national inferiority, internalized by the economically poor under globalized capitalism.[55] This blaming is particularly pronounced for women due to profoundly embedded Christian constructs of theological anthropology and ontology that justify and sustain gender inequity. It is important to recognize "symbolic violence" as the internalization of dominant ideologies as well as their foundation in oppressive religious structures of symbols, norms and archetypes.

According to feminist theologian Carmen Manuela Del Cid, the prevailing religious conceptual framework in Honduras is a deeply engrained "belief in the inferiority of women" as "an innate fact of nature," in "the eternal guilt of Eve . . . passed from generation to generation."

Women's bodies are seen as a temptation for men, and if a woman is attacked in whatever way, it will always be her fault.[56] *Mujer indecente* (indecent woman) is a common description of victims, a way to dismiss male violence, and reinforce a woman's sense of worthlessness.

Argentine queer theologian Marcella Althaus-Reid asserts "the dialectic decency/indecency is at the root of theological control of the religious behavior admissible for women. This dialectic mediates and legislates everyday life in the Latin American society."[57] Women are *indecente* who do not following traditional gender norms, they are deserving of punishment for their own good and the common good. As one Honduran woman summed it up, "The wages of sin is death." According to Althaus-Reid, this symbolic construction "works as a sophisticated machinery which pervades the public and private spheres of life for women, affecting women's economic and sexual lives . . . (it is the) ideological sacralization of a sexual economic oppressive construct which kills women and makes them into the fetish of a disconnected ontology and an exploitative form of production."[58]

According to Del Cid, we are "entangled in a great web of lies . . . throughout the history of Christianity, disowning women from their bodies, controlling almost all dimensions of their lives . . . the most tragic of all for Honduran and Central American women is (believing) the story of the irrelevance of their lives . . . which is reinforced with the ideology of the 'disposable' which has concrete expression in the permanent violence exercised against women."[59]

The theological construct of decency works together with an economic system in an ideology of disposable women. The neoliberal economic model is built upon cheap labor and fast turnover, upon a poor, young plentiful work force of women, all of whom are replaceable. In Honduras, along with the widespread growth of the maquila industry on the north coast, has come the growth in non-mainline Protestant evangelical churches, many connected to international networks based in the United States, which stress the headship of the male in family and society, as Christ is head of the Church. Women are taught to be obedient and passive according to their nature; these ideologies reinforce the workplace ethic of the multinational companies who are lured into Honduras with publicity about the huge potential employment pool of compliant young women. Pine has found a growing number of women factory workers are joining these new churches.[60] Yet, as they conform to the new work standards, disciplining their bodies to a new time clock and production quotas, women wage earners no longer fit the traditional model of "femininity" and indeed represent a challenge to patriarchy. In Pine's analysis, women are then both necessary to modern development as well as problematic.[61]

Indeed, women face frequent criticism for "social demise" in both Honduras and Mexico. They have been blamed for failing in their ability as mothers to raise healthy sons and decent daughters, to keep the social and family fabric together. They are seen as responsible for rising crime, gang violence, and widespread immorality.[62] There is a sense of annoyance at women, often expressed by Church leaders, for not fulfilling what is perceived as their natural roles of protecting and preserving the cultural moral order. Yet, it is in large part women who have responded to reconstruct the social fabric in the face of brutal violence.

The chapter's final section offers further explanation of the work of women leaders, highlighting the ways that they have drawn upon spirituality to fuel their struggles, despite the lack of support, indeed more often the resistance, intimidation and humiliation by Church and State. Women are reclaiming the humanity of the victims and the humanity of society, including perpetrators, by demanding accountability. In the process, they are reclaiming the future by offering hope for new possibilities, asserting "Life IS beautiful. We will not let the environment of insecurity and fear rob us of our capacity to love, laugh and be in solidarity."[63]

ARMED WITH UTOPIAS: WOMEN'S COMMUNITIES OF FAITH

We turn now to explore the responses of women's groups, communities of faith, in northern Mexico and Honduras, to resist and transform the violence though spirituality, religion and the arts, including public ritual, proclamation, pilgrimage, prayer, and lament.

In Mexico and Honduras, women friends, teachers, and lawyers have joined to address the immediate personal trauma of children and families, as well as the broader social trauma marked by injustice and impunity. In Mexico, the mothers of daughters killed as well as of sons wrongly accused are working together, building bridges of support. In Honduras, it has been women, many young and childless, who have mobilized in response to the violence, working to end the deaths of those whom they call sisters. In Ciudad Juárez, Marisela Ortiz has spearheaded a project of healing through the creative arts for the orphaned children of women murdered. Esther Chávez Cano, winner of the Mexico's Human Rights Award in 2008 and a longtime activist against feminicide during her lifetime, was the founder and director of Casa Amiga, the first and only battered women's shelter in Ciudad Juárez. Like many others, their commitments have involved providing services of care and healing to those suffering from violence, binding together the wounds of society at the interpersonal level while addressing the structural causes.

Throughout their struggles, women family members, friends and companions in solidarity with the victims have been incredibly imaginative in their responses to violence, creating altars, marches, murals, songs, symbols and prayers. They have followed their own liturgical calendar, commemorating Good Friday and Day of the Dead with special public services and altars to commemorate the lives of women killed.[64] Valentine's Day, International Day of Non-Violence Toward Women, and International Women's Day have become key dates for mobilization, protest and celebration; religious symbols and spiritual themes have been present throughout.[65]

The women's group, Justice for Our Daughters, in Ciudad Juárez and Chihuahua City, claim God's integral presence in their struggle: "The mothers, women of . . . hope, of struggle, of faith, are certain that our Mother Father God struggles at (our) side, and that God's name is justice, dignity, compassion."[66] This group participated with many others in a 365-kilometer, 10-day march through the desert from Chihuahua City to Ciudad Juárez. Called the "Exodus for Life," the pilgrimage is one of many examples of women's re-interpretations of Christian symbols and stories in order to draw attention to the truth of the relevance of their lives.

Voices without Echo (*Voces sin Eco*), one of the first women's groups to respond in Ciudad Juárez, called attention to the crimes by painting black crosses on pink backgrounds in public places around the city every time a woman was murdered. The symbol became synonymous with the movement, surviving repeated attempts by officials to destroy the markers.[67] Women persistently risked repainting and replacing the crosses. The cross is a symbol of unjust crucifixions, of the silence, impunity, injustice of Church and State. It is a loud lament, a demand to recognize death, turn to truth telling and join justice making. The ever-present bright pink shouts out that the victims and their allies have not disappeared and will not disappear. The black/pink cross has appeared and re-appeared in different forms and variations. Bright pink crosses with "NO +" (no more) painted in the center in black have had great resonance with women working against feminicide throughout Latin America.

In post-coup Honduras, the framing of feminicide and the demands of feminist and women's groups has shifted dramatically; the campaign against feminicide is understood and asserted now in light of a much broader political structural platform: *Ni Golpes de Estado, Ni Golpes contra las Mujeres* (Neither Abuse of the State nor Abuse of Women). Women have made up the majority of those involved in the resistance movement against the coup, an estimated 60 to 70 percent.[68] Their demand is not just for a law against feminicide, as achieved in Mexico and Guatemala, but for a Constituent Assembly to rewrite the whole constitution in order to protect, promote, and respect the rights of women and all those traditionally marginalized by an elite minority. There has been a change in consciousness. As Del Cid describes the movement for participatory democracy: the "utopias of my people are flooding the streets."[69] The dream for justice has overflowed into the public square, where masses of the population have gathered to express their opinions, exercise their citizenship and demand their rights.

With the resurgence in citizen engagement post-coup, the objectives of the Zelaya administration's campaign for "citizen empowerment" have paradoxically been met in a historically unprecedented way; Honduras is experiencing "a new civic consciousness, a cultural change," an "irreversible" social "transformation."[70] There has been a strong backlash to this civic participation, in fact, a criminalization of social protest with the collapse of democratic institutions. Del Cid asserts, "the hope of the people puts terror in the hearts of the elite who arm themselves with weapons in defense against a people armed with utopias."[71]

Underlying the religious practices of the faith communities opposing the militarization of Honduras has been a resurrection of certain aspects of liberation theology, strong in the social movements of the 1980s of progressive Christian coalitions. One key theological theme has been that of utopia, of visions that guide the faithful in the courageous and everyday works of mercy and prophetic justice. These utopian visions reflect a eschatological theology marked by the Reign of God, or the coming of the Reign of God, a Reign which is both present and not yet. Christian actors in resistance in Honduras are strongly fueled by the theological certainty that God's work is the work of justice. It is an intuitive imperative to act for justice in the face of fear and violence, in order to build peace with social equity, guided by the utopian vision.

Women involved in the resistance try to make visible the links between state violence and violence against women, advancing a sociopolitical and economic platform which includes gender equity. This has happened in a variety of ways. One example of theological creativity in women's responses can be seen in the work of the Forum of Women for Life in northern Honduras. Made up of a coalition of women's groups involved in human rights monitoring in the maquilas, economic empowerment, community organizing and human rights training, the Forum was founded in 2002 to express solidarity with women in Iraq in protest of the U.S. invasion, with gatherings in front of the Catholic Cathedral in San Pedro Sula. The Forum soon began to hold public vigils every month on feminicide, demanding state and church responses. This included carrying the pictures and calling out the names of recent victims, a kind of public lament as protest. Women, most of Catholic heritage, often placed their own shoes on the steps of the Cathedral, next to candles and crosses with women's names, as symbols of communion with victims, reclaiming the sacredness of ordinary life, reaffirming the oneness of all humanity, living and dead. These public altars recognize in an intimate way the lives of those murdered, providing the backdrop for the reciting of their names, after which all respond in unison, *"presente."* Their "Women's Litany" cries out to God: "Where are the laws? Where the authorities? So that justice is done for us? Only you are there, in the street, here with us. Because in your eyes the blood shed for every girl and woman is priceless."[72]

After the coup, in response to the sharp increase in feminicide as well as the militarization of the country, the Forum of Women for Life began to bring their theological and artistic creativity of resistance into the marches in the streets, joining with a larger coalition of women's groups on the North coast, "Women in Resistance," as well as collaborating with "Feminists in Resistance," based in the capital of Tegucigalpa. Their actions have included dressing in black as *la llorona* (the wailing women) to mourn the deaths, using ritual and prayer as a form of street theater, public education and political resistance. In one case, a woman dressed as "*Democracia*" (Woman Democracy) acted out her own death, collapsing on the street, in front of the pro-coup newspaper, *La Prensa*, a symbolic representation of the links between the murder of women and the murder of Democracy.[73] In addition, the Forum has brought their artistic public gatherings against feminicide from the Cathedral steps to the District Attorney's office in order to protest State inaction on the disappearances and murders of women, and to denounce continued death threats against women's rights defenders like themselves.

One more general outlet for theological expression in the months immediately following the coup was the coalition, "Christians in Resistance," made up of Anglicans, Mennonites, evangelicals and Catholics. Activities included collective Biblical reading and theological reflection. One event involved each denomination compiling a set of Biblical readings, including Isaiah and Paul, and proclaiming the chosen texts in turn in the central square. Women who participated asserted that the Biblical words took on new meaning, revealing their radical dimensions, their deep challenge to wise and courageous action in the face of injustice.[74]

In addition to participating in larger Christian communities of just peace, women activists in Honduras are increasingly incorporating elements of African and indigenous religions, also part of their collective heritage, into their public actions. In fact, Lenca and Garifuna women's leadership and spirituality have been critical as fuels to the resistance.[75] Part of the political struggle has involved claiming the rights to cultural and religious expression, and incorporating these religious traditions into large public meetings and demonstrations.

In sum, traditional religious practices of proclamation, of pilgrimage and lament, of prayer and ritual, have taken on new and vibrant forms in the context of feminicide in both Mexico and Honduras. They are transgressive spiritual practices, forms of trans-spiritualities, crossing the boundaries of traditional separations between public and private, secular and sacred, profane and inspired. They reflect the kinds of "trans-sacramentos" which are being used at the Mexican borderlands in the trans-sacrament of Eucharist across and through the fence, interrupting and challenging laws which do not serve life, laws which destroy in the name of justice, which protect privilege instead of persons.[76] Behind these transpiritual practices then lies a transgressive theology that disrupt transnational structures of power and builds transnational bonds of solidarity, slowly creating another world of justice and harmony. Through re-appropriating religious symbols, prayers and other practices, women have protested transnational forces of structural and symbolic violence embedded in economic, political and religious institutions, bringing international attention to their struggles for health, security and dignity. They exhibit moral agency on many levels, resisting multiple forms of patriarchy in asserting and reclaiming their humanity. Increasingly, these sorts of actions of women around the world are receiving attention from the academic, political and philanthropic spheres; exemplifying effective forms of political organizing and international diplomacy, women are recognized as "simultaneously" "political actors" and "religious practitioners" exercising both their global and local citizenship in challenging the local impacts of global forces.[77] Women's spiritual-political activism is affecting the ways both human rights and religious peacemaking are being conceptualized and supported internationally.

In the process, women are regaining their self-esteem and generating passionate energy for change, part of what Brazilian ecofeminist theologian Ivone Gebara calls a "political and religious revolutionary process" which liberates "untold forces" "from the depth of human suffering" toward new relationships based on solidarity, unity and compassion.[78] Women's political activism involves a collective spiritual awakening to interdependence, reciprocity and love. Gebara describes resurrection in terms of everyday acts of justice, gestures of tenderness, in situations of extreme duress.[79]

Spirituality is the source of strength of many women who are dedicating their lives to this struggle. This is a spirituality of collective conscience and public voice, a spirituality of creativity, which generates beauty in the process of challenging injustice, a spirituality of joyful solidarity based in responding here and now to human suffering with fearless empathy and compassionate courage. Personal and social healing are inseparable; hope and love contagious.

Scholars of the borderlands, Staudt and Coronado, assert that solidarity is based on "*compromiso*," commitment to the well-being of the community, beyond individual friendship.[80] This is friendship in the collective sense, allying with movements for social/spiritual change.

The present global crisis of violence, in all its physical, structural and symbolic manifestations, is an opportunity to weave these kinds of trans-local social fabrics that become transnational movements of justice. Think multi-locally and act multi-locally.

Feminicide is a call to create bonds of caring across national, class, racial, and sex/gender lines, to disrupt transnational systems of injustice with transnational ties of trust. We are called to move in the direction of international community based on relationships of respect and kindness.

Herein lies our hope, as part of an energy that is infinitely renewable in the common journey toward just peace. In the words of Lucha Castro:

> The sacraments of life have generated a movement of liberation and resistance. United by the communion of suffering, we denounce the social system of death. The Great Spirit is with Us!! We are strength that engenders life . . . bearers of hope, prophets that denounce the injustices, the unjust crosses! The open wounds cannot keep bleeding indefinitely. Despite the pain we have learned to sing our hymn filled with hope. . . . Ni Una Muerte Mas, Not One More Death.[81]

Adelante siempre.

NOTES

1. This essay is based on the presentation, "Resisting Militarization of U.S. Borderlands: The Case of the Coup in Honduras," at the Spring Institute for Lived Theology "Theology, Migration, and the Borderlands" at the University of San Diego, California, April 28, 2010; and the Horace De Y. Lentz Memorial Lecture, "Reclaiming the Human: Responding to Gender Violence in Mexico and Honduras," at Harvard Divinity School, Cambridge, Massachusetts, 20 March 2009.

2. United Nations, *Declaration on the Elimination of Violence Against Women.* New York: General Assembly, A/RES/48/104, 1993, Article 1.

3. Lori Heise, Mary Ellsburg, and Megan Gotttemoeller. "Ending Violence Against Women," *Population Reports.* Volume XXVII, Number 4 (1999), 1. Cited in Adriana Beltrán and Laurie Freeman, "Hidden in Plain Sight: Violence Against Women in Mexico and Guatemala," Washington Office on Latin America, March 2007: 3.

4. The United Nations *Declaration on the Elimination of Violence Against Women* asserts, "violence against women is a manifestation of historically unequal power relations between men and women, which have led to domination over and discrimination against women by men."

5. Ciudad Juárez, a city of 1.5 million people, lies across the border from El Paso, Texas.

6. "Urgent Statement on the Murder of Marisela Escobedo Ortiz, Women's Human Rights Defender of Ciudad Juárez," Women's Rights in the News, Association of Women's Rights in Development (AWID), 20 Dec 2010. http://staging.awid.org/Women-s-Rights-in-the-News/Women-s-Rights-in-the-News/Urgent-Statement-on-the-Murder-of-Marisela-Escobedo-Ortiz-women-s-human-rights-defender-of-Ciudad-Juárez, accessed 8 July 2011.

7. Guadalupe Cruz Jaimes, "Veremos que se complan compromisos para abatir feminicidio," Cimac Noticias, Nuestras Hijas de Regreso a Casa A.C., 11 November 2010. http://www.mujeresdejuarez.org/, accessed 8 July 2011. Statistics are estimates of Observatorio Justicia para Nuestras Hijas.

8. Boletina Dignas Solidarias (Associación de Mujeres por la Dignidad y la Vida) cites more than 300 feminicides in Honduras between 2003 and 2004, Boletina Electrónica No. 50, Noviembre 2004, San Salvador, El Salvador. http://www.isis.cl/Feminicidio/doc/, accessed 31 January 2006.

9. Almost half of all the feminicides reported in 2009 occurred in the three and a half months after the coup (Feministas en Resistencia, *Violaciones a Los Derechos Humanos de las Mujeres Después del Golpe de Estado en Honduras: Del 28 de Junio al 30 de Octubre del 2009.* Tegucigalpa, Honduras: Centro de Derechos de Mujeres, 2009: 25.) In just the first month after the coup (July 2009), there were a total of 51 feminicides, compared to an average of 26 per month in 2008 when the total for the year was 312 (Feministas en Resistencia, "Audiencia Sobre la Situacion de los Derechos de las Mujeres en Hondu-

ras en el Marco del Golpe de Estado." Document prepared for the Inter-American Commission on Human Rights, Regular Session 137, Testimony given by Jessica Sánchez and Adelay Carias, 2 November 2009, Washington, D.C., 4. (The total number of cases of feminicide in 2009 represented a 62 percent increase from the total number in 2008. The high level of violence against women continued into 2010 under the post-coup regime. Between the periods 2007 to 2008 and 2009 to 2010, there was an increase of 63 percent in the number of feminicides with 281 more in the latter period (Jessica Sánchez, *Impunidad: Un Grito Sin Respuesto*. Informe Final de Femicidios en Honduras, Campaña Nacional Contra los Femicidios, Tribuna de Mujeres Contra los Femicidios [Tegucigalpa, Honduras: Oxfam], 40–43).

10. Official statistics in Guatemala reported 2,273 cases of femicide in the six-year period from 2000 to 2005 (cited by Giovana Lemus, "Femicidio en Guatemala," presentation at the panel on "Crossing Boundaries: the Politics of 'Femicides' in the Americas," International Forum of the Association of Women's Rights in Development, Bangkok, Thailand, 27 October 2005.) El Salvador has also not been left unscathed. In fact, Honduras, Guatemala and El Salvador are called the "triangle of femicide" in Central America (a term cited by Miosotis Rivas Peña del Consejo de Ministras de la Mujer de Centroamérica y República Dominicana, "Integración regional en Centroamérica y República Dominicana," Simposio Internacional "La Construcción de la Paz en la Sociedad y la Religión: Practicas Feministas de Transformación Intercultural," 22 June 2011, Santo Domingo, República Dominicana.)

11. See Marcela Lagarde y de los Rios, "Por la vida y la libertad de las mujeres: Final feminicidio" Dia V-Juárez, February 2004: 8. http://www.isis.cl/Feminicidio/Juárez/pag/quessfem.htm, accessed 8 January 2005, translation by Maher.

12. Indeed, international femicide experts at the 2005 International AWID Forum stated "the violence is racialized, sexualized and discriminates on the bases of socioeconomic status and age." Program panel description of "Crossing Boundaries: the Politics of 'Femicides' in the Americas," the International Forum of the Association of Women's Rights in AWID, Bangkok, Thailand, 27 October 2005.

13. Kathleen Staudt, *Violence and Activism At the Border: Gender, Fear, and Everyday Life in Ciudad Juárez* (Austin: University of Texas Press, 2008), 7, 9, 45.

14. Kathleen Staudt and Irasema Coronado, *Fronteras No Más: Toward Social Justice at the U.S.- Mexico Border* (New York: Palgrave USA, 2002), 167.

15. Ibid., 7.

16. University of Pennsylvania, "Drug Trafficking, Violence and Mexico's Economic Future," 26 January 2011, Wharton Law and Public Policy, Knowledge@Wharton. http://knowledge.wharton.upenn.edu/article.cfm?articleid=2695, accessed 29 Sept 2012.

17. According to the Latin American Working Group (LAWG), a June 2011 "congressional report noted that *70% of the weapons* seized in Mexico in 2009 and 2010 and submitted for tracing came through the United States" (Jenny Johnson, LAWG e-letter, 12 July 2011).

18. Based on private interview with an expert on feminicide in El Paso, January 2009.

19. According to experts who have done extensive research on the feminicides in Ciudad Juárez and Chihuahua, México, such as Argentine anthropologist, Rita Laura Segato.

20. The University of Pennsylvania reports, "the U.S. has allocated US$1.5 billion over a three-year period to eliminate corruption within these countries' government institutions by funding training for police forces, security-development programs, and purchases for equipment used in the war against drugs." In "Drug Trafficking, Violence and Mexico's Economic Future," 26 January 2011, Wharton Law and Public Policy, Knowledge@Wharton. http://knowledge.wharton.upenn.edu/article.cfm?articleid=2695, accessed 1 Oct 2012.

21. Democracy Now! *The War and Peace Report*. "El Plan México y la militarización de México financiado por Estados Unidos." Interviews of Avi Lewis, Laura Carlsen and John Gibler, 31 July 2008; traducido por Gabriela Díaz Cortés en español.
22. Miguel A. De La Torre, *Trails of Hope and Terror: Testimonies on Immigration* (Maryknoll, NY: Orbis Books, 2009), 13–14.
23. María Pilar Aquino, "La Humanidad Peregrina Viviente: Migración y Experiencia Religiosa," in *Migration, Religious Experience, and Globalization* (New York: Center for Migration Studies, 2003), 103–42.
24. Rodolfo Pastor Fasquelle, "The Short Story of the Coup" Public lecture delivered at Harvard University, David Rockefeller Center for Latin American Studies, Cambridge, MA, October 2009.
25. Gloria Anzaldúa, *Borderlands/La Frontera: The New Mestiza* 3rd Edition (San Francisco: Aunt Lute Books, 2007), 19.
26. See Adrienne Pine, *Working Hard, Drinking Hard: On Violence and Survival in Honduras* (Berkeley: University of California Press, 2008), 135–36.
27. Ibid., 50.
28. Nikolas Kozloff, "Honduras: Who's the Real Drug Trafficker?" *Huffington Post World*, 16 September 2009.
29. Fasquelle, "The Short Story of the Coup."
30. Zelaya returned to Honduras on May 28, 2011 under an agreement negotiated with President Lobo, supported by the presence of the Presidents of both Colombia and Venezuela, in which all charges against him would be dropped and those who carried out the coup would also be given immunity. In late June, to mark the two-year anniversary of the coup, Zelaya announced the formation of a new political party out of the National Front of Popular Resistance, which now plans to participate in the 2013 Presidential elections. Human rights advocates are taking action to charge Honduras for "crimes against humanity" with the International Criminal Court, based on human rights violations committed by the State with impunity during and after the coup.
31. Documentation of flagrant human rights violations post-coup is extensive. See: Amnesty International, "Honduras: Human rights crisis threatens as repression increases," UK: London, August 2009; Human Rights Watch, *After the Coup: Ongoing Violence, Intimidation and Impunity in Honduras*, New York, NY, December 2010; Inter-American Commission on Human Rights, Organization of American States, *Honduras: Human Rights and the Coup D'Etat*, 30 Dec 2009, Washington, D.C.; United Nations Office of the High Commissioner for Human Rights, *Report of the United Nations High Commissioner for Human Rights on the violations of human rights in Honduras since the coup d'état on 28 June 2009*, report submitted to the UN Human Rights Council, Thirteenth Session, 3 March 2010, Geneva, Switzerland; and United Nations Human Rights Council, *Report of the Working Group on the Universal Periodic Review: Honduras*. Sixteenth Session, 4 January 2011, Geneva, Switzerland.
32. Honduras had a homicide rate of 82.1 per 100,000 in 2010 with 6,239 murders. See United Nations Office on Drugs and Crime (UNODC). *Global Study on Homicide 2011: Trends, Contexts, Data* (Vienna: UNODC, 2011), 93, 109.
33. Pine, *Working Hard, Drinking Hard*, 138–39. History of CBI, and statistics on military aid and maquila workers also cited here in Pine.
34. Pine, *Working Hard, Drinking Hard*, 141.
35. Ibid., 139–40.
36. Ibid., 61–62.
37. Cited in Pine, *Working Hard, Drinking Hard*, 58–59. See UN Special Rapporteur Asma Jahangir. "Civil and Political Rights, Including the Question of Disappearances and Summary Executions." Commission on Human Rights, Economic and Social Council, United Nations, 2002.
38. International Committee for the Peace Council's "Chiang Mai Declaration" of March 2004 summarizes the perspectives of feminist activists and religious leaders about the connections between globalization and violence against women. The document officially entitled, "Women and Religion: An Agenda for Change" was approved

unanimously by the participants at the meeting, *Women and Religions in a Globalized World: Conversations to Advance Gender Equity*, convened by the Peace Council and The Center for Health and Social Policy in Chiang Mai, Thailand from 29 February to 3 March 2004. See also the work of public health and women's rights expert, Professor Lynn Freedman of Columbia University.

39. Kathleen Staudt, *Violence and Activism at the Border: Gender, Fear, and Everyday Life in Ciudad Juárez* (Austin, Texas: University of Austin Press, 2008), 105.

40. De La Torre, *Trails of Hope and Terror*, 180.

41. Personal interview with author and colleagues, Ciudad Juárez, end January 2009.

42. Lagarde, "Por la vida y la libertad de las mujeres: Fin al feminicidio," 8. Translation by Maher.

43. Staudt, *Violence and Activism at the Border*, 33–34.

44. Estimates of Centro de Estudios de la Mujer–Honduras (CEM-H), Tegucigalpa.

45. Adriana Beltrán and Laurie Freeman, "Hidden in Plain Sight: Violence Against Women in Mexico and Guatemala," Washington Office on Latin America, March 2007: 7.

46. Ibid., 12.

47. For extensive documentation and discussion of the environment of official impunity, see Amnesty International, *Intolerable Killings: 10 Years of Abductions and Murders of Women in Ciudad Juárez and Chihuahua* (London: Amnesty International, 2003).

48. In Martha Nussbaum's book review of Catharine McKinnon, *Are Women Human? And Other International Dialogues* in *The Nation*, 31 July 2006.

49. Catharine McKinnon, *Are Women Human? And Other International Dialogues* (Cambridge: Harvard University Press, 2006).

50. As cited by Nussbaum.

51. Amnesty International, "Protection Law Fails Mexican Women," 30 January 2009. www.amenesty.org/en/news-and-updates/news/protection-law-fails-mexican-women, accessed 7 February 2009.

52. Personal interview, Ciudad Juárez, January 2009.

53. International Committee on the Peace Council, "Chiang Mai Declaration," January 2004.

54. Lucha Castro. "Las Nuevas Crucificadas de la Tierra: Feminicidios Cd. Juárez y Chihuahua, México," Justicia para Nuestras Hijas, A.C. y Centro de derechos humanos de las Mujeres, A.C. III Jornada Ecumenica, Ciudad Méndez, Rio de Janeiro, Brasil, 2005: 39. Translation by Maher.

55. Pine, *Working Hard, Drinking Hard*, 82.

56. Carmen Manuela Del Cid, "La justificación de la violencia desde la perspectiva teológica," paper presented at the panel, "Las Causas del Feminicidio," Foro de Mujeres por la Vida, San Pedro Sula, Honduras, 30 July 2003.

57. Marcella Althaus-Reid, *From Feminist Theology to Indecent Theology: Readings on Poverty, Sexual Identity and God* (London: SCM Press, 2004), 85.

58. Ibid., 87.

59. Carmen Manuela Del Cid, "Memorias Peligrosas, Mujeres Poderosas," *Revista Conspirando* 49 (Spring 2005): 24.

60. Pine, *Working Hard, Drinking Hard*, 166.

61. Ibid., 146–47, 165.

62. Pine describes the (im)morality associated with women maquila workers who subvert the gender division of labor, "a recipe for social disaster," in *Working Hard, Drinking Hard*, 146.

63. Women's Psalm, Forum of Women for Life, San Pedro Sula, Honduras, 2007. Translation by Maher.

64. Staudt describes Day of the Dead activism in Juárez, 87.

65. See Staudt on these seasonal commemorations and on the use of what she calls "quasi-religious icons," 79 ff.

66. Castro, "Las Nuevas Crucificadas de la Tierra," 27. Translation by Maher.

67. See Staudt, *Violence and Activism at the Border*, 82. Staudt asserts that pink and black have become "movement colors."
68. An estimate of Feminists in Resistance, Tegucigalpa, Honduras.
69. Carmen Manuela Del Cid, "Reflections on Honduras Post-Coup," presentation at Harvard Divinity School, Cambridge, MA, April 2009.
70. Fasquelle, "The Short Story of the Coup."
71. Del Cid, 2009, "Reflection on Honduras Post-Coup." Translation by Maher.
72. Women's Litany, Forum of Women for Life, San Pedro Sula, Honduras, 2007. Translation by Maher.
73. Based on group interviews and one-on-one conversations with participants of the Forum of Women for Life, 18–22 January 2010, San Pedro Sula, Honduras.
74. Based on conversations with Mercy Sisters/Associates, 18–22 January 2010, San Pedro Sula, Honduras.
75. See Monica Maher, "Diversidades Espirituales en Defensa de los Derechos en Honduras," CLACSO, Buenos Aires, Argentina, 2011.
76. A term coined and utilized regularly by GLBT activists of Familia Galán in Bolivia.
77. See the study at Yale funded by the Luce Foundation on "Women, Religion and Globalization: Women Living Religion." www.yale.edu/macmillan/wrg/about.htm, accessed 6 February 2008.
78. Ivone Gebara, "Women and the Mystery of Life" in *The Ecumenical Movement Tomorrow: Suggestions for Approaches and Alternatives*, eds. Marc Reuver, Friedhelm Solms, Gerrit Huizer (Kampen: Kok Publishing Company in cooperation with Geneva: WCC Publications, 1993), 195, 198–99.
79. Ivone Gebara, *Out of the Depths: Women's Experience of Evil and Salvation* (Minneapolis: Fortress Press, 2002), 121–32.
80. Kathleen Staudt and Irasema Coronado, *Fronteras No Más: Toward Social Justice at the U.S.- Mexico Border* (New York: Palgrave USA, 2002), xx.
81. Castro, "Las Nuevas Crucificadas de la Tierra," 27. Translation by Maher.

SELECTED BIBLIOGRAPHY

Althaus-Reid, Marcella. *From Feminist Theology to Indecent Theology: Readings on Poverty, Sexual Identity and God*. London: SCM Press, 2004.
De La Torre, Miguel A. *Trails of Hope and Terror: Testimonies on Immigration*. Maryknoll, NY: Orbis Books, 2009.
McKinnon, Catharine. *Are Women Human? And Other International Dialogues*. Cambridge, MA: Harvard University Press, 2006.
Pine, Adrienne. *Working Hard, Drinking Hard: On Violence and Survival in Honduras*. Berkeley: University of California Press, 2008.
Staudt, Kathleen. *Violence and Activism At the Border: Gender, Fear, and Everyday Life in Ciudad Juárez*. Austin: University of Texas Press, 2008.
Staudt, Kathleen, and Irasema Coronado. *Fronteras No Más: Toward Social Justice at the U.S.-Mexico Border*. New York: Palgrave USA, 2002.

III

The Borderlands as a Call to Action

SEVEN

The Subversive Act of Breaking Bread

How the Eucharist Transforms the Immigration Conversation

Craig Wong

On January 30, 1917, my grandmother took her seat, once again, at a small wooden table. Known to the Angel Island Immigration Station authorities as Wong Shee, my grandmother was all too familiar with this table, for it was here that she had the exhausting task of proving her worth, her value, to the interests of the United States. Seated across the table was an interrogator, who confronted her with often-redundant questions. A typical exchange went like this:

> **Interrogator:** Wong Shee, you stated before that there were eight houses in your village, and four rows. Now, with the paper clips you have used, you have arranged the village in six rows. Which is correct?
>
> **Wong Shee:** The first three rows there's only one house each. No second house.
>
> **Interrogator:** Do you mean there are really six rows instead of four?
>
> **Wong Shee:** Yes.
>
> **Interrogator:** Why do you have your village different from the way you told us it was arranged when we had the other interpreter?

Wong Shee: I did not arrange them. The other interpreter arranged them himself. I did not know what he meant.

For Wong Shee, the stakes were high. How she answered these questions meant the difference between starting a new life in America, or being deported back to China, a country in economic shambles and in the throes of a violent civil war. Moreover, she feared returning to her ruthless mother-in-law, at whose hands she suffered great abuse. Most significantly, she risked being separated indefinitely from her husband, Fong Lung Bew, who had already established himself as a legal resident, doing business as a merchant in San Francisco's Chinatown. For now, Wong Shee had to remain seated at the dreaded table, a guarded border she might never cross. The thought of this table haunted every moment of Wong Shee's detainment, a despairing existence that continued for months.

Meanwhile, just a few miles away, on the San Francisco mainland, the Chinatown Presbyterian Mission congregation drew its life from a very different table. On this table sat the elements of bread and wine, the Eucharist. Unlike the interrogation table of Angel Island, this table represented not a guarded border but a bridge that reconciled people to God, and to one another. At this table, a person did not have to prove her worth, but rather, she received her worth from a God who loves everyone despite her unworthiness. Like the interrogation table, the Eucharist was a summons to remember, but not to recall tedious details to prove one's identity but, rather, to rehearse how Christ's death on the cross gives sinners a new identity.

A TRANSFORMING SACRAMENT

In this chapter, I suggest that the Eucharist is inherently formational in a way that can transform the immigration conversation, more specifically, the way the American Church engages the immigrant community, and the policies that affect them. The Eucharist was instituted by Jesus Christ himself at the eve of His crucifixion in the "upper room," as described in all four gospels of the Bible. For example, in Luke:

> When the hour came, he took his place at the table, and the apostles with him. He said to them, "I have eagerly desired to eat this Passover with you before I suffer; for I tell you, I will not eat it until it is fulfilled in the kingdom of God." Then he took a cup, and after giving thanks he said, "Take this and divide it among yourselves; for I tell you that from now on I will not drink of the fruit of the vine until the kingdom of God comes." Then he took a loaf of bread, and when he had given thanks, he broke it and gave it to them, saying, "This is my body, which is given for you. Do this in remembrance of me." And he did the same

with the cup after supper, saying, "This cup that is poured out for you is the new covenant in my blood." (22:14–20)

Over the centuries, the Eucharist has taken a range of forms, meanings, and names, including the Lord's Supper, the Holy Feast, the breaking of bread, and the service of communion. Historic, hermeneutic tensions about the Eucharist have had to do with the manner and degree to which Jesus Christ is actually present at the table. Sadly, this debate about presence, whether understood physically, metaphysically, or symbolically, has compromised the very unity that Christ intended.

For the purposes of this chapter, I explore the implications of the Eucharist eschatologically, that is, by starting at "the end." Eschatology is the branch of Christian theology that deals with the biblical understanding of the eschaton, the ultimate "end game" where all of human history is headed. I am not concerned about how or when the end times happen, as has been the preoccupation of some theologians and authors, for example, Tim LaHaye and Jerry Jenkins of *Left Behind* fame. Rather, I am interested in what happens at the Lord's Supper as a foreshadowing of the reconciled community, depicted often in the gospels as a great banquet where the most unlikely of guests are invited (Matthew 22:1–10). Indeed, of all the New Testament metaphors used to describe life in the Kingdom of God, few are more prevalent than that of diverse peoples feasting together, sometimes enacted bodily as when Jesus has his disciples feed five thousand people on a Galilean hillside, with scant loaves and fishes (Luke 9:10–17).

Ironically, the name of the most ambitious federal immigration crackdown in our nation's history employed eschatological language, *Operation Endgame*, a sweeping ten-year plan by the U.S. Department of Homeland Security (DHS) to remove all 11 million "deportable aliens" from the country. Ostensibly created in response to post 9/11 security concerns, *Operation Endgame* coincided with the onset, and rising fears, of an economic recession. I contend that public fears and impulses underlying this massive sweep operation is subverted by the Eucharist, the breaking of bread in remembrance of the Christ's death and resurrection. This chapter, therefore, explores how the Eucharist (1) embraces, in fact demonstrates, a changing future, rather than clings to an "idyllic" past, (2) knits people together in interdependency, over and against individualistic reflexes, (3) calms our fears of scarcity so that all mouths might be fed, and (4) rehearses today, the restored humanity of the eschaton.

I will engage these Eucharistic implications for the immigration conversation by drawing from my Chinese immigrant legacy and the experiences of my worshipping community, Grace Fellowship Community Church, a predominantly Asian congregation that has been significantly shaped by its weekly practice of the Lord's Supper.

EMBODYING A RADICALLY INCLUSIVE FUTURE

My great grandfather, Fong Shew Lung, was among those considered a serious threat to millions of Anglo workers in late-1800s America. Lung's contemporaries were a hard working lot—small business owners, skilled craftsmen, teachers, and low-wage laborers who were hired by U.S. corporations to build the infrastructure of an ascending nation. However, the acceptance of the Chinese, critical as they were in building railroads and irrigation systems, was short lived. As the Gold Rush economy bottomed out, political pressure mounted to keep out all but the most productive Chinese, culminating in the infamous 1882 Chinese Exclusion Act. This law, many hoped, would be the answer to the Chinese threat, not only to American jobs, but also to public health and, most of all, the dominant Anglo culture. "Coolies," as they were referred to, were perceived as disease-ridden with strange beliefs and customs unfit for the American way of life.

Within a few years, unsatisfied by the federal government's efforts to stem the tide of Chinese immigration, the 1889 Geary Act was passed, which not only extended the term of the Chinese Exclusion Act, but added aggressive identification-based enforcement. Under the Geary Act, all Chinese were required to carry government-approved identification papers, ready to be shown when requested by a law enforcement officer. Failure to show one's papers could result in immediate arrest, imprisonment (involving forced and heavy labor), and eventual deportation.

This law instilled great fear within the Chinese community, whether or not one was "legal." Reaction to the Geary Act, among both Chinese and non-Chinese leaders, was swift and emotional. Lawyers, advocacy organizations, business interests, and common citizens pulled together in concerted opposition. The policy, they argued, was unconstitutional on the basis of cruel and unusual punishment, including the acquisition of personal property and liberty, without prior indictment or jury trial. Within four years of its passing, the controversial law was taken to the highest court in the land (*Fong Ting Yue v. the United States*). On May 15, 1893, the U.S. Supreme Court upheld the Geary Act with a vote of 5–3 on the basis that a sovereign nation has the right to deport any people or race that it wants to, that is, those it fears will bring undesirable change to the status quo.

The 2012 U.S. Supreme Court decision, therefore, to uphold the "show me your papers" portion of Arizona's infamous SB 1070 anti-immigration legislation, was a remarkable repeat of history.[1] But it was not surprising, given growing fears, among a small but powerful subset of America, of the "browning of America." Arizona state representative, Russell Pearce, one of the key champions of SB 1070, pointedly reflected this sentiment when he called undocumented immigrations "invaders": "Invaders, that's what they are! Invaders on the American sovereignty and it can't be tolerated!"[2]

Political leaders, Republican and Democratic, have often pontificated that "America is on the right side of history." This was expressed, in so many words, on September 11, 2002, when President George W. Bush maintained that the "ideal of America is the hope of all mankind . . . a light that shines in the darkness . . . the darkness will not overcome," adding that, "this hope brought millions to this harbor."[3] The Statue of Liberty served as a backdrop to his speech, a visual reminder of America's legacy as a nation of immigrants, her arms open to the world's "tired, poor and huddled masses."

Within months of the speech, *Operation Endgame* was launched, an event that not only coincided with the economic downturn, but also, intriguingly, with recent census revelation that Hispanics had surged past Blacks as the largest ethnic minority group in the country. *Operation Endgame*, unprecedented in terms of size and scope, has led to spending billions of tax dollars on the proliferation of mass detention facilities, Immigration Customs and Enforcement (I.C.E.) agents, and arrest and detainment operations everywhere, including bus depots, tacquerias, meatpacking plants, and private homes.[4]

While the DHS claims that their priority targets are felons and violent offenders, the fact remains that over half of all deported individuals do not possess such criminal records. As of the end of 2012, nearly 3 million immigrants have been deported, the majority back to Mexico, Latin American, Asia and Eastern Europe.[5] Indeed, more immigrants have been deported under President Barack Obama than in any other presidential administration in our nation's history.

So is *Operation Endgame* on the right side of history? The Eucharist paints a different picture, a counter-vision of what is to come. For Phil, a long-time member of our congregation and "closet redneck" the Eucharist confronted his sensibilities about who belongs here. Each Sunday, Phil has been provoked by the wideness of Christ's mercy. Watching individuals of every class and color walk up the aisle to the communion table, he's been struck by how "all of us are invited to His table, no matter who we are, where we come from, or how messed up we are . . . a picture of what is to come."

Embracing this radically inclusive vision of the future has prompted Phil to examine his deeply-ingrained prejudice about those who "don't play by the rules" or "earn their right to be here." However, it was clear that a transformation was at work as Phil began to grow close to Carlos, a Nicaraguan immigrant who had been regularly coming to church. Carlos had many health issues, both mental and physical, which made sustained employment difficult. He wasn't lazy; he was always looking for ways to help, whether cooking, cleaning, or setting up chairs, never asking for anything in return. He just liked to be around. One person he liked being around was Phil.

Thus, it was Phil who first noticed that Carlos was missing. No one, including Carlos's sister, knew where he was. After many phone calls, Phil discovered that Carlos had been picked up by I.C.E. and placed in a detention facility. Our first concern was his epilepsy. We were right to be concerned. When Carlos had his first epileptic seizure in detention, the guards thought he was faking. They roughed him up and put him in solitary confinement.

Concerned about the way he was being treated, we sought more information. We experienced administrative runaround, but finally tracked him down. Separated by bullet-proof glass, we prayed for Carlos and delivered greetings from members of the congregation. We gathered his medical records and made appeals for his care, but were ultimately unable to secure his release. In the end, Carlos was deported, a sad loss for his immediate kin, but also for us, his congregational family.

Phil had lost a dear brother, one with whom he had broken bread, at least for a season. Whether or not they would be reunited in their lifetime remained to be seen. In the Eucharist, however, they could embrace the eschatological hope that, ultimately, their separation was temporary, for their fellowship at the table pointed to a future reality where they would again dine together. They could anticipate the day when they would enjoy the fulfillment of the Isaianic prophecy, the true endgame, where Yahweh promises to "prepare a feast of rich food for all peoples, a banquet of aged wine; the best of meats and the finest of wines . . . and wipe away the tears from all faces, and the disgrace of his people, from all the earth" (Isaiah 25:6–8).

For a nation to resist the grain of demographic change takes tremendous amounts of resources and energy. Yet, the U.S. government has taken costly and unprecedented measures, since 2003, to build sophisticated infrastructure (e.g., border monitoring predator drones) and often-bloated bureaucracies to remove undesired populations, or at least make life so miserable for the undocumented, that they might "self-deport," in the political parlance of the day. To address the immigration challenge, as it has many other things, the U.S. government has employed coercive force as the tool of choice. What happens when Christians give in to the temptation to flex power, and how might the Eucharist offer deliverance?

EXCHANGING POWER FOR INTERDEPENDENCE

Grace Fellowship Community Church largely consists of college-educated professionals, many of whom share the classic Chinese immigrant success story—our hardworking ancestors learned not only how to please the system, but also how to reap its benefits. A journalist in 1910 paints this picture of an Asian immigrant:

> It goes to show how fast the Oriental with his thrifty ways and clever mind is gaining a place in our hearts and brotherhood and that we are at last beginning to recognize his sincere endeavor to live up to our American ideals. . . . Let the little brown man adapt to our standards and manners of life, and we are quite ready to give him a chance with our own![6]

This excerpt comes from *The Overland Monthly*, a turn-of-the century publication based in San Francisco that served as a propaganda tool by the owner of a local ship builder to rouse public support for America's imperial ambitions, in particular, her "manifest destiny" across the Pacific Ocean, through the Philippines, upon the defeat of Spain. Because his local company supplied vessels and armaments for the U.S. fleet, he had much to gain from war. Thus, his magazine championed an America on the move. The message to Chinese and other Asian immigrants was simple: Get with the program or go back home!

As the excerpt above indicates, some "Orientals" were indeed getting with the program, but obviously not all, because that same year, the government opened up the Angel Island Immigration Station where my grandmother ended up, some six years later. Having learned, from the earliest generations, how to "get with the program" of the American nationalist agenda, we've equipped ourselves with the tools of education and asset accumulation to work the system to our advantage. We've acquired what I call a "power reflex" that kicks in whenever obstacles threatened to thwart our agendas, even charitable ones. We have a strong proclivity to be problem solvers, and we bring this impulse to everything, including our relationships. In other words, we are more inclined to fix people than to join them, much less to imagine being changed by them.

And so, as a young congregation in the early 1990s, we brought this power reflex into San Francisco's Mission District, home to a majority of the city's immigrant poor, most of who came to the United States under difficult circumstances from El Salvador, Nicaragua, Guatemala, Honduras and Mexico. Wanting to be relevant, we conducted a needs assessment among the neighborhood families. Hearing that they wanted to learn English and computer skills, we launched a program called "Grace Learning *Partners*," the word in italics strategically chosen to avoid coming across paternalistically.

So why did most, after a relatively short time, stop coming? They sensed our frustration when they arrived late or came inconsistently. Also, they felt guilty knowing that their instructor had worked hard to produce lesson plans. Furthermore, when they arrived late, they often missed dinner, which was only served between the narrow window of 5:30 to 6:00 p.m. At Grace Learning *Partners*, one had to make a choice: be punctual or be hungry. More often than not, their work schedules didn't give them a choice but to be late. Insensitive to our visitors' work demands, we made it hard for them to feel welcome.

Far more destructive, however, than our cultural insensitivity, was our eyesight. When Rosita enters the doors of our church, who do I see? Do I see a poor person looking for help? An illegal immigrant who is only here to obtain free resources? An irresponsible mom who needs to get her act together? These are the questions of privileged people like me who automatically assume the role of benefactor, objectifying and dehumanizing the very people that we think we're trying to welcome.

The Eucharist, however, strips away our delusions of goodness, disabusing us of any claim to a moral high ground. We come to the table because, as is written in the book of Romans, "none is righteous, no, not one. No one understands. No one seeks for God" (Romans 3:10–11). Everyone comes to the table with nothing but a need for mercy. No one has a leg to stand on, yet all are valuable because each is loved and created by God. Biblical scholar Daniel Carroll affirms the intrinsic value of a person, and therefore every immigrant, is based on Genesis. Carroll writes, "immigrants are humans, and as such they are made in God's image. . . . [Therefore] they have an essential value and possess the potential to contribute to society through their presence, work and ideas."[7] In other words, the wealthy can receive from the indigent, the corporate executive from the migrant farm worker, and the Harvard grad from the illiterate dad. Everyone is a gift. Everyone has something to offer; everyone has something to receive. Contrary to the assumptions of our self-made individualism, we were designed to be interdependent creatures, born to need each other.

For most college-educated folks like us, conditioned at an early age to be too sure of ourselves, our greatest need is to have our perspective challenged. In one of our home gatherings, a single mom from Central America said, "I really have a hard time relating to your problems." Tatiana has struggled to survive in the United States after being physically abused and forced to flee her war-torn country. Conversely, our "struggles" were perplexing to her: stress about which home to buy, dissatisfaction with the enrichment options at our child's preschool, or boredom at the job. Having been with our congregation for more than a year, she now found the discrepancy between her experience of life and ours too difficult to stomach. She finally left the church.

Tatiana's departure was a huge loss for us. As our good friend from Nigeria, Sunday Agang, once told our congregation, "You are afflicted by your affluence." He helped us to see that the things we might consider blessings may, in fact, be our spiritual stumbling blocks. In friends like Tatiana and Sunday, we are given opportunity to see God in new ways and to witness faith that goes far deeper than our own. Resisting our power reflex, a relationship of mutual dependence can then be possible. Each one gains from the other, toward the betterment of the whole.

Cuban-American theologian Justo González explains this mutuality by looking at the Spanish word, *frontera*, which has two primary meanings, "frontier" and "border."[8] Frontier is associated with conquest, for example, the forced relocation of indigenous peoples during America's westward expansion, or the armed seizure of territory during the Mexican-American war. According to González, a frontier is typically unilateral and, therefore, inherently violent. Border, on the other hand, is bi-directional, a peaceful place of encounter where two different cultures can mingle and influence one another, resulting in a third culture.

In our church's community ministries, the shift in posture from "frontier" to "border" has meant the difference between repelling and compelling our neighbors. Humbled by our need for God, and for one another, the Eucharist sets the table for genuine interdependence. In such a space, our immigrant visitors are received as people, not projects. Strangers become friends who share stories, watch each other's children, use each other's power tools, and celebrate each other's weddings.

The Eucharist therefore raises questions about the basis of national immigration policy. How might the immigration reform conversation change if we believed that all human beings are fundamentally interdependent? That we were created to live as one family, regardless of one's place of origin, level of education, or ability to approximate a lifestyle dictated by anachronistic expectations of the classic "American Dream?" Such a radical re-orientation, of course, flies in the face of our society's bottom line, which judges a person's worth in relation to the economy, whether measured in salary, assets, or perceived ability to contribute to the nation's competitiveness in the world. This is why anti-immigrant sentiment invariably grows in times of declining prosperity.

History bears testimony to this relationship. It is why my Chinese ancestors were welcomed when the Central Pacific Railroad needed laborers, but despised when gold prospects began to dry up. Why Mexicans were welcomed across the border in the 1920s when agribusiness grew, but forcibly repatriated after the Great Depression. Why Mexicans were once again sought during the WWII farm-labor shortage through the Bracero Program, but expelled in mass numbers through Operation Wetback soon after.

This leads us to the notion of scarcity. People, and therefore governments, get ugly when operating out of a fear that there won't be enough, particularly among those who are accustomed to having plenty. What drives this fear, and how does the Eucharist transform this?

CALMING FEARS OF SCARCITY

I saw a glimpse of the transformation at a city hall public hearing. At stake was the preservation and integrity of our city's sanctuary ordinance, a set of municipal protections for undocumented residents, including the limiting of police department cooperation with federal immigration authorities, ongoing access to all social services, and due process for those accused of criminal offenses. Our then-mayor, Gavin Newsom, was under political pressure to roll back protections, and we were there to say no. Chatting about the situation outside the legislative chamber, a fellow Christian turned to me and said, "The Church needs to show the world that sharing isn't scary."

I have never forgotten that simple, yet profound, comment. Although we teach our kids early on to share, it is not something we do naturally, particularly in a culture that venerates private ownership and accommodates greed. In America, the freedom to accumulate and consume without limit is sacrosanct, and is perfectly legal regardless of how one's neighbor is doing. The bible suggests otherwise. Paul's incredulity about the Corinthians' practice of Lord's Supper drives home the point that what is legal and what is Christian are, more often than one might expect, two different things.

In his first letter to the church in Corinth, Paul is appalled by the class divisions he sees among them, particularly at their mealtimes, as the wealthy ate extravagantly while the poor went without. As New Testament theologian Richard Hays points out, what the Corinthian believers did was quite normal for that day. In Roman imperial society, it was typical for the wealthy benefactor and his close associates to lounge in the dining room while guests of lower-status gathered outside the atrium.[9] For the Christians, however, to mirror the class divisions of Roman imperial society was to "show contempt for the Church of God" (1 Cor. 11:22) and to "drink judgment against themselves" (1 Cor. 11:29). For Paul, their gathering was not for the better, but for the worse (1 Cor. 11:17). The cross had knit together these diverse Corinthians as a foreshadowing of life under Christ's coming reign, yet they were failing miserably to demonstrate it.

The problem Paul had with the Corinthians was not that some folks could afford to eat better than the others. Rather, it was that their life together fell woefully short of what Christ's death brought into being: a restored humanity, and therefore, a new economy, made possible by tearing down the "dividing wall of hostility" (Eph. 2:14–19). In such an economy, all share. Theologian Elizabeth Newman reminds us that "the Eucharist does not simply motivate Christians to practice hospitality. Rather, it is our participation in God's hospitality, as through this celebration we are enabled to become Eucharistic, extending God's offering and gift to the world."[10] Rather than live by the prevailing order, where the powerful lived in abundance while the poor feared for scarcity, Paul insisted that the Corinthian Christians practice God's hospitality, the sharing of his abundance so that everyone's needs are met, that all mouths are fed.

However, we know that the fear of scarcity is powerful and, conversely, the need for control grows the more we have. This dynamic manifests itself even in the ways we give things away. One of our parishioners made this observation about a neighboring immigrant congregation we joined at their spring cleaning day: "I'm impressed by how freely they give away their stuff to anyone who passes on the street. They're not worried about making sure everything is going to a 'good cause' the way we tend to do. They just let God do with their stuff as He chooses."

Our need to control also surfaces in our practice of home hospitality. Perhaps influenced by Martha Stewart sensibilities, our freedom to invite neighbors over for dinner is often stifled by a need we have for our homes to look "presentable." Treating our domiciles as though they're showrooms, we elevate image over relationship. Hesitant to let guests see our less-than-sparkling dining room, place settings, or even kids, we let opportunities to break bread with strangers pass us by.

Meanwhile, our immigrant friends have graciously invited us into *their* homes, despite having less room or fancy place settings. For example, a Guatemalan couple for their wedding celebration invited over thirty of us into their small flat, one shared by three families. The couple worked hard to rearrange what room they had so as to accommodate our entire group. They cooked food and we brought desert. To be sure, the gathering was cramped and a bit chaotic, but one thing was clear: most important to this couple was including us in their celebration, putting people over appearance.

We may not flaunt wealth the way, perhaps, some of the Corinthian believers did, but despite our best intentions, we remain blind to much of what life is like for our undocumented friends who labor in restaurants, harvest crops, construct buildings, watch babies, and host countless tourists. Apart from them, our local San Francisco economy would not survive. It is hard for us to relate to the challenge of having to choose between food, housing, and health care, things most of us take for granted.

Harder still is our ability to recognize our contribution to their plight. One of our Salvadoran visitors shared, "my friend's farm no longer generates enough money to support his family. The government recently accepted the U.S. dollar as the national currency. This has raised the cost of living a lot, especially for the poorest families. Only the wealthiest in El Salvador, like those who work for corporations, can afford to pay for things at American prices."

His story meshed with things we learned at a church-based citizenship fair our congregation helped out with one year. A brochure caught my attention. On the cover was a photo of the Salvadoran president shaking hands with ours. Ignorant of the negotiations taking place between these two countries, I inquired further. The Central American Free Trade Agreement had just been ratified, putting in place new economic policies that bolstered North American corporations while putting countless Salvadoran farmers out of work. Heavy-handed policies like these, our Salvadoran friends explained, are nothing new. Every year, Latino Christians in our neighborhood commemorate the life of Archbishop Oscar Romero whose work on behalf of the poor brought about his demise, assassinated in 1980 by the notorious "death squads." These specialized, lethal units were trained, in part, by U.S. military and intelligence personnel under both the Carter and Reagan administrations.

We've been privy to many such stories from our Guatemalan, Nicaraguan, Honduran, and Pilipino friends, stories we need to hear from those with whom we share the communion table. How we live, how we eat, the economic assumptions we adopt, the national imperatives we salute, all have an impact on others, for better or worse. They may be hard to hear, but stories from our border-crossing neighbors cast important light on the destructive acts of violence our government is willing to commit to preserve the "American way of life" that we all readily consume. N.T. Wright puts it this way: "When human beings refuse to use God's gift of money responsibly, they are handing over their power to Mammon, and he will take control. And when the powers take over, human beings get crushed."[11]

At the table, the Church meets the same Jesus who enabled his disciples to feed five thousand people with only a few loaves and fishes. It was Jesus who commanded his followers not to worry about what to eat, drink and wear (Matt. 6:25). Free from the fear of scarcity, the Church can engage immigration policy from a different starting point, that there is enough for everyone when we share. How might this change the conversation? To start, we might affirm municipal ordinances that ensure all residents access to services, regardless of immigration status. Or we can focus on creating livable wage jobs, and the pathways for immigrants to work legally. Or we can challenge trade policies that undermine foreign economies, which force millions to cross the desert at great risk to their lives. Or urge the redirection of funds away from extraneous border enforcement to the development of Mexico's struggling economy. In short, the Church can demonstrate that sharing isn't scary. In fact, it's simply human, the critical but missing element in today's immigration conversation.

THE ESCHATON'S RESTORED HUMANITY NOW

The Isaianic vision for what life will be like in the age to come is poetically captured in these Old Testament verses:

> The wolf shall live with the lamb; the leopard shall lie down with the kid,

The calf and the lion and the fatling together, and a little child shall lead them.
The cow and the bear shall graze; their young shall lie down together;
And the lion shall eat straw like the ox (Isaiah 11:6-7).

How could the immigration reform conversation be different if we lived not by the adversarialism of the current order but rather, in light of the future, when all humanity will be restored? What could happen if, when meeting the powers that be, we did imagine the restoration of all humanity in the eschaton, where liberals, conservatives, bureaucrats, lawyers, activists, pastors, and I.C.E. agents might well be seated together at the Great Banquet?

This eschatological vision was indeed rehearsed at a meeting with I.C.E. we hosted in our sanctuary. Two parties accustomed to vilifying each other—those charged with deporting immigrants and those who advocate for them—were seated at the table together. On one side sat the attorney general and directors of the Northern California, Hawaii and Guam field office for I.C.E.'s Enforcement and Removal Operations, and six officials from I.C.E. headquarters in Washington, DC. On the other side, were a dozen representatives of immigration advocacy organizations or congregations that serve the immigrant community.

Above us hung a church banner depicting bread and cup, a visual reminder, at least perhaps for the believers in the room, of who the true Host of the gathering was. Grace Fellowship Community Church's pastor, Reverend Doug Lee, welcomed the guests at the table, and affirmed that the Lord was present and would be at work in and through our conversation. One of the church elders, Randall Chang, recited the prayer of St. Francis, asking God to help each of us "sow love where there is hate, pardon where there is injury, and light where there is darkness, to seek to understand rather than to be understood."[12]

What followed was a conversation characterized by civility, mutual respect, and honest engagement. Perhaps for the first time, each side was able to see the other as fellow human beings, not as a faceless enemy or self-righteous rabble rouser. In a remarkable moment, after the meeting was over, one of the I.C.E. officials walked up to a group of religious leaders, pulled out his wallet, and produced not his federal badge, but a laminated card of the Prayer of St. Francis. "I carry this prayer around everywhere I go," he shared with us. We now meet with his staff quarterly to continue dialogue about our concerns regarding I.C.E.

These meetings, and their tenor, have been a picture of what is possible when the Eucharist is our starting point. There will continue to be seismic differences in the outcomes that each side wants, and the enforcement reforms we seek will be slow in coming. As I.C.E. agents regularly remind us, "We're just doing our job." But we are learning what it means for our humanity to be restored, for we recognize that the "strangers in our midst" are not only our immigrant friends from Mexico, El Salvador, or Burma, but also the I.C.E. agents who show up for work every day to support their families. They too are dehumanized by a broken system held captive to the fallen powers and principalities in need of Christ's redemption.

A SENSE OF URGENCY

In my neighborhood, Steve Li, a college student with dreams of becoming a nurse, had a rude awakening. As one local paper described the scene:

> It was around 7 a.m. on September 15, 2010. Steve Li was in his pajamas when he heard a loud knock on the door and woke up his mom to see if she was expecting anyone. No, she said. The knocking continued, and she got up to answer while Li went into the bathroom. That's when five officers dressed in black rushed into the small San Francisco apartment and, in a flurry, began searching—for passports, identification cards, wallets. They swung open the bathroom door and found Li brushing his teeth. Get dressed, they demanded. "What are you doing here? Why are you in my house?" Li asked. As Li's mother dressed in her room, officers sat him down in the kitchen and informed him that he would be deported from the United States. They took him outside, searched and handcuffed him, and put him into a black van with dark-tinted windows. Li was on his way to a holding cell at the San Francisco headquarters of the federal Immigration and Customs Enforcement agency. Half an hour earlier, he had been getting ready for school at San Francisco's City College.[13]

But there was more to the story. As fellow congregation members and other community leaders gathered in our sanctuary to learn what happened, Steve shared about how I.C.E. agents had intimidated him that morning, using baseless threats and promises, into revealing the whereabouts of his father. Both of his parents, unbeknownst to him, had ended up being handcuffed and placed in two separate black vans after he had been taken away. Each of them was locked up in separate cells, one from the other, in a Sacramento county jail, with no way of knowing where the others were, let alone to communicate with them.

Although his parents were released within a couple weeks, Li was transferred to the I.C.E. detention facility in Phoenix, Arizona, where he remained for nearly two months before a public outcry, including a concerted appeal from the faith community, eventually won him a temporary reprieve. In the meantime, the ordeal dealt a heavy blow to Li's family, as his parents' employment was jeopardized and his nursing education was put on hold.

This incident served, particularly among many in San Francisco's Chinese community, as a painful flashback to Angel Island's notorious legacy, where tens of thousands of ordinary, hard-working Chinese were incarcerated like common criminals, intentionally isolated from loved ones, and left to despair in the shadows of an unknown fate. What my grandmother experienced in 1916, and what happened to the Li family nearly a century later, offers yet another picture of how America's dark immigration history repeats itself.

But what happened to Steve Li in particular exposes an even darker reality, in that he would have been better off had he been college student in 1882! While the Exclusion Act barred all Chinese laborers, skilled or unskilled, from the country, it assumed that any immigrant who was here for the purpose of attending school was worthy of inclusion. In other words, even in the shadow of an egregious federal law of race-based exclusion, all students were still welcome.

Sadly, as of the time of this writing, all efforts to pass legislation to give undocumented students some form of legal status—for example, the Dream Act—have failed. Only a 2012 administrative order issued by the executive branch, called Deferred Action for Child Arrivals or DACA, has made possible any sort of relief, albeit temporary, for students like Steve Li whose simple goal is to acquire skills and knowledge to join the American workforce.

What does it say, then, of a nation who is willing to detain and deport even law-abiding *students* from our borders? Or a democracy that votes down laws to accept a class of immigrants that were deemed an asset over a hundred years ago, an era that was far less progressive than it presumably is today? The Li story reveals an unsettling moral setback in U.S. immigration policy, an increased callousness with regard to how we treat the strangers in our midst. This should heighten the American church's sense of urgency, to more deeply inculcate her counter-narrative that can expose, judge, and even reverse the dehumanizing momentum of a social system subjugated under the golden calves of free market capitalism and radical individualism.

EPILOGUE

America has power, but not justice.
In prison, we were victimized as if we were guilty.
Given no opportunity to explain, it was really brutal.
I bow my head in reflection but there is nothing I can do.
Imprisoned in the wooden building day after day,
My freedom withheld; how can I bear to talk about it?
I look to see who is happy but they only sit quietly.
I am anxious and depressed and cannot fall asleep.
The days are long and bottle constantly empty;
My sad mood, even so, is not dispelled.
Nights are long and the pillow cold; who can pity my loneliness?

After experiencing such loneliness and sorrow,
Why not just return home and learn to plow the fields?

These words, forever etched on the barrack walls of Angel Island, are not attributable to my grandmother, but they very well could have been. Carved in Chinese characters, multitudinous poems and political polemics were written by detainees as a way not only to express frustration, but to while away the hours of a seemingly endless and demoralizing existence. As the months of her imprisonment wore on, Wong Shee began to seriously consider taking her own life, a desperate move that several others before her had chosen.

Were it not for the Christians at the Chinatown Presbyterian Mission home, this chapter could not have been written. Mission superintendent, J.H. Laughlin, along with Ethel Higgins and Donaldina Cameron, tirelessly advocated for my grandmother's release, providing character references, establishing the veracity (which, according to policy, only a white person was allowed to do) of her husband's and father's claim to be merchants, and paying for medicine to treat her bout of trachoma. Dozens of respectfully written letters, immortalized in microfiche in the National Archives, bear witness to this amazing labor of love that saved my grandmother, and countless other immigrants who shared her fate. My mother, Pearl Wong, and I are forever indebted.

There is much more about the saints of the Chinatown Presbyterian Mission that I want to learn about—for example, their liturgical practices, their communal life, and their theology of public witness. But this I do know: that they welcomed the changing color of America while others feared it, intertwined their lives with a people very different than themselves, gave generously of their time and resources for the sake of the whole, and treated with dignity even the *captors* of their loved ones. In other words, they lived as the Eucharistic community, a people marked by a subversive generosity, interdependence, humaneness, and a joyous anticipation of the radically-inclusive future.

In the breaking of bread, the Church rehearses in the here and now, the reality of God's good future, proclaiming and embodying the hope of Christ until he returns, when "a great multitude . . . from every nation, from all tribes and peoples and languages, standing before the throne and before the lamb . . . cry out in a loud voice, saying 'Salvation belongs to our God who is seated on the throne, and to the Lamb!'" (Revelation 7:9).

NOTES

1. Adam Lipnak, "Blocking Parts of Arizona Law, Justices Allow Its Centerpiece," *New York Times* (June 26, 2012), available at: http://www.nytimes.com/2012/06/26/us/supreme-court-rejects-part-of-arizona-immigration-law.html?_r=0.

2. Rusell Pearce quoted in Ted Robbins, "The Man Behind Arizona's Toughest Immigrant Laws," National Public Radio's *Morning Edition* (March 12, 2008), available at: http://www.npr.org/templates/story/story.php?storyId=88125098.

3. George W. Bush, quoted in Jacklin A. Elliot, "What Have We Done With Hope? A Brief History," in *Interdisciplinay Perspectives on Hope*, Ed. Jacklin A. Elliot (Hauppauge, NY: Nova Science Publishers, 2004), 38.

4. Sadhbh Walshe, "Operation Endgame and the Profitable Purge of Legal Immigrants," *The Guardian* (July 11, 2012), available at: http://www.guardian.co.uk/commentisfree/2012/jul/11/operation-endgame-purge-legal-immigrants.

5. U.S. Immigration and Customs Enforcement publishes these numbers: http://www.ice.gov/secure_communities/get-the-facts.htm (accessed July 8, 2011).

6. Billee Glynn, "Lights Reminiscent: The Orientals and Portola," *The Overland Monthly* 55 (January–June 1910): 204.

7. M. Daniel Carroll R., *Christians at the Border: Immigration, the Church, and the Bible* (Grand Rapids, MI: Baker Academic, 2008), 67.

8. Justo L. González, *Santa Biblia: The Bible Through Hispanic Eyes* (Nashville, TN: Abingdon Press, 1996), 84–85.

9. Richard B. Hays, *First Corinthians: A Bible Commentary for Teaching and Preaching* (Louisville: John Knox Press, 1997), 196.

10. Elizabeth Newman, *Untamed Hospitality: Welcoming God and Other Strangers* (Grand Rapids, MI: Brazos Press, 2007), 149.

11. N.T. Wright, *Following Jesus: Biblical Reflections on Discipleship* (Grand Rapids, MI: Eerdmans, 1995), 18.

12. A prayer attributed to St. Francis of Assisi in *La Clochette*, 1912.

13. Lisette Mejia, "Life as an Undocumented Student, Part I," *Mission Local* (July 12, 2012), available at: http://missionlocal.org/2012/07/life-as-an-undocumented-student-part-i/.

SELECTED BIBLIOGRAPHY

Carroll R., M. Daniel. *Christians at the Border: Immigration, the Church, and the Bible*. Grand Rapids, MI: Baker Academic, 2008.

González, Justo L. *Santa Biblia: The Bible Through Hispanic Eyes*. Nashville, TN: Abingdon Press, 1996.

Mejia, Lisette. "Life as an Undocumented Student, Part I." *Mission Local* (July 12, 2012). Available at: http://missionlocal.org/2012/07/life-as-an-undocumented-student-part-i/.

Newman, Elizabeth. *Untamed Hospitality: Welcoming God and Other Strangers*. Grand Rapids, MI: Brazos Press, 2007.

Wright, N.T. *Following Jesus: Biblical Reflections on Discipleship*. Grand Rapids, MI: Eerdmans, 1995.

EIGHT

A Divided Friendship: Friendship Park

The Past, Present, and Future of the U.S.-Mexico Border

John Fanestil

At the westernmost end of the U.S.-Mexico border, a small cement plaza sits atop a bluff overlooking the Pacific Ocean. For generations people from both nations have met at this location to visit with family and friends. Locals call it "Friendship Park."

The cement plaza at Friendship Park encircles a stone monument, its base sitting half in the United States and half in Mexico, bearing bold inscriptions on either side: "Boundary of the United States" and "Punto Límite de la República de México." The monument marks the spot where a bi-national commission began the arduous task of demarcating the international boundary at the end of the U.S.-Mexico War. The Treaty of Guadalupe-Hidalgo, signed on February 2, 1848, brought an end to hostilities and created the U.S.-Mexico Boundary Commission to address outstanding territorial disputes. The treaty stipulated that the western terminus of the new boundary should begin "one Spanish league south of the southernmost tip of San Diego Bay." The next year, after considerable bickering, the members of the Boundary Commission had chosen the bluff now known as Monument Mesa as the place to begin their work.

According to Charles W. Hughes, members of the Boundary Commission met at this location on October 10, 1849, and ordered the burial of a hermetically sealed bottle containing "a sworn statement, in both Spanish and English, declaring 'that the demarcation of boundary between the United States and Mexican Republic shall commence at this point.'"[1] The commissioners also placed a temporary post to mark the spot and agreed upon arrangements for the manufacture of a permanent monument. In March 1851, the permanent monument was completed in New York, and it was shipped in four pieces, together weighing over 8 tons, to San Francisco. The next month the pieces were shipped to San Diego aboard the schooner Annette. Hughes concludes the story of the monument's placement:

> Upon the monument's arrival in San Diego, military personnel transported the pieces down to south end of the port on a flat-bottom barge before transferring them to gun carriages for delivery to the bluff overlooking the Pacific Ocean. The monument was installed on a masonry foundation six feet square on top and extending three feet below the earth's surface to prevent settling. . . . News reports about the dedication called it a "splendid marble monument." Except for a brief two-week period in 1894, this monument has stood on the line . . . identifying the beginning of the boundary shared by Mexico and the United States.[2]

For over a century after the border was established, no barriers of any kind existed at this location. Visitors from Mexico and the United States frequented the Monument undeterred by the ever-changing and often contentious relationship between Mexico and the United States. As late as the 1960s, the international boundary atop Monument Mesa was marked by nothing more than a few cement posts and a low-hanging metal chain. Old-timers in San Diego remember hauling their bicycles over the chain to cruise the streets of Tijuana for the day, before returning by the same method to the United States.

On August 18, 1971, when then–First Lady Pat Nixon inaugurated the surrounding area as California's Border Field State Park, the international boundary at Friendship Park was marked by just three strands of barbed wire. After planting a tree at the center of Monument Mesa to mark the opening of the State Park, Mrs. Nixon walked to the monument on the border and asked her to security detail to cut the barbed wire fence so she could wade into the adoring crowd that had assembled on the Mexican side. "I hope there won't be a fence here for too long," she is reported to have said.[3]

In 1994, as part of a larger plan to fortify hundreds of miles of our nation's southern border, what was then a chain-link border fence at Friendship Park was replaced by steel metal panels, salvaged from the landing mats of retired U.S. aircraft carriers. Still, in recognition of the venue's historic function as a bi-national meeting place, panels of metal grate were installed on either side of the Monument, with openings wide enough for a child to slip a hand through, or an adult a few fingers. Across the ensuing decade, the Army Corps of Engineers struggled in vain to stabilize a fence on the beach below Monument Mesa. Tall metal posts, pile-driven close together into the sand, shifted constantly over time, creating gaps through which people darted back and forth across the border, under the watchful eye of a Border Patrol agent stationed permanently atop the mesa.

Despite the continuing imposition of evermore hardware atop Monument Mesa, people from both nations continued to frequent the spot—for its historic significance, for the spectacular ocean view, and for the simple, irreducible pleasure of visiting with family and friends. Because Friendship Park is difficult to get to on the U.S. side of the line—the only road providing vehicle access is flooded for several months each year, and it takes at least thirty minutes to hike to the park by foot—it never became a heavily-trafficked tourist destination. But it has remained a treasured meeting place, especially for people separated from their loved ones by immigration status. People awaiting rulings on their immigration hearings; people on parole or probation; people awaiting the arrival of a new passport—all were commonly told by authorities that they could not leave the territory of the United States. If their loved ones living in Mexico couldn't get a visa to enter the United States, Friendship Park became the only place in the world where people like these could see each other in the flesh.

Until very recently, on a typical Saturday or Sunday, dozens of people could be found at Friendship Park, visiting with family and friends. Across the years I have seen grandmothers meet newborn grandchildren, newlyweds introduce their in-laws and dying people say goodbye to their loved ones through the grated fence atop Monument Mesa. And I have seen children play tag and lovers exchange passionate kisses through the poles on the beach.

* * *

The seeds of Friendship Park's desecration were sown in the aftermath of the terrorist attacks of September 11, 2001, when members of Congress who had long championed cracking down on illegal immigration succeeded in portraying control of the southwest border as a matter of national security. Never mind that the men who attacked the World Trade Center and the Pentagon did not enter the United States from Mexico. Never mind that no known terrorist ever has. The psychic needs of an aggrieved nation matched nicely with the desire to limit Mexican migration to the United States—a desire shared to varying degrees by a majority of Americans for a wide variety of reasons. Post-9/11, the idea that the nation's security depended on "securing the border" became axiomatic for politicians of all ideological persuasions.

The Bush administration institutionalized the axiom in 2003, when the U.S. Border Patrol and other immigration-related agencies were placed under the purview of the newly created Department of Homeland Security (DHS). The result was more than mere bureaucratic reshuffling: all matters pertaining to life on the border were now cast in the light of national security. The strategies of heightened vigilance and beefed-up enforcement came to trump all others in U.S. border policy.

Champions of "border security" achieved a significant breakthrough in 2005 when Congress attached a rider to the Real ID Act granting to the Secretary of the Department of Homeland Security (then Michael Chertoff) the authority to waive any and all laws deemed necessary to expedite construction of supplemental fencing along the border. Human rights, interfaith and environmental organizations mobilized in protest, calling the Real ID Act an abdication of Congress's constitutional responsibility to exercise oversight of the executive branch. Suits were filed contesting the constitutionality of the DHS waiver authority.

On April 1, 2008, Chertoff exercised the authority granted to him by Congress and waived more than thirty-five federal, state, and local laws and regulations.[4] In announcing the waivers, Chertoff made clear that the executive branch would claim carte blanche to do whatever it took to complete construction. "I reserve the authority," Chertoff wrote, "to make further waivers from time to time as I may determine to be necessary." In June the Supreme Court refused to hear an appeal of the last legal case challenging the waiver authority—the Real ID Act had withstood legal challenges and retained the force of law.[5] With the last legal obstacle cleared out of the way, DHS officials moved quickly to meet a Congressional deadline for the construction of additional barriers along the border, including in Friendship Park.

In San Diego, the pace of construction accelerated dramatically through the summer of 2008. The urban corridor connecting San Diego and Tijuana had already been double-fenced, but immediately DHS contractors launched the construction of triple-fencing along the westernmost 3.5 miles of the border. To meet the stated goal of completing the project by year-end, DHS condemned over 150 acres of San Diego County and California State land; in this case to condemn means that the federal government takes the land to use for whatever purpose it desires. A $59 million "design-build" contract was awarded to the Kiewit Corporation, which designed the project and built it on a timetable allowing no room for public review of any kind.[6] Cutting into the mesa tops and filling the canyons as they worked their way to the coast, Kiewit workers relocated millions of cubic yards of earth, transforming what were alternating canyons and mesa tops into rolling hills. After reinforcing the existing border fence, Kiewit erected a second fence that is 20 feet high, made of concrete pylons with steel mesh angled at the top. Between these two barriers they laid a patrol road made of decomposed granite, allowing for rapid movement of Border Patrol vehicles along the border.

That summer it became clear that San Diego Border Patrol intended to extend the second border wall across the face of Friendship Park. The wall would run ninety feet to the north of the international boundary, all the way to the Pacific Ocean, eliminating public access to the historic meeting place atop Monument Mesa and to the international boundary on the beach below. We, who are aficionados of the park, were stunned. We knew San Diego Border Patrol had concerns about drug-smuggling and illegal border-crossings at the location, but this kind of illegal activity was well-controlled by routine surveillance and interdiction. We had assumed that the totality of the law enforcement strategy for Friendship Park would not be predicated on the illegal conduct of a few. We had assumed that some accommodation would be made for the vast majority of visitors to the park, who respected and honored the park's intended purpose.

Surely, we thought, there must be some room for friendship in the complex formula of U.S. border policy.

* * *

The idea of Friendship Park's closure just didn't sit right with me. And it didn't sit right with Dan or Christian or Pedro or Jill or Jaime or Catherine or Enrique . . . or any of the other people who came together to form the "Friends of Friendship Park."[7] The coalition emerged spontaneously as people who cared about the park first mobilized in hopes of stopping the construction of the second border wall. When that effort failed, we turned our attention to a more narrow goal—preserving public access to the park.

The idea of serving communion at Friendship Park came to me after leaders from the Friends of Friendship Park convened a bi-national vigil at the park on June 1, 2008. I am an ordained Methodist minister who had served as pastor of a border church in Calexico for four years. Although my professional life had led me to become the leader of a social justice organization that focuses on immigrant and border communities in San Diego and Tijuana, I continued to serve Communion when the opportunity presented itself. The bi-national vigil proved to be such an opportunity. For this event we planned to share a "love feast," a modified version of communion that avoided complicated liturgical issues of how to share a formal sacrament with an ecumenical crowd. As we made our preparations, Border Patrol agents informed us—for the first time ever in our years of gathering at this location—that we were not to pass items through the fence. Doing so, we were told, would constitute a "customs violation." On that day we decided to adhere to this new restriction, and in an act of lament, those of us in the United States ate our bread in silence, as we looked through the fence at our friends in Mexico, who went without.

Two months later, on August 3, we gathered again, and this time I couldn't bring myself to tolerate what seemed to me a farcical prohibition. People had been breaking bread at Friendship Park for a long, long time, I thought. It seemed only fitting that the park should host the sacrament of communion, too. I was well aware from the outset that passing bread and juice through the fence would be considered a provocation by Border Patrol agents on duty at the park.

Still, I was determined to celebrate the sacrament. "What have we come to as a nation," I asked the crowd assembled, "when breaking bread together—the simplest and most common act of human solidarity— is deemed an illegal act?"

I consecrated the bread and juice and passed them through the fence to a colleague from a church in Tijuana. People formed into two lines, one in each country, and came forward solemnly to receive communion. People were given the choice of receiving the elements from either celebrant, the people on the U.S. side having been forewarned that by taking a small piece of tortilla through the fence they would be breaking the law. One by one, my friends on the U.S. side shook their heads at me as they approached the serving station and reached out their hands to receive the body of Christ through the fence. I sat silently with tortilla in hand, as my colleague from Tijuana, separated from me by twelve inches and an international boundary, served the entire assembly.

The following Sunday I returned to Friendship Park, and I continued the weekly practice of celebrating communion there for the next six months. Each time, Border Patrol agents looked the other way as I served the elements to people on both sides of the border, choosing not to enforce the newly announced ban on passing things through the fence.[8]

Tensions began to mount. On December 23, 2008, Customs and Border Protection declared Friendship Park a construction zone and posted signs stating that anyone entering the park would be charged with trespassing on federal land. I was determined to continue serving communion, however, and for the next several weeks, my friends and I simply climbed around the barriers of plastic mesh that Border Patrol had put in place. I set up my cup and plate, consecrated the elements and served communion to people from both nations. It was clear we were headed for a showdown: when would the Border Patrol begin to enforce their ban on public access?

The answer, it turns out, was February 21, 2009. On that day I had moved the communion celebration to Saturday for a reason that any pastor can understand: I wanted to make the choir happy. A fabulous choir, composed of singers from both countries, wanted to perform at Friendship Park. Because most of the singers had standing obligations on Sunday, they asked for the event to be held on Saturday. I was quick to oblige.

As we approached the border that Saturday afternoon, we were met by dozens of Border Patrol agents, who formed a human wall to stop our progress about 90 feet from the border fence. The choir assembled and sang the Fauré Requiem as we had planned, the music blasting from a sound system our friends had set up in Tijuana, performing admirably, despite having to compete with whistles, shouts and bullhorn blasts from a small group of anti-immigrant protestors who tried to hi-jack the gathering. The protestors' inimitable combination of hatred and incivility was no match for the choir, the performance concluding with a stunning soprano solo—the *Pie Jesu*, "at the feet of Jesus"—sung from a distance in Tijuana.

After the requiem and a few prayers, I shared a brief message with the congregation. I recalled the gospel story in which Jesus goes to a mountaintop with his closest disciples. After Jesus is transfigured in dazzling light, Peter proposes that they erect tents atop the mountain and simply stay put. I drew the analogy to the love that so many of us feel for the United States, the land our forebears called "a shining city on a hill."

But can a city on a hill still truly shine if it has walls built around it? I asked. This is the great temptation of patriotism—there is a fine line between love of country and the demonization of "the other." The desire to secure the United States at all costs is akin to Peter's desire to stay up on the mountaintop with Jesus. As the Bible story makes clear, God has other things in mind for Jesus and those who find in him a kindred spirit. Jesus came down off the mountaintop and set out on his journey to Jerusalem, resisting at every step along the way all human efforts to build walls between God and God's people.

Having concluded my brief sermon, I then offered communion to the 150 or so who had gathered in the United States. I then turned to the south, intending to serve the many hundreds of people who had assembled in Tijuana.

My way was blocked by a Border Patrol agent, who was determined to make an impression. "You don't want to do this," he shouted at me, unsnapping compartments on his uniform—to handcuffs, then mace.

I told him that all I wanted to do was serve communion, and another agent nearby shouted, "Go to Tijuana if you want to serve communion. You're supposed to be a man of God. Obey the law!"

This was no time for a teach-in about civil disobedience. Instead I simply tried to step forward, cup in one hand and tortilla in the other. "I just want to serve communion," I said.

The lead agent stepped in front of me, holding out his hand. "If you bump into me," he shouted, "you'll be charged with assaulting an officer."

I've since learned from a lawyer that my actions did not come anywhere near the threshold for constituting assault, but in the moment I didn't know that this was the case.

"So if I try to walk past you, and I bump into you, I'll be charged with assault?" I asked.

"That's right," he said.

"Then I guess you'll have to arrest me," I replied, "because I'm going to serve communion."

"OK, I will," he said. "Turn around and put your hands behind your back."

I did as I was told and the lead agent then instructed a colleague to remove me from the premises. "Take him out of the park," he said.[9]

In retrospect I should have asked if I was being arrested, and on what charge. By allowing myself to be detained and removed from the park, I let the Border Patrol agent off the hook from having to press charges against me.

As the agent escorted me up the hillside that overlooks the beach at Friendship Park, we began to exchange pleasantries.

"If it weren't for all this mess, it really would be a beautiful day, wouldn't it?" I said.

"Yeah," he replied. "What did you have to go and do all that for?"

"I didn't mean any disrespect to you or your colleagues," I explained. "Our problem isn't with you guys, we know you are just following orders. Our problem is with the policy, with the decision to shut down the park."

"The ones who ruin it," the agent replied, "are the bad guys who pass all kinds of crap through the fence."

"I understand that," I said, "but that's exactly the problem. There's got to be a way to distinguish between the bad guys and the good guys." (The comment is an apt summation of my core critique of the entirety of U.S. border policy.)

The agent shrugged.

We sat atop the mesa, the agent and I, looking down on the beach. Later I learned that another of my friends, Dan Watman, was also removed from the beach by Border Patrol. After that, as Border Patrol agents maintained their solid human wall, the leaders of our group decided to stand down.

That Saturday marked a new era in the history of Friendship Park—and the history of the U.S.-Mexico border. For the first time in the park's 160-year history, U.S. citizens were forcibly prevented from approaching the border fence on the top of the mesa.

* * *

Serving communion at Friendship Park has confirmed for me three things: the fundamental disconnect between both popular and political understandings of the U.S.-Mexico border and the lived reality of the people who live on that border, the inherently political claims of the Christian sacraments, and the enduring symbolism of "Friendship Park."

The first decade of the twenty-first century saw the federal government of the United States recast the U.S.-Mexico border as a battleground in the war on terror. In doing so it dramatically altered the physical and social landscape of the borderlands. Over one third of the border's 1,952 miles are now covered by double or triple barriers. Due south of San Diego border walls now cut not just through Friendship Park, but also through the Tijuana Estuary, an internationally-recognized wetlands and wildlife preserve.[10] In eastern San Diego County, DHS contractors blasted their way through the Otay Mountain Wilderness to erect border walls where the mountains themselves are an overwhelming deterrent to illegal border crossing.[11] In Arizona federal officials pressured wildlife managers to approve new border walls in the Buenos Aires National Wildlife Refuge, and border wall construction in Nogales caused millions of dollars of flood damage in the neighboring town of Nogales, Mexico.[12] In Texas, border walls have cut off entire communities from the Rio Grande River and decimated dozens of private landholdings, many of which have been occupied by the same families for generations.[13]

If the border really were the frightening place that some make it out to be, it might have made sense for the DHS to raze the border landscape, reducing it to nothing more than a "theater of operations" for law enforcement personnel. Popular media in the United States routinely portray the U.S.-Mexico border as a desolate place marred by violence and lawlessness. And with few exceptions the elected and appointed officials who are responsible for shaping U.S. border policy have little personal experience with the borderlands and the people who live here.

But the people who live along the border know the borderlands are not the fearsome place that pundits and politicians would make them out to be. The borderlands are beautiful and complicated, layered in history, home to ecological and cultural treasures. Above all, they are marked by profound human encounter. On the border cultures clash and collide, but they also mingle and dance and embrace.

People have been traversing what are now the U.S.-Mexico borderlands for centuries—millennia, in fact—and as a consequence of this vast history, these lands are crisscrossed by the roots and branches of millions of family trees. They have continued to do so since the United States and Mexico first appointed a commission to draw what are, in fact, quite arbitrary lines on maps and then transpose these lines onto the land. And they will continue to do so long after the changing demography of northern Mexico and the southwest United States gives rise to political changes in both nations that will render these lines obsolete.

This is why I felt so compelled to serve communion at Friendship Park—because it was a small act within my power to express solidarity with the families who routinely met there, each one a living witness to the arbitrariness of the international boundary.

Of course not everyone approved of my decision to introduce the sacrament of communion into the environment of ever-increasing conflict at Friendship Park. Most vehement in their disapproval were the anti-immigrant protesters who spewed hate and venom on me and others who attempted to gain access to the park on the day Border Patrol decided to enforce their ban. The agents themselves (with their shouts of "Obey the law!") made clear that they, too, felt my actions were at best a misguided expression—at worst, a betrayal—of the Christian faith. But even some among the choir and congregation that day wondered afterward whether my decision to take the sacrament into the conflicted environment of Friendship Park had subordinated the religious meaning of the sacrament to the political objectives of demonstrating my opposition to U.S. border policy.

As I see it, though, my practice of serving communion at Friendship Park served to juxtapose in sharp relief the inherently universal demands of the Christian sacraments and the inherently restrictive demands of the nation-state. In my Methodist tradition, we interpret the liturgy of communion to demand that the sacrament be served at an "open table," meaning any who desire to be reconciled to God through the giving and receiving of the elements are to be included. Each time I celebrated communion at Friendship Park, I made clear to the crowd assembled on both sides of the border that there was no expectation for anyone to participate, but that all were welcome. In doing so, I like to think I was acting in ways consistent with the very origins of the Methodist movement, whose founders—the brothers John and Charles Wesley and other reform-minded clerics in the Church of England—counted among their commitments that of taking the sacraments to people who were not receiving them within the established worship services of the scruple-minded church. I also like to think I was acting in ways consistent with the ministry of Jesus, who is portrayed in the Christians scriptures as constantly at odds with both the civil and religious authorities of his day.

Among those who participated regularly in the communion services I presided over at Friendship Park was a young homeless man, Adrian, who was living on the beach right there in Tijuana, while his family saved the money to hire a *coyote* to bring him to join them in the United States. Another regular, Oscar, was deported in early 2008 and came to communion each week to meet up with his wife, a U.S. citizen living in San Diego. I saw both Adrian and Oscar waiting and watching in Tijuana on that Saturday I was turned forcibly away from Friendship Park. The logic of the Eucharist demanded that I offer them a piece of tortilla and a swig of juice. The logic of the nation-state cast my attempt to do so as a small, but significant, threat to our national security. I find this conflict inevitable and ultimately untenable, as do millions of others the world over who in myriad ways refuse to allow the claims of the state to trump the claims of their faith.

At the end of the day, finally, I can't resist the lure of the symbol that is Friendship Park. The park's closure captured the attention of national media—including *The New York Times*, the *Washington Post*, the *Los An-*

geles Times, and National Public Radio, and film crews from around the world.[14] Even the conservative hometown newspaper, the *San Diego Union-Tribune*, trumpeted the cause, concluding in a lead editorial that the decision to re-open the park, "coming at a time when the border is being reinforced like a hostile demilitarized zone, would be a powerful reminder that the United States and Mexico are not the combatants of 1846–1848, but rather are friends and neighbors."[15]

I believe our struggle to save Friendship Park gained so much attention because the park stands as a symbol of the borderlands and border people that local residents know and love. Like millions of others whose lives and relationships straddle the international boundary, I know the U.S.-Mexico border can be a place where human beings meet, a place of friendship, a place of communion.

I have also come to think of Friendship Park as the "birthplace" of the borderlands, both because of its initial creation, and also because the border is continually being re-defined at this location. Time and again, as the U.S. government has sought to transform the popular understanding of what the border is meant to be, it has sought to impress this new understanding upon the mesa where the U.S.-Mexico Boundary Commission first met over a century and half ago. Echoes of these transformations can be heard in the slang that Mexicans use to talk about the international boundary. Once a wide open frontier (*la frontera*), the work initiated by Guadalupe-Hidalgo eventually recast the border in the popular imagination as a line (*la linea*). In the twentieth century, this line was marked first by wire (*el alambre*) and then by a fence (*el cerco*). By the end of the century the fences on almost a third of the border's length had been reinforced with barriers of many different kinds—panels of steel mesh, cement posts driven six feet deep in the soil, recycled landing mats from retired U.S. battleships. For most residents of the region, the border had become a wall (*el muro*).

Like the others that came before them, these words ("the wall," *el muro*) will not have the final say at Friendship Park. The U.S.-Mexico border is nothing if not ever-changing. In the two and a half years since those agents first enforced a ban on public access to the historic meeting place atop Monument Mesa, the Friends of Friendship Park have engaged in long, drawn-out and mostly behind-the-scenes negotiations with San Diego Border Patrol. The result is a compromise plan for modifying the walls at Friendship Park. Sometime in late 2011 or early 2012 a large rolling gate will be installed in the second wall, the one standing ninety feet to the north of the border. When this gate is rolled back, which we are promised will happen at regular hours each weekend, people will once again be allowed to approach the international boundary at this historic location. For now the fence on either side of the Monument will be made of a very fine mesh, permeable enough to allow a line of sight into Mexico, but woven so tight that not even a strip of tortilla will be able to pass.[16]

EPILOGUE

Indeed, the border is ever changing. As this book goes to press, I have recently begun serving communion again at Friendship Park. Through a long and cumbersome process of negotiations lasting almost three years, leaders from the Friends of Friendship Park community coalition have engaged with Border Patrol officials and we have secured a commitment from San Diego Border Patrol to staff the park for "open hours" year-round on Saturdays and Sundays from 10:00 a.m. to 2:00 p.m. This regular schedule means that families and friends can once again count on the park being open if they make arrangements to meet.

As I began to offer the communion elements once more at the wall, I was reminded that the U.S.-Mexico border can indeed be a place of communion. As I write this now, the words echo in my ears and in my soul, a kind of bilingual chant which speaks the promise of a brighter future for the people of both nations:

Take, eat. This is my body, broken for you.
Toma la copa. Este es el sangre de Cristo, derramado para ti, para el perdon de los pecados.
Do this in memory of me.
Hazlo en memoria de mi.

NOTES

1. Charles W. Hughes, "'La Mojonera' and the Marking of California's U.S.-Mexico Boundary Line, 1849-1851," *The Journal of San Diego History* 53 (Summer 2007), 126–47.
2. Ibid., 142.
3. Joseph Nevins, "Pat Nixon at the U.S.-Mexico Border," New American Media (August 21, 2008), http://news.newamericamedia.org/news/view_article.html?article_id=555f6a6f5b0c8684b9e0451c9d85f5b1.
4. Department of Homeland Security, "DHS Exercises Waiver Authority to Expedite Advancement in Border Security" (release date: April 1, 2008), http://www.dhs.gov/xnews/releases/pr_1207080713748.shtm.

"The Real ID Act of 2005" HR 1268, May 11, 2005, Section 102(c) reads "Notwithstanding any other provision of law, the Secretary of Homeland Security shall have the authority to waive all legal requirements such Secretary, in such Secretary's sole discretion, determines necessary to ensure expeditious construction of the barriers and roads under this section." http://frwebgate.access.gpo.gov/cgi-bin/getdoc.cgi?dbname=109_cong_public_laws&docid=f:publ013.109.pdf (accessed December 30, 2008).

For accounts of DHS using Real ID to waive laws, see Suzanne Gamboa, "Homeland Chief Waives Laws to Restart Border Fence Work," *San Diego Union Tribune* October 23, 2007, www.signonsandiego.com/uniontrib/20071023/news_1n23fence.html (accessed December 30, 2008). See also Eileen Sullivan, "US Invokes Legal Waivers To Complete Border Fence," *San Diego Union Tribune* (April 2, 2008), www.signonsandiego.com/uniontrib/20080402/news1n2fence.html (accessed December 30,

2008); Adam Lipnak, "Power to Build Fence Is Above US Law" *New York Times* April 8, 2008 (accessed December 30, 2008); Julia Preston, "Environmental Laws Waived To Press Work on Border Fence," *New York Times* (October 23, 2007), www.nytimes.com/2007/10/23/us/23fence.html?scp=7&sq= chertoff%20border%20fence%20waive%20laws&st=cse (accessed December 30, 2008).

5. Leslie Berenstein, "Border Fence Case Rejected: Supreme Court Allows Construction to Proceed," *San Diego Union Tribune* (June 24, 2008), http://www.signonsandiego.com/uniontrib/20080624/news_1n24fence.html (accessed July 25, 2011).

6. Leslie Berenstein, "Officials Celebrate Patching of Notorious Gap in Border," *San Diego Union-Tribune* (July 7, 2009). http://www.signonsandiego.com/news/2009/jul/07/officials-celebrate-patching-notorious-gap-border.

7. For more, see http://friendshippark.org.

8. For more on my experience of serving communion at Friendship Park see: Fanestil, John, "Border Crossing: Communion at San Diego's Friendship Park," *The Christian Century*, (October 7, 2008). http://www.christiancentury.org/article/2008-10/border-crossing.

9. For a news report on the final showdown, see Crabtree, Penni, "Meeting Place Sealed Off: Border Patrol Prohibits access to Friendship Park," *San Diego Union-Tribune* (February 22, 2009). http://www.signonsandiego.com/news/2009/feb/22/1m22park23590-meeting-place-sealed/. For a video of the stand-off with border patrol, see http://www.youtube.com/watch?v=DyCeSRDLeuk.

10. April Reese, "Border Fence: Smuggler's Gulch Project a "Disaster" for Estuary, Critics Say," *E&E Publishing* (January 15, 2009). http://www.eenews.net/public/Landletter/2009/01/15/1 (accessed July 25, 2011).

11. Connell Dunning, "Draft Environmental Impact Statement for the Proposed Construction, Operation, and Maintenance of the Proposed Tactical Infrastructure, U.S. Border Patrol San Diego Sector, California" (February 25, 2008). http://www.epa.gov/region9/nepa/letters/prop-constr-ops-prop-tact-infra-sdiego-brdr-deis.pdf (accessed July 25, 2011).

12. "Wildlife Manager Pressured on Border Wall," Union of Concerned Scientists: Citizens and Scientists for Environmental Solutions (February 20, 2009). http://www.ucsusa.org/scientific_integrity/abuses_of_science/border-wall.html (accessed July 25, 2011).

13. Marjorie Childress, "Path of the Border Wall Cuts off Land Grant Heir's Property," *New Mexico Independent* (April 17, 2009). http://newmexicoindependent.com/25220/path-of-the-border-wall-cuts-off-land-grant-heirs-property (accessed July 25, 2011).

14. Randal C. Archibold, "New Fence Will Split a Border Park," *New York Times* (October 21, 2008), http://www.nytimes.com/2008/10/22/us/22border.html?_r=4&oref=slogin&oref=slogin (accessed July 25, 2011); Ashley Surdin, "A Growing Divide at the Border," *Washington Post* (October 19, 2008), http://www.washingtonpost.com/wp-dyn/content/article/2008/10/18/AR2008101801690.html (accessed July 25, 2011); Jason Beaubien, "Fence Supplants 'Friendship' at US-Mexico Border," *Day to Day* (February 10, 2009), http://www.npr.org/templates/story/story.php?storyId=100155361 (accessed July 25, 2011).

15. The Editors, "Distant Neighbors: Homeland Security Should reopen Friendship Park at border," *San Diego Union Tribune* (June 2, 2009), http://www.signonsandiego.com/news/2009/jun/02/distant-neighbors/ (accessed July 25, 2011).

16. For a news report on the 2011 compromise, see Elizabeth Aguilera, "Border Patrol and Friendship Park advocates compromise on design," *San Diego Union-Tribune* (February 28, 2011), http://www.signonsandiego.com/news/2011/feb/28/border-patrol-and-friendship-park-advocates-compro/.

SELECTED BIBLIOGRAPHY

Dunning, Connell. "Draft Environmental Impact Statement for the Proposed Construction, Operation, and Maintenance of the Proposed Tactical Infrastructure, U.S. Border Patrol San Diego Sector, California." February 25, 2008. United States Environmental Protection Agency. Available at http://www.epa.gov/region9/nepa/letters/prop-constr-ops-prop-tact-infra-sdiego-brdr-deis.pdf.

Fanestil, John. "Border Crossing: Communion at Friendship Park" *Christian Century* 125, no. 20 (October 7, 2008): 22–25.

Hughes, Charles W. "'La Mojonera' and the Marking of California's U.S.-Mexico Boundary Line, 1849–1851," *The Journal of San Diego History* 53 (Summer, 2007): 126–47.

NINE

Vicissitudes of the Margins

An HIV/AIDS Theological Journey

Ángel F. Méndez Montoya

Vicissitude is "a quality or state of being changeable," implying mutability, a "natural change or mutation visible in nature or in human affairs." It can also refer to a "favorable or unfavorable event or situation that occurs by chance: a fluctuation of state or condition: [such as] the vicissitudes of daily life; a difficulty or hardship attendant on a way of life, a career, or a course of action usually beyond one's control."[1] Vicissitudes are part of my life, and in this chapter I want to present my experiences of hardship and elation as an example of a life on the margins and how such a life can be appreciated as a theological location (a *locus theologicus*). I am inviting the reader to think about a theology *en conjunto* (jointly), a queer theology amid hardship and chaos, a theology in the midst of a constant flux and marked by migration and expulsion. I do so as a queer and hybrid theologian. I am a Mexican, gay, HIV-positive Dominican brother from the U.S. Southern Dominican Province. I was born in the borderland of Mexicali, Baja California, near the monstrous wall (*el muro*) that divides Mexican and U.S. territories.

VICISSITUDES OF A LIFE JOURNEY: BACKGROUND

It was not easy to be gay *en la frontera* (on the border). If we understand the term "vicissitude" as something that contains an internal paradox—that is, something that is simultaneously harsh and soft, sweet and sour, saddening and rejoicing—then I have experienced a life full of paradoxes.

Back in the late sixties and early seventies, while growing up in Mexicali, I experienced the hardships of a violent macho culture. Although I believe I was aware of my gay orientation since early childhood, I nevertheless had to learn to hide it, make it invisible, and never talk about my homosexual feelings with family or friends. Hiding behind a mask offers protection within a hating and unwelcoming environment. As an adolescent, I had to learn the discipline of masking my sexual orientation in order to be accepted. But I still enjoyed a supportive life growing up in *la frontera*. I experienced real love and caring from my parents and family, knowing that they accepted me just the way I am. We seldom talked about sexuality at home, yet I am grateful for the love my parents, family, and close friends showed through their actions.

Living between Mexicali and Calexico made me aware of borders and walls. We Mexicans were never fully accepted on the other side of the border, since for most U.S. citizens we have always been the Other. Yet, we are nonetheless a valuable commodity for U.S. economic growth, as customers as well as laborers under harsh and abusive conditions. I became used to the constant flux of people coming and going from Mexico to the United States. Some were crossing the border with documents, but many without, looking for some improvement or following the fictitious dream of the American way of life. Others crossed the border to escape persecution and harassment, including many gay Latinos and lesbian Latinas who moved away from their homelands where they suffered discrimination.

My life drastically changed at the age of seventeen when I moved from my small border town to Mexico City. Perhaps escaping from my own sexuality—although we never fully know God's deepest intentions—I joined the Mexican Dominicans. Since early childhood, as a Catholic I was deeply drawn toward God and the sacred, liturgical performance, community making, and the intertwining of faith and reason. My home parish was run by Dominicans, and since the age of twelve I studied pastoral and liturgical theology, church history, and the Bible. A true sense of mystery spoke to my vocation of responding to an earlier call to God's voice and sharing God's message of love and compassion with others. However, at that time, some of the Mexican Dominicans in charge of formation were ruthlessly homophobic, and I ended up leaving the Dominican community as I was beginning to accept my homosexuality. James Alison, a gay Catholic priest and former Dominican, points out that the homophobia inside the houses of religious formation is often a consequence of pathological self-hatred, having learned to lie to oneself and to live a lie. I was aware of those mechanisms, and by God's grace this pathological attitude did not devastate me. I learned to accept myself as one of God's beloved children in spite of being in the midst of hatred, rejection and harassment.

The transition from life in a religious house to secular life did not embitter my soul. On the contrary, I knew God was ever near and that I had still much to learn about God and myself, beyond the framework and walls of a religious institution. At that time, leaving the Order was a blessing, for I encountered two great loves in my life: philosophy and dance, another queer hybrid that has shaped my thinking and life. I started a Bachelor Program in Philosophy at the National Autonomous University of Mexico, taking philosophy classes in the mornings and training in modern dance in the afternoons. If vicissitude is understood as a situation that occurs haphazardly, here I encountered it again. Dance happened by chance, something I cannot fully understand through reason, but only with my heart. Life became a joyful fusion of critical thinking and body awareness. It was precisely this interweaving that deepened my search for the divine, for it did not lessen my *appetitus* for God but rather opened up new ways of understanding and experiencing God. I was truly happy and felt blessed being gay and experiencing a divine "queer love."

In 1993, I re-entered the Order with the U.S. Southern Dominicans Province. I decided that being gay should not be a hindrance to follow my call. Unfortunately, back in 1985, when I shared this view during the interview with the vocation's director of the Mexican Province, he promptly replied that being a homosexual was a terrible impairment, similar to being blind or deaf, and that by no means would I be accepted in the Mexican Province. Once again I was marginalized, excluded, and unwelcome. The Christian experience of cross and resurrection, however, gave me hope for life ahead of me, and so I trusted God's queer designs.

I interrupted my university studies when the professional demands as a dancer left me without enough time for my academic education. But I knew deep in my heart that one day I would return to academia. Unexpectedly, I received an invitation to enroll in a Bachelor Program in Dance at the University of Texas, Austin, and to work with the university's professional Sharir-Bustamante Dance Company. In Austin, I was delighted to meet Dominican brothers, who invited me to live with them while studying at the university. The welcoming spirit of the Superior gave me the opportunity to bring together dance, academic study, community and pastoral life. The brothers in Austin do not discriminate against gay people, and they encouraged me to continue dancing and to discern my vocation as a Dominican. This follows a great religious tradition of Dominican brothers and sisters who understand the arts as a way of preaching God's good news.

In the years following 1993, as a Dominican student, I developed a sense of being at peace with my sexuality, while learning to integrate dance, philosophy, and theology with prayer and community, including pastoral work with the Latino communities in Denver and St. Louis. My experience as a Latino in the United States had somehow been privileged, in part because I was in an academic environment and enjoyed a religious status, as opposed to the vast majority of Latinos and Latinas who are vulnerable and easily exploited—as the history of U.S.-Latin American political and economic relations so clearly reveals. Despite this privilege, I was never blind to the reality of exploitation and injustice; my pastoral experience among *mis hermanos y hermanas* made it possible to ground myself in my people's tears and laughter. These experiences later helped me to face another life challenge.

In 2001, I learned of my HIV-positive status while beginning my doctoral studies at the University of Virginia. As part of the U.S. residence application process, I was required to undergo an HIV test, and it was then that I received the painful results. I lack words to express the devastation I felt. Because of misinformed legal advice, the residency application that my Province had filed was rejected. For various reasons, I ended up overstaying my visa for eighteen months before I asked my Provincial for permission to leave the country and complete my doctoral dissertation elsewhere. Fortunately, I was able to do so as a scholar in residence at Cambridge University, England, with Professor John Milbank as dissertation director. I was also blessed by the hospitality of the Cambridge Dominicans, where I lived in an environment of prayer, community, study, and pastoral life—an ideal space for completing my dissertation. After obtaining the doctoral degree, I returned to my homeland, and have since been working in Mexico City as a professor of philosophy and theology.

Because I am HIV-positive, I was rejected by the U.S. government; and because I overstayed my visa, I had to face a ten-year bar disallowing me to enter U.S. territory. The HIV inadmissibility policy was eventually lifted in 2010, but back in 2005, while in England, I had applied for a waiver to enter the United States in order to present a paper at the General Meeting of the Academy of Catholic Hispanic Theologians in the United States. But my application was denied, partially on the suspicion that I might overstay again. Yet, despite being barred from entering the United States, we managed to transcend the borders by delivering the paper virtually at the meeting of Catholic Hispanic theologians. Years later, I received another invitation to participate in a national meeting with the Project on Lived Theology held at the University of San Diego and scheduled in April 2010. Though the inadmissibility law had been lifted by that time and although we submitted another application for entering the United States, the reply from the U.S. embassy did not arrive in time and we were forced again to hold a videoconference. In July 2010, after innumerable bureaucratic steps, I finally received a permit to enter the country. I hope that this is just the beginning of a process of healing a deep wound not only in my life, but also in the lives and hearts of many others who may have been through a similar trial of immigration processes as an HIV-positive person.

HOMOSEXUALITY AND HIV: THE INADMISSIBLE OTHER

Based on my experience, I can state that practices and methods of discrimination still persist in the United States. Although some gay rights have been slowly included in U.S. policies, gay, lesbian, bisexual, and transgender people are not always welcome. HIV came to be known as a homosexual disease, although increasing numbers of heterosexuals are becoming HIV-positive on a worldwide scale. Nevertheless, HIV still confirms a cultural stigma that marks homosexuality as a disease. Fundamentalist Christians rally against gay people in the streets and claim that HIV is a divine punishment for their sinful homosexual condition. There are cities and villages where gay people are openly unwelcome. They are constantly harassed, in some cases terrorized, tortured, and killed. Not to accept HIV people in the United States is a reflection of a policy of inadmissibility, a practice of anti-hospitality that defies Christian values. It is the leper, who needs to be kept at bay and a distance, away from our secured borders.

What is the Christian response to such violent stigmatization? As Christians we learn to see the crucified and resurrected Christ in the marginalized and the most vulnerable (see Matthew 25). The delaying of my application surely had to do with the condition of being Mexican, gay, and HIV-positive—a condition Marcella Althaus-Reid called "triple outsider."[2] As the Biblical narratives challenge us to repeat God's gift of hospitality with each other, particularly with the stranger, can we recognize the presence of God in the alien Other, the one who is inadmissible?

QUEER THEOLOGY AND BORDER-THINKING: A QUEER DECOLONIAL ALTERNATIVE

One could argue that all Christian theology is in itself already "queer." It proclaims a God who became flesh, died, and was resurrected: a God who, contrary to the "normal" cycle of religious violence, reverses that cycle from within rather than from the outside by offering peace, reconciliation, and hospitality, rather than destruction and hostility. As Christians, we believe in a queer God, who cannot ultimately be subsumed under a linguistic description, for God is ineffable, a name beyond all names, a deep mystery and infinite love that cannot be fully grasped by human insight or reasoning alone. That is why faith becomes an extravagance, the locus of receiving divine grace, a divine gift that drives us to desire to know God. As Catherine Pickstock rightly argues in her essay "Eros and Emergence," our desire for God reveals His/Her being already present among us, fulfilling in our present the original divine desire to be near us, a desire that comes from a primordial past but also promises a future eschatological union. It gives meaning to a search for God in the present, nourishing our human *appetitus* for God.³ Such a union of human and divine desires illustrates our perpetual condition of being on the border of our human condition, *la frontera* between divine and human agency. However, *al otro lado del muro*, on the other side of the human frontier, we find a hospitable inclusive God, who is always ready to welcome us and to share divinity with us, making us participants of His/Her divine love. On the other side of divinity, we find ourselves in a place without walls, becoming neither alien nor any longer the Other vis-à-vis God, but one with God in an all-loving divine embrace. Through incarnation, God also subverts the boundaries between divinity and humanity and radicalizes His/Her intimate and immanent relationship without leaving transcendence behind. God actually reveals divinity as already analogically contained in all creation: God's kenotic descent as our bounteous ascent to Him/Her through the resurrected Christ and in the company of the Holy Spirit. This total affinity of God and creation, particularly expressed in the midst of our human condition, displays affinity and love within the Trinitarian community's perfect and perpetual exchange of gifts. Reciprocity is expressed by a relational, ever-dynamic, ever-living God. Colonial Christianity forgot and betrayed this welcoming divine logic and constructed instead its own logic of excluding the Other, as Enrique Dussel has so rightly stated.⁴ The construction and invention of Latin America is paradigmatic of this geopolitics of exclusion and the extortion and domination of indigenous people.

The Mexican-U.S. political relations still reproduce this same colonizing logic, whereby Mexicans are dominated by a country that excludes and exploits them. The exclusion of gay people, particularly those who—like myself—are HIV-positive, illustrates this violent practice that colonizes the Other and labels us as inadmissible. In the midst of this chaotic, hostile and hurtful reality, how can we perform a truly Christian decolonizing practice rooted in a vision of a Trinitarian God that subverts the geopolitical and "ontological" borderlands? A practice that welcomes everyone, and particularly those who are outcast?

BETWEEN SUBVERSION AND EMERGENCE: THE VICISSITUDES OF THE MARGINS

The cross reverses our daily violent and crucifying practices, transforming violence into peace and forgiveness, bringing about eternal life from within the realm of death. The crucified God is the expression of God's ultimate solidarity with those who are crucified in our midst. God's kenosis is not nullifying or self-annihilating but subversively brings about plenitude where there is lack. It affirms and welcomes where there is rejection and marginalization. This subversive divine love is a counter-practice to the coercive politics of the migratory regulations of nation-states. In the midst of a rapidly globalized and globalizing world under the dominant empire of neoliberalism and a capitalist practice of desire based on rivalry and competition (a pathological erotics of desire as absolute consumption and domination of the Other), God's practice of love and inclusion emerges and gives birth to a new erotic-agapeic union, the ecclesial human-divine community, a community that springs from practices of inclusion and hospitality.

My hybrid condition of being Mexican, Dominican, gay, and HIV-positive is subversive as it also pushes me further to the margins. I must confess that this is a painful place to be, but I refuse to be victimized. Like everyone else, I am a child of God. For within the vicissitudes of my story of marginalization, I have encountered incredible support from family, friends, and colleagues. And in that human embrace I have found God's own embrace. Paradoxically, I have come across laughter where tears had been overflowing. Regardless of repeated rejection, even in my own homeland, where, on a daily basis, there is direct and indirect discrimination against gay people and particularly against people living with HIV, much hope abides in me. Sadly, the Mexican Catholic clergy is no exception to this discriminatory attitude, with the result that I continue to suffer discrimination at the hands of the homophobic sectors of the Church in Mexico. I also face discrimination within academic and institutional circles, including those who claim to uphold Christian values and principles. At times, the secular world tends to be more welcoming. Small niches and communities within and outside the Church have given me enormous support, which sustains me and keeps me full of hope. In their support and care, I also encounter God.

NOTES

1. http://www.merriam-webster.com/dictionary/vicissitudes.
2. Marcella Althaus-Reid, *The Queer God* (New York: Routledge, 2003), 160.
3. See Catherine Pickstock, "*Eros and Emergence*," in Gerard Loughlin (ed.), *Queer Theology: Rethinking the Western Body* (Oxford: Blackwell Publishing, 2007).
4. See Enrique Dussel, *1492: el encubrimiento del otro. Hacia el origen del "mito de la Modernidad*," Conferencias de Frankfurt, October 1991, Colección Académica, No. Uno (La Paz, Bolivia: Plural editores, Centro de Información para el Desarrollo, CID, Facultad de Humanidades y Ciencias de la Educación, Universidad Mayor de San Andrés, 1994).

SELECTED BIBLIOGRAPHY

Althaus-Reid, Marcella. *The Queer God*. New York: Routledge, 2003.
Loughlin, Gerard, ed. *Queer Theology: Rethinking the Western Body*. Oxford: Blackwell Publishing, 2007.

Index

AFSC. *See* American Friends Service Committee
Althaus Reid, Marcella, 131, 181
American Friends Service Committee (AFSC), 100, 111
American Gothic, 65
Amnesty International, 129
Angel Island, 145, 146, 151, 158, 159–160
Anzaldúa, Gloria, 8, 37
Army Corps of Engineers, 101, 102
Asociación Tepeyac de New York, 92–93, 96. *See also comité guadalupano*

Bañuelas, Arturo, 35
Basilica of our Lady of San Juan del Valle, 90–92
Bedford, Nancy, 34
Bersin, Alan, 114
Bible. *See Index of Bible Passages*
biblical interpretation, 41–42, 45–46, 59, 60, 67, 71, 135
Boeing Co., 113
Bolton, Eugene, 7, 8
border: between human and divine, 181; border crossing deaths, 3–4, 93, 108–109; as idol, 22; as imaginary line, 19; as motif, 36–43, 75, 92, 99; vigilantism on border, 105; wall, 164, 166, 170, 173, 174, 177. *See also* border policy in U.S.; deaths at the border; Minutemen; U.S.-Mexico border; violence, normalization of
Border Industrialization Program, 123
borderlands: concept of, 7–9; Galilee as, 38; historiography of, 7–8; religious practices in, 81–96; theology of, 36–34, 182; transnational, 123, 126; U.S.-Mexico borderlands, 170–171, 177

Border Patrol, 6, 19, 100, 101, 102, 105, 109–110, 110–112, 168, 169–170
border policy in U.S., 3, 113–114; environmental impact, 114; use of technology, 113. *See also* deterrence; Operation Gatekeeper; Secure Borders Initiative
Bush, George, 102, 110, 145, 165

Cabeza de Vaca, Alvar Nuñez, 87
CAFTA. *See* Central American Free Trade Agreement
Carroll, Daniel, 152
Castle Garden, 61, 62
Casto, Lucha, 137
catholicity, 27–28, 29
Central American Free Trade Agreement (CAFTA), 125
Chávez, César, 82
Chávez Cano, Esther, 132
Chertoff, Michael, 166
Chihuahua City, 122, 128, 133
Chinese Exclusion Act of 1882, 63, 148, 159
Christian churches in U.S., 21
Christian theology: dogmatic, 19, 21–22; of migration, 33; systematic, 20. *See also* catholicity; Christians, as pilgrim people; Christology; contextual theology; Crucifixion; ecclesiology; eschatology; feminist liberation theologies; idolatry; image of God; queer theology; Reign of God; theological anthropology; theology of migration; theology of reparations; Trinity
Christians: Episcopalians, 20; as immigrants, 20, 60, 74; Pentecostals, 20; as pilgrim people, 21–22, 23, 27,

29; Roman Catholics, 20; in the U.S., 20. See also Methodism
Christology, 38
citizenship, 26, 35, 37, 42, 44, 104; in the Bible, 1, 74; cultural citizenship, 93, 96; history of in U.S., 6–7, 81; legal citizenship, 82, 93
city on a hill, 169
Clinton, Bill, 106–107
colonialism, 42, 81, 85, 87, 127, 130, 182. See also postcolonial studies
colonias, 91
comité guadalupano, 92–94, 97. See also Asociación Tepeyac de New York
communion at the border, 112, 167–170, 171–172, 174. See also Eucharist
consumerism, 154, 155
contextual theology, 34, 35, 42, 46, 47
Cornelius, Wayne, 3
Coronado, Irasema, 128, 136
coyote, 101
Crucifixion, 182
curanderismo, 86, 86–89

Davila, Maria Teresa (MT), 47
deaths at the border, 104, 107–108, 109, 111–112. See also border crossing deaths
Defense Authorization Acts of 1990 and 1991, 103
Del Cid, Carmel Manuela, 130, 131
deportation, 149, 150, 159
deterrence, 2–6, 107–109
detention of immigrants, 149–150, 150, 158
Department of Homeland Security (DHS), 4, 110, 111, 113, 114, 149, 165–166
DHS. See Department of Homeland Security
diaspora: as motif, 35–36, 42, 43–44, 47; Cuban, 41; Puerto Rican, 44–46, 53n59
Díaz, Miguel, 35
Dominicans, 177, 178–180, 183
Dream Act, 159
drug trafficking, 39, 124
Dunn, Timothy, 103, 104

ecclesiology, 27, 29
Elizondo, Virgilio, 35, 38
Ellis Island, 61, 63
eschatology, 147, 149, 152, 154, 156–157
Eucharist, 112, 135, 146–147, 156, 157, 160. See also communion at the border
exile, 35, 39, 41, 42–43, 70
Exodus, 34

Fanestil, John, 112
feminicide, 121, 122, 123; connection to domestic violence, 128; official government response to, 128; women's response to, 128–129, 130, 132–137. See also violence against women
feminist liberation theologies, 121
Fidencio, Niño, 88
Flores, Juan, 44, 45, 48
Forum of Women for Life, 134–135
Francis, St., 157
Friendship Park, 100, 112–113, 163–174
Friends of Friendship Park, 172–173
frontera, 35, 36, 37, 153, 173, 177, 181
frontier, 153, 181
Frost, Robert, 99

Gadsen Purchase (1853), 102
GAO. See Government Accounting Office
Gálvez, Alyshia, 94
gay and lesbian, discrimination against, 177–179
Geary Act of 1889, 148
Gebara, Ivone, 136
gender violence, 121–132. See also violence against women
globalization, 24–27, 28, 29, 46, 123, 182
Goizueta, Roberto, 38
González, Justo, 40, 41, 153
Government Accounting Office (GAO), 3, 113
Guadalupe, Our Lady of, 95–96

Hays, Richard, 154
healing. See curanderismo; limpia
Hernández, Esequiel, 104, 109
Hernández, Esther, 95–96

Hispanic identity, 35, 49n3, 66, 67, 95, 104, 109, 149
historiography, 7, 8
HIV status, connection to immigration status, 180–181, 182
Honduras: 2009 coup, 125; U.S. remittances from, 124; U.S. involvement with, 124–125. *See also* feminicide; Zelaya Rosales, Manuel; Palmerola (Soto Cano)
hospitality, 45, 73, 118n53, 127, 154–155, 180, 182
human rights, 100, 107, 109–110, 111–112, 128, 134
hybridity, 37–38, 45, 46, 49n3, 82, 177, 179, 183

ICE. *See* Immigration and Customs Enforcement
idolatry, 22, 23
illegal alien, 4, 37, 82, 96, 105, 112, 152, 168
Illegal Immigration Reform and Immigrant Responsibility Act, 106
image of God, 23, 68–69
immigrants to the United States: anti-immigrant groups respond to, 105–106; anti-immigrant rhetoric, 4–5, 6, 39, 58, 62–63, 73, 105–106, 127, 148; from China, 63–73, 146, 147–148, 158–159, 160; from Cuba, 35, 39, 40, 40–41; as economic refugees, 124; from Germany, 61–62, 73; from Ireland, 62, 73; from Italy, 62, 64, 73; from Mexico, 1, 89, 92; use of public services, 106; who are Christians, 20
immigration: biblical perspectives on, 57–76; connection to crime rates, 104; public attitudes about, 99; raids, 39, 96, 110, 118n44; reporting on, 4–5; and theology, 19–31, 145–159
Immigration Act of 1917, 6
Immigration and Customs Enforcement (ICE), 110, 112, 114, 149, 157, 158
Immigration and Naturalization Service (INS), 106, 109

immigration policy, 6, 71, 81–82, 94, 106, 180–181. *See also* Immigration Act of 1917; Chinese Exclusion Act of 1882; Dream Act; Illegal Immigration Reform and Immigrant Responsibility Act; Immigration Reform and Control Act; Naturalization Act of 1790; Naturalization Act of 1870; Proposition 187 (California); Proposition 200 (Arizona); SB 1070 (Arizona)
immigration reform, 1, 82, 83, 93, 99, 153, 157, 159
Immigration Reform and Control Act, 103
impunity, 39, 110, 111, 125, 127
INS. *See* Immigration and Naturalization Service
Isasi-Díaz, Ada María, 41, 43
Israel's Law, 71, 72–73, 74

Jaramillo, Don Pedro, 88
Jesus, as a refugee, 74
Jiménez, Maria, 109
Joint Task Force 6, 104
Juárez, Mexico, 39, 122, 123, 128, 129, 132, 133
Justice for our Daughters, 133

Kiewit Corporation, 166

Latino/a theology, 19, 30n1, 33–49
Latinos/as: in borderlands, 82, 91; gay and lesbian, 178; identity of, 4, 35, 179; religious population, 1, 20, 155; as voters, 114
liberation theology, 34, 134, 137
limpia, 85
Lockheed Martin, 113
locus theologicus, 33, 177
love: commandment to love foreigner, 30n4, 73; commandment to love neighbor, 22, 28–29, 73, 157; of country, 169; for Cuba, 41; God's love for human beings, 152, 181; God's love for immigrants, 73–74, 146; God's love for poor, 91; queer, 179; spiritualities of, 122, 130, 132,

136
love feast, 167

majority culture, 59, 60, 65, 68, 70, 73, 74, 76
manifest destiny, 102, 115n3, 151
maquiladoras, 107, 123, 124, 125
Marcos, Sylvia, 84–85
Marine Corps of the United States, 104
Matsuoka, Fumitaka, 34, 49
McKinnon, Catherine, 128, 130
Medina, Néstor, 38
"The Mending Wall", 99
Mérida Initiative, 124
Mesoamerican cosmology, 84, 85, 86, 87, 89
mestizaje, 38, 82
mestizo/a, 37, 38, 67, 95
Methodism, 172
Mexican-American War of 1846-1848, 5, 81, 102, 123, 163
Mexican Revolution, 6, 107
Minutemen, 105–106, 116n23
mujerista theology, 41, 43

NAFTA. *See* North American Free Trade Agreement
Nahuas, 84–86, 87, 89, 96, 97n14
Naturalization Act of 1790, 6
Naturalization Act of 1870, 6
neoliberal economics, 107, 121, 123, 125, 126, 131, 182
Nevins, Joseph, 4
Newman, Elizabeth, 154
Newsom, Gavin, 154
New York City, 40, 43, 44, 45, 92, 93, 94
Nicaragua: Sandinista government, 124
Nixon, Pat, 113, 164
North American Free Trade Agreement (NAFTA), 5, 107, 123–124
Nussbaum, Martha, 128
Nuyorican, 35, 38, 43, 45, 47, 53n60

Obama, Barack: and border policy, 102–103, 114; and immigration policy, 102–103
Operation Endgame, 147, 149

Operation Gatekeeper, 107, 108, 117n32, 164
Ortiz, Marisela, 132

Palmerola (Soto Cano), 124–125
Personal Responsibility and Work Opportunity Reconciliation Act of 1996, 106. *See also* welfare reform
Pew Hispanic Center and the Pew Forum on Religion and Public Life, 1
Phan, Peter, 34
Pickstock, Catherine, 181
Pine, Adrienne, 126, 130, 131
Pineda-Madrid, Nancy, 35, 39
Posada Sin Fronteras, 112–113, 118n53
Posse Comitatus Statute of 1879, 103
postcolonial studies, 48
power reflex, 151–152
preferential option for the poor, 38
Proposition 187 (California), 5, 105, 106
Proposition 200 (Arizona), 82
Proposition 209 (California), 106
Proposition 227 (California), 106
Puerto Rico, 43, 44

queer experience, 179
queer God, 181
queer theology, 181–183

race: creation of, 37; determines U.S. citizenship, 6–7, 37; history of race relations, 82–99; intersectionality with other categories of experience, 47, 81, 88, 92, 123; post-racialism, 47; and U.S. immigration policy, 6–7, 148, 159
racial binary (black/white), 53n60, 95
racial hierarchies, 96
racial hybridity, 82, 95
racially underrepresented scholars, 33, 38
racial politics, 91, 94
racism, 34, 81, 82–83, 86; directed at immigrants, 37, 148; in immigration policy, 6; in theology, 34. *See also* immigrants, anti-immigrant rhetoric

Reagan, Ronald, 114, 124; and border policy, 103; and immigration policy, 103; and military aid to Central American, 125; and trade policy, 107
Real ID Act, 166
Reign of God, 21, 23, 29, 134, 154
religion: folk religion, 87; indigenous religion, 135; lived religion, 83, 122; lived theology, 9; religious imagination, 83, 90, 92, 96; women's religious imagination, 122. *See also* Christian theology
remittances, 124
rite of passage, 94
Rodríguez, Luis Rivera, 46, 47
Roman Catholic Church, 88
Roman Catholicism, 85
Ruiz, Jean-Pierre, 38, 43, 45–46, 47

San Diego, 2, 3, 5, 11, 13n7, 22, 36, 99–115, 163–174
San Ysidro, 5, 100, 101, 111
Sandoval, Chela, 95
SB 1070 (Arizona), 82, 148
Secure Borders Initiative, 113–114
Segovia, Fernando, 42, 43
September 11, 2001 attacks on U.S., connection with immigration enforcement, 110, 113–114, 147, 149, 165
social location, 9, 42, 100–101, 149–152, 150, 155–156, 177–181, 183
sojourner, 60, 73, 76
Solivan, Samuel, 44
spirituality, 136
Staudt, Kathleen, 123, 128, 136
stranger, welcoming the, 28, 181
structural inequality, 121, 127
structural violence, 123, 126
Sugirtharajah, R.S., 33–34
symbolic violence, 130

theological anthropology, 130
theology of migration, 34–35, 36
theology of reparations, 127
Tijuana, 3, 5, 6, 36, 100, 101, 107, 164, 166–168, 172

Torres, Eliseo, 86, 87, 88
transnational, 25, 46, 47, 95, 96, 123, 127, 135, 136
transparency, 110, 114
Treaty of Hidalgo, 5, 7, 50n16, 102, 123, 163
Trinity, 181–182
Turner, Victor, 94
Turner thesis, 8

Urrea, Teresa, 82
U.S.-Mexico border: history of, 5–6, 81, 102, 112–113, 163–165; militarization of, 96, 100, 102, 103, 104, 107; security, 99; U.S.-Mexico Boundary Commission, 89, 163–169; violence on, 101, 102, 108

vicissitude, 177, 179, 183
violence, normalization of, 101, 115n2, 127
violence against women, 121–132; church responses in Honduras to, 130, 130; church responses in Mexico to, 129, 130; civil society organizations responses to, 132–134; Honduran government response to, 129, 130; Mexican government responses to, 129; political responses to, 133; theological responses to, 132–137; theological roots of, 130–132. *See also* gender violence
Voices without Echo, 133

War on Drugs, 103, 104
War on Terror, 110, 113–114
welfare reform,. *See also* Personal Responsibility and Work Opportunity Reconciliation Act of 1996 106
Wilson, Pete, 105, 106

Zelaya Rosales, Manuel, 125, 134, 139n30

Index of Bible Passages

Genesis 1, 68
Genesis 1:26–28, 68
Genesis 2:15, 60
Genesis 2:18, 68
Genesis 11:31, 69
Genesis 12, 45
Genesis 12:1–5, 69
Genesis 23, 69
Genesis 37, 69
Genesis 39, 69
Genesis 40–41, 69
Genesis 42, 69
Genesis 42:23, 69
Genesis 47, 69

Exodus, 70
Exodus 1–2, 70
Exodus 5, 70
Exodus 12:35–49, 73
Exodus 20:10, 72
Exodus 22:21, 73
Exodus 23:9, 73
Exodus 23:12, 72

Leviticus 16:29, 73
Leviticus 19:9–10, 72
Leviticus 19:18, 73
Leviticus 19:33–34, 60, 73

Numbers 9:14, 73

Deuteronomy 1:16–17, 72
Deuteronomy 5:14, 72
Deuteronomy 10:12–22, 73
Deuteronomy 14:28–29, 72
Deuteronomy 16:14, 73
Deuteronomy 24:14–22, 72
Deuteronomy 24:17–18, 73
Deuteronomy 26:11, 73
Deuteronomy 27:19, 72

Ruth 2:5–7, 70
Ruth 4, 70

Ezra 7–10, 71

Nehemiah 1, 71

Esther 2:7, 71

Isaiah 11:6–7, 156–157
Isaiah 25:6–8, 150
Isaiah 58:7, 73

Lamentations, 41

Matthew 2:13–18, 74
Matthew 19:16–19, 73
Matthew 22:1–10, 147
Matthew 25, 181
Matthew 25:31–36, 60, 74

Luke 9:10–17, 147
Luke 10:25–37, 74
Luke 14:12–14, 75
Luke 17:11–19, 74
Luke 22:14–20, 146
1 Corinthians 11:17, 154
1 Corinthians 11:22, 154
1 Corinthians 11:29, 154

Romans 3:10–11, 152
Romans 13, 68
Romans 13:1–5, 75

Ephesians 2:14–19, 154
1 Timothy 3:2, 75

Titus 1:8, 74

Philemon 3:20, 74

Hebrews 13:2, 75
Hebrews 13:14, 74

1 Peter 1:1, 74
1 Peter 2:11, 74

About the Contributors

Sarah Azaransky teaches in the Department of Theology and Religious Studies at the University of San Diego. She is author of *The Dream is Freedom: Pauli Murray and American Democratic Faith* (Oxford, 2011).

M. Daniel Carroll R. (Rodas) is Distinguished Professor of Old Testament at Denver Seminary and adjunct professor at El Seminario Teológico Centroamericano in Guatemala City, Guatemala. His latest books are *Christians at the Border: Immigration, the Church and the Bible* (Baker Academic, 2008) and *Global Voices: Reading the Bible in the Majority World* (Hendrickson, 2012), which he coedited. In addition to his work in the fields of Old Testament social ethics and the prophetic literature, he has contributed to several publications on the topic of immigration. Dr. Carroll Rodas is half-Guatemalan and is involved in Hispanic ministry.

Orlando O. Espín is professor of theology and religious studies at the University of San Diego. He earned a dual doctorate in systematic and practical theology at the Catholic University of Rio de Janeiro, Brazil. Espín has specialized in the study of popular religion, as well as in study of culture, interculturality and traditioning. He is author or editor of nine books and coedited an award-winning dictionary of theology and religious studies. He has published over 450 articles in U.S., European, and Latin American professional journals, and more than 50 book chapters. He has received several national and international awards, including an honorary doctorate and an honorary professorship.

John Fanestil is an ordained elder in the California-Pacific Annual Conference of the United Methodist Church and the executive director of Foundation for Change, a social justice foundation working in border and immigrant communities of the San Diego/Tijuana region. Fanestil is a graduate of Dartmouth College, Oxford University, where he studied as a Rhodes Scholar, and the Claremont School of Theology. From 1992 to 2005 he served as the pastor of United Methodist Churches in Southern California, including four years at the bilingual United Methodist congregation in the border town of Calexico. He is author of *Mrs. Hunter's Happy Death: Lessons on Living from People Preparing to Die* (Doubleday, 2006) and his writing has been featured in *The Christian Century* and the *San Diego Union-Tribune*.

Daisy L. Machado is academic dean and professor of the history of Christianity at Union Theological Seminary, New York City. Born in Cuba and raised in New York City, Dr. Machado considers herself a borderlands dweller learning from childhood the importance and risks of crossing borders—racial, linguistic, religious, and political. She has been teaching about the Texas/Mexico border for more than fourteen years, helping her students see firsthand the struggles of *colonia* residents on the both sides of *la frontera*.

Monica Maher, PhD, is former associate director at Harvard University of the University Committee on Human Rights Studies and currently a research professor in the Program of Gender and Culture Studies at the Latin American Faculty of Social Sciences (FLACSO) in Quito, Ecuador. A Christian social ethicist, Dr. Maher has taught at Harvard Divinity School and Union Theological Seminary. Named a 2004 Fulbright New Century Scholar on the Empowerment of Women, she has worked on women's rights with international organizations throughout Latin America.

Ángel F. Méndez Montoya is a Lay Dominican Brother from the Province of Saint Martín de Porres, United States. He holds a BA in dance, an MA in philosophy, an MA in theology, and an MDiv and a PhD in philosophical theology from the University of Virginia. He wrote his dissertation at Cambridge University as a scholar in residence, which was published under the title, *The Theology of Food: Eating and the Eucharist* (Wiley-Blackwell, 2009). This work was nominated for the Michael Ramsey Prize in 2011. In 2010, this same book was published in Spanish by Editorial JUS, in Mexico City, under the title *Festín del deseo: hacia una teología alimentaria*. He currently teaches theology, philosophy and cultural studies at several universities in Mexico City, and gives lectures primarily in Mexico, Latin America, the United States, and Europe.

Carmen Nanko-Fernández is associate professor of Pastoral Ministry and director of the Ecumenical Doctor of Ministry program at the Catholic Theological Union, Chicago, Illinois. She served as President of the Academy of Catholic Hispanic Theologians of the United States (ACHTUS) and is the author of *Theologizing en Espanglish: Context, Community, and Ministry* (Orbis Books, 2010). Her publications focus on Latin@ theologies, Catholic social teaching, interreligious and intercultural relations, im/migration, and the intersections between faith and popular culture with particular attention to béisbol. Born and raised in the Bronx, New York, she views teología through what she calls a decidedly "huban@" lens—that is, Hispanic and urban. In 2012, ACTUS awarded her the Virgilio Elizondo Award for "Distinguished achievement in theology, in keeping with the mission of the Academy."

Pedro Rios is director of the American Friends Service Committee's U.S./ Mexico Border Program and is chairperson for the San Diego Immigrant Rights Consortium, a coalition of more than twenty-five different organizations in San Diego working to support the rights of immigrants. In his current position, Rios oversees a program that documents abuses by law enforcement agencies, working with cross-sectional community groups, advocating for policy change, and interacting with migrant communities. A native San Diegan, Rios holds an MA in Ethnic Studies from San Francisco State University.

Craig Wong is executive director of Grace Urban Ministries (GUM), a church-based nonprofit in San Francisco's Mission District that connects congregations and community partners to serve vulnerable communities, including ministries of health, education, family support, and immigrant advocacy. Wong is a member of the advisory board of the Christian Community Development Association, a national organization that equips churches and nonprofits in urban ministry. He also serves on the board of Dayspring Technologies, a faith-based web technology firm. Wong is a columnist for PRISM, a publication of Evangelicals for Social Action. He and his wife raise four children in San Francisco.